L. M. Jackson

THE MESMERIST'S APPRENTICE

arrow books

Published by Arrow Books 2009

1 3 5 7 9 10 8 6 4 2

First published in Great Britain in 2008 by William Heinemann

Arrow Books
The Random House Group Limited
20 Vauxhall Bridge Road, London, SW1V 2SA

www.rbooks.co.uk

Addresses for companies within The Random House Group Limited can
be found at: www.randomhouse.co.uk/offices.htm

The Random House Group Limited Reg. No. 954009

A CIP catalogue record for this book
is available from the British Library

ISBN 9780099498421

The Random House Group Limited supports The Forest Stewardship
Council (FSC), the leading international forest certification organisation.
All our titles that are printed on Greenpeace approved FSC certified
paper carry the FSC logo. Our paper procurement policy can be found at
www.rbooks.co.uk/environment

Typeset by Palimpsest Book Production Limited,
Grangemouth, Stirlingshire
Printed and bound in Great Britain by
CPI Cox & Wyman, Reading, RG1 8EX

The Mesmerist's Apprentice

PROLOGUE

The coffee-house was a small establishment, situated upon the corner of Liquorpond Street and Leather Lane. In fact, to be quite accurate, it was not so much on a corner as a kink in the road. For the streets of Saffron Hill had a tendency to intersect at unlikely, inconvenient angles and the northerly end of Leather Lane was no exception, terminating in a peculiar sloping piazza, plagued by loose cobbles, littered with cabbage leaves and herring-bones, the detritus of the market. The spot bore no particular name – being too asymmetrical and lopsided to be a 'square', and far too open to be a 'court' – but the market crowds were predisposed to swirl and eddy around its precincts, until trickling downhill along sundry obscure tributaries that meandered in the direction of the Middlesex House of Correction or Smithfield. It was, therefore, however undistinguished, a good location for a business, especially one savouring of mocha.

The coffee-house in question – Sarah Tanner's New Dining and Coffee Rooms – was squeezed between the premises of H. Nicolls, Tobacconist, whose front was all but hidden by the coster's barrow that had a seemingly permanent claim on the pavement outside, and Brecknell's Wax Chandlers, whose window advertised

1

'botanic transparent' at ten pence per pound, and the sale of colza oil by gallon or pint. Unfortunately, neither Mr. Nicolls nor Mrs. Brecknell (a robust widow of some twenty years standing) had much time for their neighbour, not since the dramatic conflagration which had laid waste to the old Dining and Coffee Rooms the previous year and threatened to doom their respective stocks of weed and wax to premature ignition. True, no great harm had been done to their property, but there were gossips amongst the coster-women who had claimed the accidental blaze was Mrs. Tanner's own doing; that she had come home *dead drunk*, and sent the fateful oil-lamp flying *in an awful fit*. Sarah Tanner herself had said nothing to correct the rumour and if her miraculous escape from the fire had only fuelled the impression, in certain corners of the market, that *it was the luck of the devil with that woman*, then the ensuing reconstruction of the Dining and Coffee Rooms – within three months of its fiery destruction – only served to make matters worse.

In fairness, it was hard to say precisely what the coster-women objected to in the proprietress of the coffee-shop. Despite the rumours, she had no great fondness for liquour: she was but rarely seen in the Bottle of Hay, the nearest public-house, and not known to frequent any of the local beer-shops. She was well-spoken, polite, and made herself agreeable to all her customers, from the most condescending of junior clerks to the humblest street-hawker. She had a face which any self-respecting gentleman of the press would have dubbed *interesting* and which lesser men of the coster fraternity called *pretty as a picture*. And if she kept her past something of a mystery, she was not alone in that – not in the vicinity of Leather Lane, at least, not by a long chalk. Possibly it came down to petty jealousy, for she did have a fine figure. Indeed, since no-one knew how Mrs. Tanner had come by her shop at such a young age, or revived it from the ashes with such speed, there was a good degree of speculation of the worst sort.

And yet Mrs. Tanner was not entirely without friends in the market, if only because she did a good deal of trade in the way of comestibles, and paid her bills promptly. Furthermore, when the New Dining and Coffee Rooms re-opened, it did so with a full complement of former employees: Mrs. Hinchley, its redoubtable plain cook; Ralph Grundy, the old man who had served as its waiter; and a young general skivvy by the name of Norah Smallwood, reputed to be the proprietress's cousin. There was a decent complement of customers too: for few men in the vicinity of Leather Lane, whether costers or otherwise, put their wives' scruples above the demands of an empty stomach. Mrs. Hinchley's breakfast, in particular, enjoyed the enviable reputation of being *a reg'lar blow-out at a knock-down price* and there was not a man in the market who would hear a word against it.

At least, not until the trouble began.

CHAPTER ONE

Norah Smallwood leant casually over the counter and glanced at her employer's newspaper. If there was one thing that perplexed her about the owner of the New Dining and Coffee Rooms, it was the general interest she took in the daily press. It made sense to collect the abandoned papers that accumulated in the coffee-house's little booths: that was a wise economy, since the fried fish stall on the corner of Baldwin's Gardens paid ready money for wrapping. But to read the tiny print in the meantime; to take any pleasure in the inky notices and reports of the *Morning Chronicle* or *Daily News* – well, that seemed quite unnatural in a woman. For her own part, although she had been taught to read, she found it something of a chore to attempt even the most straightforward of penny romances that were hawked around the market.

Every rule, however, has an exception. And although Norah felt a broad disdain for most forms of literature, she maintained an healthy interest in one branch of the art: the lively notices of public amusements that graced the front page of every newspaper. Thus, as her eyes alighted upon a particular advertisement, she paused in her rather desultory efforts at cleaning.

'Is that tomorrow?' she said.

Sarah Tanner stopped reading and laid down the paper, rather pointedly. If the proprietress of the New Dining and Coffee Rooms had grown fond of Norah Smallwood – which was undoubtedly the case – she occasionally found her company a little too convivial. She preferred to treasure the rare quiet moments, when there were no customers at the counter and the occupants of the shop's little booths enjoyed their food and drink in solitary contemplation. In short, she slightly resented the interruption.

'What?'

'There,' said Norah, pointing. 'That's tomorrow, ain't it? What's it say?'

The item in question was a modest advertisement that lay half-way down the front page of the newspaper.

MESMERISM AND ITS ANALOGOUS PHENOMENA, PHYSICAL AND PSYCHICAL – Prof. FELTON will demonstrate the workings of the New Science at the Mechanics' Institution, Southampton Row, 28th April, commencing at eight o'clock. The lecture will examine the transference of health and incorporate a curious and interesting experiment. Gallery 3d.; reserved seats 1s. Members of the Institution admitted half-price. Private consultation from eleven until three o'clock.

'It says,' replied Mrs. Tanner, 'that anyone fool enough to part with threepence, to see some kitchenmaid faking a jig half-asleep, should go to Southampton Row tomorrow night.'

'Well, I'd go,' said Norah, doggedly ignoring the sarcasm, 'if I had threepence handy.'

'Then it's a good thing you don't. Besides, you're in a daze half the time as it is; it would look well if you came back magnetised. Now, unless I'm much mistaken,' said Mrs. Tanner, pointing, 'that table hasn't seen a dish-cloth all week – if it's not too much trouble?'

Norah Smallwood looked rather sullenly at her employer, and turned her back, muttering something that incorporated the words 'like a slave'. Sarah Tanner smiled a wry smile, and reached to pick up the paper once more. Her attention, however, was distracted by one of her customers who sat in the booth by the window. He was a young man – no, she thought to herself, not much more than a boy – in plain working clothes, with a thick head of brown curls and rather angular cheekbones. He was not from the market, she was sure of it. She did not know his face, and neither did he wear the polished bluchers or colourful neckerchief which were the fashion amongst the coster-boys. There was nothing so unusual in that, but there was something odd in his manner. In particular, his food, a penny plate of hashed beef, was hardly touched, though it had sat upon the table for several minutes. Moreover, as he took up a mouthful on his fork, he seemed to masticate it with a curious thoughtfulness.

His eyes suddenly caught Sarah Tanner's as she looked at him.

'Here, missus,' he said, volubly enough for his voice to carry across the room, and the other diners to stare in his direction, 'this ain't up to much.'

Mrs. Tanner raised her eye-brows.

'I mean to say,' he continued, unabashed, 'you can pepper it up all you like, but you can't expect a fellow to eat it.'

'What you going on about?' demanded Norah, on her employer's behalf, with an indignant vehemence that caused a couple of the diners, both costers, to chuckle, doubtless anticipating an amusing *to-do*. Mrs. Tanner cast an admonitory glance in her direction.

'Are you saying there's something wrong with it?'

'Well, there ain't much right with it, missus,' insisted the boy. 'My belly's all twistin' up, and I ain't had more than a couple of morsels. What do you call it again?'

'Beef hash,' replied Mrs. Tanner calmly.

'Well, *you* might call it that,' said the boy, grimacing and spitting a mouthful of food back on to his plate, 'but I know a bit of horse-meat when I has it.'

'It's off a good leg of beef that we've been serving all morning, and no complaints.'

'That ain't my affair,' observed the boy. 'Maybe their gullets was so choked up, they didn't have half a chance.'

Mrs. Tanner looked over at her other customers. To her annoyance, if not surprise, the pair of costers who sat nearby suddenly seemed to contemplate their own plates with a degree of suspicion. She stepped out from behind the counter and walked over to the boy. He was no more than fifteen years old, despite his cocksure demeanour, and not particularly tall for his age.

'Hook it,' she said, firmly. 'Before I call a copper.'

'Here's a fine thing!' exclaimed the boy, seemingly affronted. 'Poison a fellow and chuck him out!'

'Look here, I don't know who you are,' she said, lowering her voice, 'but you won't get a penny from me for this cheap dodge, not if you drop down dead on the spot and half of London gets to hear about it. Now, hook it.'

'Dodge?!' exclaimed the boy, deliberately loud. 'Now it ain't enough to poison a fellow but call him a liar an' all! Here – take your bleedin' penny for your hash and I hope it chokes you – if that horse-meat don't choke you first!'

And, before Mrs. Tanner could say a word, the boy stood up, pulled a penny from his waistcoat pocket, shoved it into her hand, stalked from his seat to the door, and slammed it behind him.

'Must be wrong in the head,' said Norah, disdainfully.

Norah's employer shook her head, looking at the penny. 'I don't think so. Go and find Ralph – he's out the back.'

'What do you want him for?' asked Norah.

'Tell him he's in charge,' said Sarah Tanner, grabbing her shawl from the hook behind the counter. 'I'm just going out.'

———

Sarah Tanner stepped outside the shop and headed down Leather Lane, following in the boy's footsteps.

It was almost mid-day, and most of the costers' barrows were emptying, with the exception of a solitary vendor who seemed to have acquired two barrels of herring, whose aroma – a little too ripe for popular taste – filled the street. The market, however, was still crowded. For there were a host of lesser dealers upon the lane whose stock-in-trade were less perishable items. They filled the pavements around the barrows, occasionally interpolating their own little cart or sometimes simply laying a cloth upon the ground. Dealers in 'fancy goods', 'plain goods' – and, if truth be told, goods that were no good to anyone – who sold everything from curtain-hooks to candles, patent remedies to pin-cushions. They always attracted a curious crowd and, in consequence, it was no easy matter to spot an individual amongst them.

Nonetheless, after a few minutes, when she had almost given up hope, she saw the self-same boy. He was loitering upon the edge of the market, near a small hand-barrow, propped upon the pavement so as to render it horizontal. The goods for sale were, as far as she could make out, of the 'fancy' kind – cheap jewellery, scarf-pins and brooches – not the sort to entice the average youth. But there were several interested parties already there, including a middle-aged gentleman of the shabby-genteel variety, bending over in earnest contemplation of the equally shabby wares, perhaps choosing an affordable gift for an elderly mother or long-suffering spouse.

She watched the boy edge forward. Instinctively, she stepped back behind the nearest barrow. For, in that instant, she had a good idea what would happen next.

There!

Even a seasoned police constable might have over-looked it. But she knew the movements of a practised pickpocket; and – if only for the briefest instant – she saw the glint of metal in his fingers, as a watch passed from one waistcoat pocket to another.

The boy then walked on briskly, but not so quickly as to attract attention. She followed, on the opposite side of the road, negotiating the various makeshift stalls. The boy slowed his steps to a casual sauntering pace and it was a simple matter to catch up with him. She waited for the right moment, dodging the crowd.

Then she reached out and grabbed hold of him.

'Eh!' the boy protested, instantly wriggling free. A look of angry indignation passed across his face; but it dissipated the second he saw his assailant.

'You! I thought you was a Peeler!'

'I'll fetch one if you like,' said Sarah Tanner.

'Well, you do that, missus. I ain't the party what's poisoning other parties, am I now?' he said, merrily. 'What do you want with us, anyhow?'

'You know there was nothing wrong with that meat. What are you playing at?'

'Playing?' said the boy. 'I ain't playing, darlin'. Straight as they come.'

'Is that so?'

'Just!' exclaimed the boy, visibly amused by the entire exchange.

'Then,' continued Mrs. Tanner, holding out her closed hand and opening it, 'what's this?'

The boy looked down and immediately put a hand to his own waistcoat pocket. For, before him, lay the very watch which had only recently passed into his own possession. His mouth fell open, then, after a second or two, he broke into uncontrollable laughter.

'That's a proper facer, that is!' he exclaimed, wiping his eyes. 'I thought you was playing the high and mighty, when you must be the best prig this side of Holborn – I didn't feel a bleedin' thing. Just! Well, I'm pleased to make your acquaintance, missus, honest I am.'

'I doubt there's much honest about you,' said Sarah Tanner, warily. 'Do you want the watch back?'

'If you like,' shrugged the boy, 'it was only a lark.'

'Is that what you'll tell the magistrate?'

'What, are you going to give me in charge, then, is that it?' said the boy, with a chuckle. 'Nah, you keep it, missus. I bet you've got an uncle or two who can give it a good home, eh?'

'I might do. I could get a good price on it. Let's say I give you half if you tell me what that business in my shop was all about.'

10

The boy merely smirked and shook his head.

'Pleasure, though, missus – charmed!'

And, with a cheerful nod, he raised a hand to his cap and made to walk off. Sarah Tanner, without giving the matter much thought, grabbed hold of the boy's arm. But as he turned round, the youth took hold of her hand with his own, and looked her in the eye. All the good humour had drained from his face, to be replaced with a cold, malevolent stare.

'I'll keep away from your little shop, darlin', out of courtesy. But don't interfere with the Brass Band, 'cos we're not the boys to take it, see?'

And with those words, his cocksure smile returned, and he darted into the crowd.

Sarah Tanner let him go. There was something so unnerving in the way he had looked at her, she had little inclination to follow. Instead, she turned and walked back in the direction of the New Dining and Coffee Rooms.

And, half-way down Leather Lane, she casually dropped a certain watch into the waistcoat pocket of a certain shabby gentleman.

CHAPTER TWO

'Well, what time is it, then?' said Ralph Grundy.

The elderly waiter stood near the plate-glass window of the coffee-house, his face almost pressed up against the glass, peering out along the market. It was growing dark outside and the naphtha man was doing a brisk trade with his oil-cans, working his way amongst the costers who kept up an evening trade. Bargains were struck – with some haggling over measures – and, one by one, the lamps, which dangled from rough-and-ready awnings, or odd spars of wood, flared into life. The bituminous scent of the oil, meanwhile, carried on the breeze, potent enough to make the old man wrinkle his nose in disgust.

'It's just gone seven, Ralph,' replied Sarah Tanner. 'Didn't you hear it strike?'

'Reckon not. Anyhow, I'm right, ain't I? It's like I told you. I'll swear, missus, we ain't seen a soul step through that door for a good hour.'

'Not quite that,' said Mrs. Tanner.

'He ain't far wrong,' muttered Norah, who sat rather forlornly in one of the shop's little booths, tying back the ribbon in her hair for the third or fourth time in as many minutes. 'I ain't served a morsel all afternoon, not since you sent Mrs. H. home.'

12

'It's this business with the meat, missus,' persisted the old man. 'You know what folk are like round these parts, once word gets round. Only takes some fool to have a belly-ache and they'll swear blind you're on the gee-gee dodge; and they won't stick that. They're particular about their meat, even if they ain't particular about nothing else.'

'That boy yesterday wasn't ill,' insisted Mrs. Tanner. 'And there was nothing wrong with that meat. We'd have heard about it, if there was – he wasn't the only one who ate it. If there's any "dodge" here, we're victims of it.'

'The truth of it don't matter a jot,' said Ralph, punctuating his sentence with a derisive snort. 'Certain persons get talking; they ain't got nothing better to do. Besides, it ain't just a question of that boy. If it were just him, it'd be forgotten by now, like you say. But I've heard things down the market; and last time I set foot in the Bottle of Hay, too.'

'What "things"?' asked Mrs. Tanner.

'Well, we get all our meat from Sanders, don't we?'

'He's a decent butcher.'

'Ah, well,' said the old man, 'maybe he is and maybe he ain't. That's a matter of opinion. Only there's been rumours—'

'I ain't heard nothing,' interjected Norah Smallwood.

'Well, most likely you don't stop flapping your gums long enough to listen,' said Ralph, tetchily. 'Anyhow, there's been rumours this last week or so that he's taking horse-flesh off flying knackers, and putting it in his germans to bulk up the weight.'

'And why would he need to do that?' asked Mrs. Tanner. 'He makes a good living.'

'Still makes for a cheaper sausage, though, don't it,

missus?' said Ralph. 'All grist to the mill. Talking of which, I heard something else last night and all, what was going round the Bottle.'

'In the bottom of a bottle, more like,' muttered Norah.

'I ain't vouching for it,' said Ralph, ignoring her remark. 'But I heard old Sanders went and put gas in his cellar last week; and now there's some machine and all, which he sets a-going during the night; and a ramp down the back.'

'A ramp?' said Sarah Tanner, none the wiser.

'As might suit any old horses,' said the old man, significantly, 'what no-one had no more use for.'

───

It was a half-hour later, when Mrs. Tanner made a resolution, quit her shop and walked down Leather Lane. There was a hint of fog, and the damp air seemed to render the costers' lamps a particularly warm orange, casting a hazy, flattering glow over their barrows of produce. Her destination was not the street market, however, but one of the shops that overlooked it, situated upon the corner of Dorrington Street, marked out by an exposed pipe that shot a flickering jet of flame into the night air – namely the premises of '*Geo. Sanders, Pork Butcher*'.

The shop was one of the grandest upon the street, and the sign which made reference to pork was patently misleading; for Mr. Sanders – or possibly Mr. Sanders' ancestors – had long since ventured beyond the porcine. Thus, several legs of mutton and beef shared space with the hanging hams and loops of sausages that formed an artful, if rather grisly curtain, inside the butcher's twin windows. Moreover, lying upon trestle tables on the pavement, sheep's trotters nestled next to the blackest of black puddings; and even a tray of oysters had mysteriously come to rest beside them. In short, Mr. George Sanders was a general dealer in the meat line; and he was – or, at least, he had always been considered – a respectable one. For, although the gutters outside generally ran with blood, there was always a light sprinkling of sawdust upon the pavement.

Mrs. Tanner peered into the shop; there was a gas-light inside and she could make out the proprietor himself, dressed in the customary duck apron and leggings of his trade, and a rather dirty-looking individual, clad in greasy oilskins, a canvas sack slung over his shoulder. She could tell from their manner that they were engaged in finalising some transaction. Feigning interest in the trotters, she waited until it was done and the man in oilskins had departed. Once the butcher was alone, she walked inside.

Mr. Sanders, a large, burly-armed man, with rather extravagant side-whiskers, broke into a smile.

'Mrs. Tanner! Bless me! A bit late in the day for you, ain't it? I'm about to close up but I'm sure I can oblige you. What can I get you, ma'am, eh? Running short on your beef, is it? Or is it the ham? I said to your girl last week, didn't I? You get through more ham than that in a weekend!'

Sarah Tanner, somewhat embarrassed by the butcher's rather exaggerated enthusiasm for her custom, smiled back.

'We are a little short,' she said. 'But, first, may I ask you something?'

The butcher's cheerful smile quivered, then crumbled entirely.

'Don't tell me!' he exclaimed bitterly. 'Not you and all! That's it, I'm ruined!'

'You've heard the rumours, then?' she inquired.

'Heard them! Oh, I've heard them all right! Criminal, is what it is – lies! Damned lies! I'd sooner eat my own mother, God rest her dear departed soul, than lay hands on horse-meat – any man who knows me will swear it.'

'I believe you,' said Mrs. Tanner. The butcher, however, did not brighten at the intelligence.

'Do you now, ma'am? That's something, I suppose, although it won't keep me and the missus in clover. See, I ain't seen a single body set foot through that door all afternoon, 'cepting you and old Hopkins. And he weren't too happy with me neither.'

'Hopkins?'

'Don't you know him, ma'am? I suppose no reason why you should. A bone-boiler; glue-man. Only I ain't hardly got nothing for him; hardly worth his trouble. I ain't shifting the meat, see? Anyhow,' he continued, rather despondently, 'I don't suppose you want to hear my troubles.'

'It is not so much that . . .'

Sarah Tanner halted, mid-sentence. For, as she spoke, there was a loud clatter from outside the shop; a volley of curses and shouts, audible above the general hub-bub of the nocturnal market.

'Damn me!' exclaimed Mr. Sanders. 'What is it now?'

The butcher grabbed a cleaver which lay on a nearby slab, and darted outside into the darkened street, with neither a 'by your leave' or 'beg pardon' to his would-be customer. Sarah Tanner followed him.

The source of the confusion was not directly outside the shop, but round the corner on Dorrington Street – a street in name only, little more than an alley – by the wooden gate which led to the butcher's back yard. The bone-boiler's cart and horse were tied to a lamp-post that adjoined the wall and the animal was shifting uneasily in its harness. The unfortunate Mr. Hopkins, meanwhile, lay sprawled in the gutter, his canvas bag split open, and his meagre haul of bones – cleaned of all but the most stubborn scraps of flesh – scattered along the dirty cobbles. Worse still, he was surrounded by a gang of half-a-dozen boys, none older than sixteen years. One held a thigh-bone with which he prodded his victim, whilst all six chanted in unison.

'Horse-meat! Horse-meat!'

Sarah Tanner looked at the group. She already recognised the leader who held the bone – she had only spoken to him the previous day. She glanced at the butcher and noticed that a crowd of passers-by was gathering behind them.

'Here!' shouted the boy, calling to the crowd with the same confidence with which he had addressed the diners in the coffee-house. 'That one over there, he does for them, and this fellow here clears it up. Ain't that prime! How much for the whole horse, eh? How much is it?'

The boys renewed their chant; the crowd, in the way of London crowds faced with two sides to an argument, respectfully waited for the arrival of Her Majesty's Police; or a twist in the unfolding drama. They were gratified in the latter respect, as George Sanders, his face incandescent with anger, ran forward, waiving his blood-stained cleaver wildly above his head.

The gang of boys hesitated; a tremor of uncertainty passing across their faces. There was no doubting that the apoplectic rage in the butcher's countenance was authentic. With a nod from their leader, they turned and bolted down the street, with a few choice curses cast over their shoulders for good measure. In a matter of seconds, their figures became hazy and indistinct in the damp night air, then vanished altogether.

Mr. Sanders, for his part, though a rugged, healthy individual in his own way, had no great turn of speed. After an ineffectual effort, he reluctantly abandoned the pursuit, flinging his cleaver clattering down upon the pavement. It was only then, as his rage subsided, that he became aware of the motley crowd of market-goers who had watched the whole spectacle from a safe distance. He hurried back to the bone-boiler, who was just levering himself to his feet.

'Tell them, Bill Hopkins,' said the butcher, pleading, gesturing towards the crowd, 'tell them it's a nonsense – tell them! You know bones, don't you? Tell them!'

The bone-boiler, however, nursing a bruise upon his temple, merely spat upon the ground, untied his horse and climbed up into the driver's seat.

'You won't catch me here again, Sanders,' said Hopkins, at last. 'That's all I'm saying.'

And with that, the bone-boiler set off down the street.

⁓

'I'll gut the little swine,' muttered the butcher. 'I'll swing for them; mark my words. If it's the last thing I do.'

It was a few minutes later that Sarah Tanner stood once more in George Sanders' shop. The return to his premises had done nothing to calm the butcher's nerves. For the slabs and trays of meat had been overturned in his absence; a pile of old paper, ready to be used as wrapping, had been flung wildly about the room; sausages pulled off their hooks and trampled down into the mess.

'You'll have to go elsewhere tonight, missus,' said

the butcher, collecting his thoughts. His anger, however, seemed to lift him a little. 'I'll be open again tomorrow, mind. Mark my words. They won't beat George Sanders down. Not on my life, they won't.'

Mrs. Tanner nodded sympathetically, though she was preoccupied by her own thoughts.

'Have you seen those boys before?' she asked.

'I don't reckon I have,' said the butcher. 'But if I seem them again—'

'I mean, I don't think they're local boys, that's all,' Mrs. Tanner continued, thinking out loud. 'So what do they care about Leather Lane meat?'

George Sanders wearily shook his head in mute despair, gazing at the wreckage around him.

Sarah Tanner frowned, and turned to leave.

'Do you have any enemies, Mr. Sanders?' she asked, pausing by the door.

'That's just it,' said the butcher, anger and frustration making his voice positively quaver. 'I ain't got an enemy in the whole world!'

She shrugged.

'Well, I rather think you do.'

CHAPTER THREE

Sarah Tanner stared thoughtfully at the newly lit fire that burnt in her bedroom grate. It was her custom to warm the room a good hour before she closed the shop. She maintained this indulgence, even though the presence of Norah Smallwood as her lodger guaranteed that she rarely went directly to bed – for there was always some piece of market gossip, or some fine point concerning the outward appearance of an eligible young coster, upon which Norah was happy to propound her views; and the conversation could last well into the small hours of the morning, especially if aided by a drop of warm gin. In truth, Mrs. Tanner rather enjoyed the young girl's company; and though she did not confide her own innermost thoughts with the same readiness as Norah, a friendship of sorts had grown between the proprietress of the coffee-shop and her garrulous young tenant.

There was a friendship, too, between Mrs. Tanner and Ralph Grundy, though the old man retained his naturally morose and curmudgeonly character. Indeed, as a noise from the street outside startled her from her reverie, her first thoughts were of the waiter, who had taken a night's leave from the New Dining and Coffee Rooms. Upon such occasions, it was not utterly unknown for the old man, having spent an evening in the tap-room of the Bottle of Hay, to pay his respects to his employer before heading homewards; nor was it unknown for him to occasionally collide with sundry obstacles along the way.

She walked to the window, pulling back the curtain, but there was no-one to be seen. It occurred to her that the noise from the public-house, just out of sight, a couple of hundred yards down the Lane, was a little more boisterous than usual.

Idly, she sat down at her dressing-table and opened one of the drawers. It was not some item for her evening toilette which she retrieved, however, but a care-worn scrap of printed paper, that she read to herself:

MARRIAGE IN HIGH LIFE. – The marriage of the Hon. Arthur Stallworth DeSalle, eldest son of the Viscount DeSalle, with Miss Arabella Montague, the beautiful and accomplished daughter of Mr. J. S. Montague of Eaton-square, Belgravia, was solemnized yesterday in the Church of St. James's, Piccadilly, in the presence of a very numerous circle of the immediate connexions of both families. The Lord Bishop of London was in attendance to perform the service. The bride was attended by a train of six bridesmaids, similarly attired in pale sea-green glacé silk, with flounces and jackets *en suite*. The bride was beautifully robed in a superb dress of white watered silk, with Brussels lace flounces and trimmings. A veil of the same order and a wreath of orange blossom completed her costume . . .

She put the scrap down. She almost knew the words by heart, though it still galled her to read them. She briefly wondered why she did not crumple it up and throw it upon the fire. But, instead, as always, she replaced it in the drawer. The cutting – so she told herself – served as a valuable reminder: that she had left her old life utterly behind her; and that a certain young man, for whom she once had a certain tenderness, was utterly lost to her.

She closed the drawer. Then, after a moment's quiet reflection, she left the room and went down the narrow staircase that led to the shop. She found it quite empty, but for Norah Smallwood, stationed behind the counter.

'Reckon we should close early,' said the waitress, with a rather defeated air.

'We close at twelve,' replied Sarah Tanner, mechanically.

'No-one seems to mind we're open.'

'I can't help that,' said Mrs. Tanner.

'It's not like there's anything wrong with the meat, anyhow,' muttered Norah. 'But if it carries on like this, you'll have to find another butcher, missus. How long's it been? Four days now, I reckon. Take tonight! Hardly anyone's bought a bite of food all evening; and those that have all look at it queer. One fellow even asked us if it was Sanders' meat, and then turned his nose up.'

'Not until I know what's going on,' replied Mrs. Tanner. 'I'm damned if I'll be done out of my livelihood by some ridiculous rumour.'

Norah shrugged. 'I reckon Sanders will, though, from what I hear. Now, I'll tell you what he needs! Did you hear about York's?'

'York's?'

'The cheese-shop,' persisted Norah, 'the one on Saffron Hill, by Evans's – you know.'

'I don't make it my business to hear the comings

22

and goings of cheesemongers,' replied Mrs. Tanner, a little distracted; for the rather riotous noise from the Bottle of Hay could still be heard outside, louder still.

Norah Tanner raised her eye-brows at her employer's response, as if to say that *she* didn't consider herself too good not to hear about anyone. But she let the matter pass and carried on.

'A gentleman came in to his little shop, last week – that's what I heard, anyhow – respectable – and he says – straight out – "My good man, how much for everything in the place – all your wares?" So old York reckons he's chaffing him, so he says, "Twenty pounds, sir," – and you'll never guess what . . .'

'I give up.'

'He only paid him the money. Had everything in the shop on the spot, put it all on a waggon, and drove off.'

'Is that so?' replied Mrs. Tanner, still not quite attending, walking over to the shop-window.

'Said it was for a bet. Lord knows what sort of bet that was – but I suppose that's what some swells are like, when they've had a few . . . Here! Are you even listening to me?'

Mrs. Tanner's reply was forestalled by her opening the shop-door. For, from the other side of the road, she had spied Ralph Grundy hurrying back along the market, looking not so much inebriated as breathless and agitated.

'Missus!' exclaimed the old man. 'You better hurry – I'll swear an oath on it, they're going to string him up.'

'Who?'

'Sanders!'

'I don't know who started it,' said Ralph, as they hurried together along the lane, 'but everyone was talking on it, and saying how it was a crying shame to have his sort in the market.'

'Sanders?' asked Mrs. Tanner.

'Who else? And then one fellow says another fellow told him that he'd seen him taking an old horse round the back, all sly and quiet.'

'He has a horse – a chestnut mare.'

'Ah, well,' continued the old man, 'that's what I said. But then another fellow chips in, and says he saw it too, and it was definitely a black 'un and no mistake. Then someone else said he heard that machine of his a-grindin' again all night.'

'Didn't anyone speak up for him?'

'Joe Drummond said it weren't likely; he's got a good head on his shoulders; but then old Teach went out – he didn't say nothing – and when he came back, he said he'd been down to the shop, which was all shuttered up like, but he heard the machine going full pelt.'

'I can guess the rest,' muttered Mrs. Tanner.

'They're all going down there, missus,' continued Ralph, 'and their women-folk too. Must be two dozen of 'em or more. All this about horse-meat fires them up. I mean to say, it's the beer talking, with most of 'em, but I wouldn't want to be in Sanders' shoes, not if you paid us.'

'It's all nonsense,' exclaimed Sarah Tanner, exasperated.

'Still,' replied the old man, breathless, 'I'm glad it ain't my neck they're after.'

They soon approached the butcher's premises. The gas jet in front had long since been extinguished, and the windows shuttered, but the sound of an incensed

24

crowd, engaged in noisy animated discussion, could be heard from the back of the shop. Hurrying round the corner, they found the wooden gate to the butcher's yard was wide open, creaking upon its hinges. In the yard stood a group of locals, one of whom carried a lantern, hurriedly requisitioned from the Bottle of Hay. The focus of their attention was the rear of the shop and, in particular, the drop of some six feet or more between the yard and the butcher's cellar.

'Only one thing for it, if he won't come out,' said one of the women present, a ruddy-cheeked female whom Mrs. Tanner recognised from the market. 'You go at it, Jim.'

Her remark was addressed to a burly coster, something of a giant amongst his fellows, at six feet or more in height. The man looked around him. From the encouraging words and shouts which followed, it seemed that there was a consensus that he should, indeed, 'go at it', and with a will. Consequently, a path was cleared; the coster took a deep breath, and ran towards the back of the butcher's premises, in the manner of a bull charging a gate.

Mrs. Tanner edged through the crowd of on-lookers. It was only then that she could make out that the coster had gone down the ramp that – as the rumour had correctly stated – led to the back of the butcher's cellar. She felt a tremor of uncertainty in her own mind: for there was no doubting that the planks were fitted with cross-pieces, nailed every eighteen inches or so, designed to provide a steady footing for an animal.

'That'll do it all right,' murmured Ralph Grundy, who stood behind his employer, as half-a-dozen more men followed down the slope.

And, before Mrs. Tanner could reply, the old man's

prediction proved correct: the bolted wooden doors that led into the butcher's basement sprung off their hinges, as the large coster flew at them, shoulder first. The other men followed, pursued by their wives, sons and daughters, and all the other stragglers that formed the angry mob. They hailed the coster's success with a rousing, if somewhat inebriated, cheer.

Sarah Tanner briefly wondered if she could push to the front, but the space was plainly too small to accommodate the irate crowd – at least, under such shambolic circumstances. Instead, she crouched down in the yard, and peered over the heads of the assembled throng who had descended into the cellar. It was an unexceptionable, tidy-looking basement – albeit a large space with a high ceiling – and did not resemble any slaughter-house with which she was familiar. Sanders and his wife, the former defensively brandishing a knife, the latter in her night-dress, stood at one end of the room, plainly terrified by the Lane's would-be vigilantes. Towards the centre, however, was the focus of the crowd's attention: a brand-new cast-iron meat grinder; and tethered to its crank-shaft, pausing in its trudge round the room, snorting in surprise, was the ageing placid horse that drove the mechanism – the butcher's own chestnut mare.

It was plain to even the most drunken of the rioters that the animal in question suffered from nothing more than a somewhat wearisome nocturnal routine – namely that of circling the cold cellar in harness, to drive the grinder.

Chaos followed. Some, to their credit, appeared shame-faced, a couple going so far as to attempt an apology to the butcher and his wife; others broke out into drunken laughter; others simply turned round and made to leave. The words and movements of each man and woman seemed to interfere with the intentions of their nearest neighbours. As Sarah Tanner watched, with a mixture of relief and amusement, she felt a tap on her shoulder and turned to see Ralph Grundy gesturing upwards.

'There! Look at that!'

She followed the old man's gaze. Although the night sky was clouded, a dim light shone from the windows of the upper floors of Sanders' shop and she could just make out the focus of his attention: an attic window, some three storeys up, lay wide open, and a small figure of a man – or was it a boy? – scrambled along the roof, moving with consummate ease, grasping the chimney for support then skidding further along, half on the roof, half on the guttering.

Then the figure disappeared from sight.

Mrs. Tanner got up and ran back through the yard, into the narrow confines of Dorrington Street, with Ralph Grundy not far behind. She paused and stood still, motioning for the old man to do likewise; for she could hear the sound of footsteps above. Then, suddenly, there was a blur of motion and a noisy clattering upon the tiles.

Ralph Grundy blinked in astonishment. The figure had jumped – crossing from the butcher's gutter to the roof of one of the ageing tenements which lined the southern side of the alley.

'It's bleedin' Spring-heeled Jack!' exclaimed the old man.

'It's no phantom,' insisted Mrs. Tanner. 'Listen, will you do something for me?'

'What?' said the old man.

'Go back and try and speak to Sanders. Tell him what you just saw, and say I'd like a word with him. Tell him I've got an idea – well, half an idea, anyhow – what's going on.'

27

'And what are you going to do, missus?' asked Ralph.

'What do you think?' said Mrs. Tanner, as she began to run along the pavement, following the distant sound of footsteps, somewhere upon the rooftops above.

CHAPTER FOUR

Sarah Tanner caught sight of the figure only once, for the briefest of moments. She relied for her pursuit upon the clatter of boots upon the bricks and slates. But she knew it would only be a matter of time before he selected a way down, a low wall or out-house that led into a yard or court; and then it would be impossible to guess his direction. The figure moved quickly, determinedly; there was nothing cautious or timid in his progress. She wondered whether he could hear her following: her own feet splashed in the viscous mud that lined much of the road, and the sound seemed to echo from one end of the deserted alley to the other.

He did not jump again, although the first turning off Dorrington Street was narrow enough. Instead, as far as she could fathom, he turned south, still negotiating the rooftops with ease, into the warren of narrow lanes that ran between Dorrington Street and Holborn. She heard a cry of complaint; an angry shout from a sleepless tenant; a decrepit sash window thrown open with a head poking into the street: all served to confirm the burglar's progress.

She knew the little district well enough. Known as Brooke's Market, it was considered a poor one, even by the standards of Leather Lane, being the residence of a good many sweeps, dust-yard workers and other scavengers, who seemed to find something homely and sympathetic in its cluttered, dingy arteries. The 'Market' itself was simply a central clearing amidst the distinctly rickety tenements that surrounded it, with a small public-house at one end and a beer-shop at the other. She felt sure that it suited her purpose more than her quarry. Upon the north side, the buildings were, despite their wretched condition, more substantial brick-built dwellings, whilst upon the south, they yielded to twin rows of ancient houses, all but hovels, constructed of little more than weatherboard and tar. It was, she concluded, a spot where even an agile man would have to quit the rooftops.

She hurried onwards, increasingly uncertain whether she could still make out the footsteps. There was hardly a soul upon the streets; the only exception being a pair of men with hang-dog expressions, loitering upon a corner, sharing a single pipe of tobacco, oblivious to her progress. As she turned the corner into the open space of Brooke's Market, with its solitary gas-lamp – a failed effort by the parish to 'improve' the district – she instantly regretted her rather impetuous entrance. There, immediately before her, lounging by an upturned barrow, a rotten-looking article that must have lain there abandoned for some months, was the same gang of boys who had persecuted the unfortunate bone-boiler. Seven in number, they turned as a group and gazed in her direction. The gas-light shone upon their faces and she noted that they looked neither so lean nor ill-fed as many of the boys that passed by her coffee-house. Their clothes, moreover, even bordered upon the 'swell'. Several had pristine white neckerchiefs and a watch-chain in their waistcoat pockets.

'What you lookin' at, darlin'?' asked a dark-haired youth; the others chuckled.

'Nothing,' said Sarah Tanner. She looked back at the boy, meeting his impertinent gaze. She noticed that all the youths wore an identical brass ring on the little finger of their right hand. Her mind went back to the boy in the market, their leader, who appeared to be absent from the group.

'I expect you're this "Brass Band" I've been hearing about,' she said, cautiously, watching for their reaction.

Several of the boys looked at their fellows in surprise. The dark-haired youth, however, seemed less flustered than his colleagues.

'What if we are?' he asked.

'I met a pal of yours a couple of days ago,' replied Mrs. Tanner. 'Said I served him horse-meat.'

The boys laughed again amongst themselves – giggled, if truth be told. But the dark-haired youth nodded his head in recognition.

'Now I know who you are! Jem told us about you – drew a click-thimble on him without him clueing to it. Now that's something, missus, if you knew Jem Cranks. Not many gets round Jem.'

'Where is he, then, your friend Jem?'

'Oh, I'll expect he'll roll up when he likes,' said the youth, with a sly smirk.

'Then maybe you can tell me, while you're waiting – what's your game with George Sanders? I know you're after something. Tell us what's the lay, and I won't blab a word. I'm no great friend of his; I might even be able to help you out.'

The boy, however, merely shook his head. But Sarah Tanner noticed that, as she spoke, he glanced upwards.

At the same time, one of the group, a skinny youth,

more timid-looking than his fellows, shouted out, 'Watch out!'

Instinctively, Sarah Tanner stepped back. She felt a rush of air by her face, as something flew past her cheek and scudded into the cobbles, breaking into several pieces.

She peered at the ground – it was the cracked remains of an old grey slate, flung from above.

'That's your second warning, missus,' said a familiar voice.

She knew the speaker – it was the boys' leader – Jem Cranks by name, if she could trust his comrade – plainly the same boy she had been following, perched upon the rooftops. She peered heavenwards, but he had already vanished from view. Meanwhile, as she looked back into the market, the Brass Band themselves had begun to saunter off with deliberate youthful langour, the dark-haired youth looking back at her with a disdainful stare. She noticed that the boy who had shouted a warning was surrounded by his peers; one casually kicked his shin, whilst another jabbed at his ribs.

She hesitated. At least, she reasoned, she knew the identity of the burglar; but there was little chance of following the gang unobserved.

A woman stepped out from a nearby house.

'What's all the row? Ain't a body got a right to their sleep?'

'Just some boys,' said Sarah Tanner.

And, without further explanation, she turned back and headed towards Leather Lane.

~

Ralph Grundy met his employer upon the corner of Dorrington Street, outside the butcher's shop.

'Well, I suppose you came back after all,' said the old man.

'Did you think I wouldn't?' asked Mrs. Tanner.

'I've given up second-guessing on your account long ago, missus. Ain't no purpose to it.'

'I haven't been gone more than half an hour. Did you speak to Sanders?'

'Told you I would, didn't I?' said the old man. 'Even though I had to wait on half the market clearing out!'

'And what did he say?'

'Spoke to him not two minutes ago. Said he's obliged, but he's had enough of excitement for one night; and if you wants a word, come back in the morning.'

Sarah Tanner sighed, but nodded acquiescence. 'I suppose I can't blame him for that. Did you tell him about the burglary?'

'That's just it, missus,' said Ralph, as his employer began walking back down Leather Lane. 'I was telling him and his missus comes down and says someone's been through the whole house, turning out drawers, opening cupboards – must have been when the trouble all started.'

'Did they take anything?'

'Not a thing! She was quite put out – left her jewel-box and everything. Said it was like her rings weren't good enough!'

'She's a fool,' said Sarah Tanner, distractedly. 'I've seen them, they're all paste. Never mind that. It's not her blessed rings they're after.'

'Never mind?' said the old man. 'After I stands here not knowing whether you're alive or dead! And you tell us not to mind! Ain't you going to tell us what happened? Did you catch up with him?'

'After a fashion.'

'Who was it then?'

'It was just who I thought – the horse-meat boy – and I met his little friends. They call themselves the "Brass Band". I think they fancy they're swell mobsmen. Lord! None of them hardly old enough to strop a razor.'

'That don't mean nothing, missus. A boy that age can have the devil in him, mark my words.'

'You sound like you speak from experience, Ralph.'

'Well, here we are, anyhow,' muttered the waiter, changing the subject as they came back to the New Dining and Coffee Rooms. 'Here – you said you had an idea what this is all about, didn't you?'

'Maybe,' she replied. And, without another word, she walked briskly indoors. The coffee-house itself was still empty, and Norah Smallwood stood alone behind the counter.

'What's going on, then?' she asked her employer. 'Tell us!'

'Have we got any bacon left?' said Mrs. Tanner, ignoring the question.

'Bacon?' said Norah, rather confused. 'Are you hungry?'

'Have we got any left?' persisted Mrs. Tanner. 'From Sanders?'

'There's a good two pound of it in the larder,' replied Norah, perplexed. 'Seeing as how no-one's eating it.'

'Well, that may do,' said Mrs. Tanner and proceeded towards the back of the shop, and Mrs. Hinchley's larder – a small cupboard adjoining the kitchen. Ralph Grundy and Norah Smallwood followed close behind, watching with bemused interest as their employer retrieved the bacon, gently pulling it from its paper, and laying it upon the wooden shelf.

'This ain't about bacon?' said the old man, incredulously.

'Not quite,' said Mrs. Tanner, taking the paper and walking back into the shop, holding it up to the orange glow of the oil-lamp. 'Yes, there you are – that's a decent hand, I'll swear it. Smudged and faint, true, but it's still there.'

'Hang on, missus, are you saying it's the wrappers they're after?'

'Yes, I believe I am,' said Sarah Tanner. 'And first thing tomorrow, we ask George Sanders where he gets his waste paper.'

CHAPTER FIVE

The morning after the horse-meat riot, Sarah Tanner found the butcher's premises filled with customers. Some, present the previous night, had determined to show their sincere repentance via the purchase of half a pound of germans. Others, who had missed the excitement entirely, wanted to hear the fullest particulars from the wronged man. In short, the residents of Leather Lane were not the sort to bear a grudge; and if George Sanders was happy to say nothing about the damage to his cellar doors, his livelihood and his reputation, they would condescend to renew their patronage. The butcher, therefore, having given the matter some thought, played his part and laughed the matter off. In fact, he was so successful in renewing relations with his customers, that Mrs. Tanner was obliged to wait a full half-hour before she found him on his own.

'Well, things seem to have improved,' she said, looking round the shop.

'Ah, it's you, missus,' said the butcher, picking up a mop that he kept to clean the stone floor. 'I ain't saying. I suppose a fellow should count himself lucky; but the wife swears she won't set foot down here again, and Lord knows how much trade I've lost.'

'I'm sorry to hear that.'

'Well, what's done is done. I hope last night was an end to it. To tell the truth, after that treatment, I'd throw it all in for tuppence. But I suppose a fellow must make his living or he'll starve.'

'I gather you were robbed last night too.'

'Robbed?' said the butcher, scratching his head. 'Ah, Grundy said you'd seen someone on the tiles. There was someone here all right – turned us inside out. Only we weren't robbed of nothing; I checked this morning to be double sure. Queer, ain't it? Did you see his face?'

'Ah. No, I didn't, I'm afraid. But I've half an idea what he was after.'

'Well, that's still twice as much as I do, missus.'

'Tell me,' she went on, 'did you hear about what happened at York's last week?'

'York? The fellow who bought all his blasted cheese?' asked the butcher. 'I did that! So did my missus, more's the pity!'

'How do you mean?'

'The very same fellow came in here; it was the same day, I reckon. I sent him packing – thought it was all some gent's idea of a prank. I expect he got his meat somewhere else. Sounds like I lost twenty pound into the bargain. My missus, well, she weren't happy.'

'I don't think he was after the meat,' said Mrs. Tanner. 'I think it was the paper.'

'The paper?' said the butcher, uncomprehending.

'Where do you get your wrapping from?'

'Well, I get it here and there,' said the butcher, a little evasively.

'You can be honest with me, Mr. Sanders,' she said, in a confidential tone.

'To tell the truth, missus,' said the butcher, after a

37

short pause, 'two weeks back, I bought a load off a young lad who came round. He only wanted one and six for ten pound of it; good paper too; I couldn't refuse him.'

She raised her eye-brows. 'Rather a bargain. Didn't you ask where it came from?'

'He told me that he was clerking for a solicitor's down Gray's Inn; that he got the waste as perks.'

'Well, I rather think, Mr. Sanders,' she replied, 'whether he had rights to it or not, there was something in the paper; something that shouldn't have got thrown out. I got thinking when I saw what they did to your shop the other night; they were waiting for you to clear out – that's what all the commotion was about, mark my words. So I went down to York's cheese-shop this morning. They got their paper from the same boy.'

'But then, they only had to ask, missus,' said the butcher, uncertain. 'I wouldn't object to 'em buying the paper back; or taking it, come to that, if it weren't regular and above board. Nor would anyone in their right mind. What was all that business about a "bet" and all?'

'That I can't say,' said Mrs. Tanner. 'Now, tell me, do you have any of it left?'

'I suppose I do,' replied the butcher. 'I'd hardly started using it. Why?'

'Because I intend to find out who's been interfering in your affairs,' said Mrs. Tanner, firmly, 'and in mine.'

A quarter-hour after concluding her conversation with George Sanders, Sarah Tanner stepped cautiously down Feathers Court, Holborn. It was a mean, narrow little road, a half-mile westwards from Leather Lane.

Her caution was not due to the residents – who seemed principally to be ragged children who played happily in the mud-clotted gutters – but the lines of wet washing that hung from one side of the street to the other, upon the first and second storeys. There was always something of the laundry about Feathers Court and she had forgotten that an umbrella was a wise accompaniment to any visit.

Her object was a tumbledown, tired-looking old house, whose roof seemed to sag under its own weight, and whose front door bore only a few cracked flakes of old paint to testify to a once lustrous dark blue coat. The sign above was, however, still legible: *Chas. Merryweather & Son, Bookseller and Law Stationer.*

She tried the door and walked inside.

'Who calls?' demanded a voice, rather theatrically, from inside the front parlour.

'The Queen of Sheba,' answered Mrs. Tanner in turn, and stepped from the hall into the room.

The room was a smoke-filled one, a fug of rich tobacco pungent in the air. The walls for the most part were lined with books; and, to one side, lay a desk upon which piles of documents and letters had been precariously heaped up with little caution. The owner of the premises, a substantial gentleman of ruby complexion and bald pate, sat in a comfortable chair by the fire, though there was no blaze, wrapped in a great winter coat. He rose to greet his visitor.

'Miss Mills!' exclaimed Charles Merryweather. 'We are honoured! I would know that delightful voice anywhere. You've come to cheer an old man, I hope. Please, do take a seat. Would you care for some port?'

Sarah Tanner sat down in the proffered armchair, refusing the drink.

'It's Mrs. Tanner now,' she said. 'And you're not *that* old.'

'I feel it, my dear Mrs. Whoever-you-like. You will always be Sarah Mills to Chas Merryweather, but I will do my utmost to remember. Pray, forgive the coat – I have felt cold all spring. The perils of being a humble scribe, I fear. One simply does not exercise the limbs with sufficient vigour; the vital fluids become sluggish and grudging. Now, do remind me, how long has it been? When did we last meet?'

'A year ago. You know it full well.'

'Ah yes, Mr. Ferntower and his daughter. I heard how that turned out, my dear, remarkable! But now a twelvemonth has passed and we have lived as distant to one another as if you were the Antipodes and I the Arctic – although the rooms in this wretched hovel come close in temperature.'

'You could light a fire.'

'On the third day of May! During the hours of daylight! I am not made of gold, my dear. Still, you are here now. What news do you bring?'

'My little shop is open again,' replied Mrs. Tanner. 'You must pay us a visit; there's always a good meal waiting for you, if you care to have it.'

'Ah! The coffee-house! I heard that little story too. The phoenix from the ashes! But, my dear, do you serve venison?'

'No,' she replied with a smile.

'Fillet of beef?'

'No.'

'Then, with regret, I must humbly decline your generosity. You know I have a very particular consti-tution; very particular. Now, let us cease this chatter

– charming though it is – I am sure you have a purpose. I have never known you to pay morning calls without a purpose.'

'A favour, Charlie. Although, I can pay a shilling or two, if you like.'

'That would be most agreeable,' replied Mr. Merryweather. 'But how might I oblige?'

'I've had some trouble at the shop. A gang of boys who think they're flash.'

'I'm sure you're capable of setting them straight, my dear,' said Mr. Merryweather, with a smile.

'They're not local; they call themselves the "Brass Band". I was wondering whether you'd heard of them.'

'Not that I recall. But I can make discreet inquiries.'

'If you would. And there's another matter,' said Mrs. Tanner, pulling a folded sheet of paper from her dress's pocket, and handing it to Merryweather. 'Probably part and parcel, in fact.'

'What's this, my dear?' said Merryweather, with a rather affected sniff. 'Why, I do believe it smells of bacon grease.'

'Most likely. It's been sitting in the back of a butcher's for two weeks. But it's from a lawyer's office, probably Gray's Inn or thereabouts. I want to know which one.'

Mr. Merryweather peered at the weathered-looking document and laughed. 'Sarah, forgive me, I know there are gentlemen at Greenwich Fair who claim to divine a young man's intentions from his scribble, but I'm not an astrologer; and you are not some love-sick kitchen-maid.'

'I never said you were. If you read it properly, there's half-a-dozen names in there – I can't make it all out, but it sounds like part of a suit; maybe something that got to Chancery. If someone from

41

the court were to look at it, they might well know the parties—'

'And their lawyers,' interrupted Mr. Merryweather. 'Yes, you're quite right, of course. I always said you were an intelligent woman, Sarah.'

'You speak like we're a rarity, Charlie.'

'It's a rare and precious gift, my dear, in either sex. Now, as to the small matter of remuneration?'

'Two bob?'

'Call it three, my dear? And then maybe I can start a fire tomorrow.'

Sarah Tanner smiled ruefully, taking her purse from her pocket. 'Well, I wouldn't want you to freeze to death.'

'I am most glad to hear it,' said Charles Merryweather, taking the money.

⬤

It was a little before mid-day when Sarah Tanner returned to the New Dining and Coffee Rooms. She was pleased to note that there were several plates of food before diners in the little booths, and the shop seemed almost as busy as it had done a few days previously. Before she could say a word, however, Norah Smallwood ran forward, and pushed an envelope into her hands.

'A letter came for you,' said the waitress, excitedly.

Although written correspondence to the coffee-house was uncommon, Mrs. Tanner wondered what could prompt such unchecked enthusiasm. But then she looked down at the fine Manila envelope, and recognised the precise, rather elegant hand that had written the address.

'It's from *him*, ain't it?' said Norah. 'After all this time!'

She trifled with the idea of putting the envelope aside, and affecting disinterest, promising to read it later; she could picture the open-mouthed look upon Norah's face. Instead, with a nod to Ralph Grundy, she made no excuse for absenting herself from the shop, and went directly to her room. She could no more put the letter in her pocket than a burning coal.

She opened it with hurried, nervous fingers and read the contents.

The Reform Club,
Pall Mall
3rd May

Dear Sarah,

After all that has passed between us, I hardly know in what manner to begin this letter. We have both made a promise that we should not interfere in the other's future happiness. I have steadfastly kept my side of the bargain this past year, and you have kept yours.

Nonetheless, you acknowledged yourself in my debt after I assisted you at Avery Row. Moreover, if you recall, you placed yourself in the position of an 'old friend' when you came to *me* for aid. It is upon just such a footing that I write to you now.

To be brief, I seek your practical help – help which I fear no other can provide – in a peculiar and delicate situation.

Perhaps it is foolish of me to ask for your assistance couched in such terms? I hesitate to attempt to renew our connection. You must know of my changed domestic circumstances; and I am sure that will not help my cause. At least, I should add,

43

the matter does not concern my wife – please do not consider me so insensible to your sentiments.

If you cannot or will not reply, I shall understand your forbearance.

Otherwise you may write to me at the Reform.

Yours,

    Arthur DeSalle

Sarah Tanner stared at the letter. She read it a second, then a third time. The mere sight of the handwriting of her former lover brought back a flood of memories.

Then, abruptly, she crumpled it between her fingers.

'"Please do not consider me so insensible to your sentiments"!' she exclaimed to herself. 'How very kind!'

CHAPTER SIX

A second letter arrived at the New Dining and Coffee Rooms in the afternoon post of the following day. Norah Smallwood was visibly disappointed to note that its author – if the tatty and crumpled envelope was any indication – was not Arthur DeSalle. Ralph Grundy was overheard to remark that 'something was up', declaring that he 'had a nose for it'. Mrs. Tanner, for her part, took the same precaution of retiring to her room before reading the letter's contents.

Charles F. Merryweather, Esq.,
13 Feathers Court,
Holborn
4th May

My dearest Sarah,
    (May I address you thus? I trust there is no need for stifling formality in our correspondence. No, we know each other too well for that, do we not?)
    You have entrusted me with two inquiries which, I am glad to report, have not proved unduly onerous.
    Let us begin with the 'Brass Band'. I must write

that I am grateful that I have never made the acquaintance of these young gentlemen; and I would advise you – if you pardon my presumption – to give them, in the nautical idiom, a 'wide berth'. I cannot speak for the origin of their *nom de guerre*, but they are not of a musical bent. I am informed, by one who knows, that they are Lambeth boys, natives of The Walk; an honest a gang of young roughs as you might hope to meet. A couple are considered 'prime' amongst the local fraternity; good for fanlight jumping and house-cracking – one such goes by the name of Cranks and may be considered their 'king'. For the most part, however, they are common rampers – preying upon inebriates with bludgeon or garrotte – such is their reputation, at least. Their 'ground' is Lambeth and Vauxhall, and they are known to frequent the Gardens. I am led to believe that three or four of them presently reside in Horsemonger Lane gaol. Unfortunately, The Walk breeds idle youths in sufficient quantity for their number rarely to be much depleted.

I trust that is sufficient? I cannot account for their presence in the Lane.

Your second request, the item bearing an unpalatable odour, was a little more difficult. Fortunately, I was able to consult an old friend familiar with the Lord Chancellor's court. Your guess was quite correct: a suit in Chancery. It was a case, however, which came to a settlement some years ago (something of a phenomenon in that infamous hall of justice): a trivial matter of a small inheritance, no more than a few hundred, to a man-servant's widow, tied up in a quarrel over an estate, disputed, but finally paid in full.

Now, my dear, how can this be of interest to you? I cannot imagine!

You asked most particularly for the lawyers. Very well, I have not failed you. A certain Mr. Tinnams of Guildford, Surrey, for the widow; a Mr. Wilmot of Dovey's Chambers, Theobald's Road, Gray's Inn, for the family.

Now, I have laid the facts before you and I do not think you can find fault with my efforts. I will not ask that you vouchsafe your purpose in discovering this peculiar information – nor how it pertains to the Lambeth roughs – but if I can offer any further assistance, I hope you will inquire of,

Your old friend and warm admirer,
Charles Fairview Merryweather

Sarah Tanner put the letter down and stared idly out of the bedroom window. Then, at last, coming to a decision, she walked over to the wardrobe beside her bed, and flicked through the half-dozen dresses inside. None were particularly extravagant in cloth or trimming, but she selected a demure black silk that would not be unsuited to a respectable widow subsisting upon a modest income.

It would, she decided, give a better impression.

It was a short walk from Leather Lane to Dovey's Chambers, the latter being situated upon the corner of Theobald's Road and Lamb's Conduit Street, a couple of hundred yards beyond the legal warren of nearby Gray's Inn. The building itself was an unpretentious classical affair of three storeys, with a small but neat iron-railed area descending to the basement, and a black-painted front door boasting both white stucco pilasters and a matching pediment of modest dimensions. Sarah Tanner noted four bell-pulls by the entrance, but found that none were marked.

She rang the topmost and waited.

The distant tinkling of the bell was answered, in due course, by a care-worn functionary of an indiscriminate sort. Too old to be an errand boy; too stout to be a footman; too ignorant to be a clerk; a man of middling years. A man of little ambition, she imagined, who 'did' for the various residents of Dovey's Chambers.

'Which office?' he said bluntly, opening the door, and surveying his female visitor with a gimlet eye.

'Is there more than one?'

'Several.'

'Mr. Wilmot's, if you please,' she replied. 'I do not have an appointment. Do you think he might spare me a moment?'

The functionary seemed to smile the briefest of smiles, as if finding the question somehow amusing.

'A moment? Oh, I couldn't say, ma'am. I ain't the man to ask. But I'll take you up to his clerk, if you like.'

Mrs. Tanner agreed to the proposition and the functionary obliged. She followed him upstairs three flights, to the upper floor of the building. There, she was directed to a varnished oak door, bearing a brass-plate with the name *J. Wilmot, Attorney and Solicitor*. The man knocked in a business-like manner, opened the door and, with his realm of influence terminating at the doorway, he immediately turned and began to descend the stairs.

The office was a plain room, the walls panelled, with two rather dirty sash windows providing only a

modicum of daylight. The decoration was of a practical nature – a clock which hung between the two
windows; a musty bookcase of legal knowledge that
looked as if it had been untouched for some years;
and sundry wooden cabinets that filled almost an entire
wall. There were two workers present: a clerk in his
early twenties, a handsome, fresh-faced young man
who sat by the window, guarding his master's inner
chamber; and another youth, somewhat younger,
hunched over a smaller desk, upon the opposite side
of the room. The first clerk raised his head from his
work and hurriedly got down from the tall stool upon
which he was perched.

'May I be of some service, ma'am?'

Mrs. Tanner smiled politely, but there was something about the second clerk, who remained at his
seat, that drew her attention. A flash of recognition
struck her, as the young man looked up from his
work. She knew his face: it was the boy who had
warned her of the falling slate the night before last,
in Brooke's Market. For his part, the boy hurriedly
turned his face away, crouching nervously over the
papers before him.

The first clerk, perhaps noticing her abstraction,
repeated his question.

'Ma'am? How can I assist you?'

Mrs. Tanner collected her thoughts. 'I am sorry –
you must forgive me, Mr. —'

'Biggs, ma'am.'

'You must forgive me, Mr. Biggs. I have come to
seek an interview with your employer.'

'You do not have an appointment with Mr. Wilmot,
ma'am?'

'No, I regret I do not.'

'He does not receive callers without appointments

as a rule, ma'am. May I inquire as to the matter you wish to discuss with him?'

'I am afraid not,' replied Mrs. Tanner. 'You may tell him that it is most pressing; and that it is confidential.'

The clerk was about to reply, when disturbed by an indistinct noise from the inner office. He cleared his throat and began again.

'Unfortunately, I am afraid Mr. Wilmot is . . .'

Here, the clerk stammered, a flush of embarrassment suffusing his face. For the noise from the inner office became most audible: loud snoring.

'I am afraid,' persisted the clerk, 'Mr. Wilmot is indisposed this afternoon.'

Sarah Tanner glanced at the clerk. Not only was the sound of snoring now quite obvious, but, as a gust of wind rattled the sash windows, she could suddenly smell the distinct aroma of brandy wafting from the same direction. She smiled politely.

'I see. Perhaps I might come back later?'

'I'd suggest tomorrow morning, ma'am,' replied the clerk, with a renewed blush on his cheeks. 'Mornings are preferable – though I cannot promise he will see you.'

'I see,' said Mrs. Tanner. 'Well, I am afraid I do not have a card, but you may say "Mrs. Tanner" called. And I shall call again, rest assured.'

'If you like, ma'am,' replied the clerk, plainly a little curious about the woman before him. 'I will pass on the message.'

Sarah Tanner nodded and bid the clerk good day. The other clerk – the boy she had seen in Brooke's Market – did not so much as glance in her direction, though she watched him closely as she turned to leave.

She stopped upon the landing, then descended the

stairs. By the time she had reached the front door, she had had an idea.

———

It was at dusk, later that day, when Sarah Tanner returned to the corner of Lamb's Conduit Street and Theobald's Road. She had, however, undergone something of a transformation in the meantime. Gone was the respectable black dress and in its place was a mottled mauve garment of faded cotton, visible beneath a tatty woollen shawl, wrapped around her head and shoulders, artfully concealing her face. She clutched in her hand a few sprigs of dry lavender, and could easily have passed for a flower-girl. The only flaw in her simple disguise was that she did not importune any passer-by but merely loitered upon the corner, occasionally moving a little further along the road, and then back again. All the while, she kept a close watch upon Dovey's Chambers.

As night fell, the building began to empty. There was no universal rush, for each office within belonged to a different master; and each believed to a greater or lesser degree in expenditure upon gas or candles, to carry work onwards into the hours of twilight. Nonetheless, Mrs. Tanner was rewarded, after half an hour or so of waiting, by the appearance of the solicitor's young clerk, who quit the front door by himself, turned up his collar, and began to walk briskly eastwards. She waited for him to progress a few yards along the road, then followed.

The boy's route took him along the northern border of Gray's Inn, in the direction of Leather Lane. For a while, she thought that he might actually walk down Liquorpond Street and past the very door of the New Dining and Coffee Rooms. Instead, he turned south, going along Portpool Lane and Hatton Wall, then down the sloping lane that led to Clerkenwell Green.

It was on the Green – 'green' in name only, having long since been paved and cobbled by the City of London – that the boy paused, seemingly distracted by the aroma of green-peas and hot eels that emanated from a stall upon the busy road-side. There were already a half-dozen men and boys standing around the stall-keeper, spooning pieces of the fish from chipped cups, filled with salty liquor. As the clerk dipped into his pocket, to estimate what morsels he might afford for his supper, Mrs. Tanner walked up beside him, lowering her shawl about her shoulders.

'Hungry?' she said, casually.

The boy, startled, gazed at his interrogator. There was no mistaking the look of anxiety upon his face, as he recognised her. She wondered whether he was contemplating running.

'What if I am? What do you mean, following us here?' he said at last, with rather unconvincing bravado.

'I don't mean you any harm, if that's what you think,' she replied. 'But I expect you saw me at your office this afternoon?'

'Well, what if I did?'

'I'll bet you were worried what I might say.'

'No, I weren't. What do I care?'

Sarah Tanner fought hard to restrain a smile; there was something almost comical in the youth's ripostes. He had none of Jem Cranks's swagger or menace; there was something pathetic in his efforts at self-assurance; an unconvincing quaver in his voice which utterly belied his words.

'Here,' she continued, nodding towards the stall, 'let me get you something and we can have a little talk. I don't suppose it can do you any harm to hear me out?'

The boy contemplated the offer. The scent of peppered vinegar hung heavy in the air.

'All right,' he said.

CHAPTER SEVEN

Sarah Tanner looked over her shoulder, whilst the eel-man, resplendent in a white hat wreathed in black crape, scooped two cups from his rather rusty-looking fish-kettle. She had half expected the young clerk to bolt, as soon as her back was turned. Instead, he sat upon the steps of the nearby Session House, watching her, but looking decidedly ill-at-ease.

Reassured that her money would not be entirely wasted, she paid the street-seller a penny and walked over to the boy, sitting down beside him on the court steps. He accepted the cup of eels and spoon with little grace, taking it warily from her hand, without a word of gratitude, as if he feared it might be poisoned.

'What's your name?' she asked, as the boy teased a piece of meat from the liquor.

'What's it to you?'

'Come, be civil at least. You know I can find it out. I only have to inquire at the office.'

The boy reflected on the proposition, and seemed to concede its logic.

'Charlie. Charlie Grubb.'

'Well, I have a theory, Charlie,' continued Mrs. Tanner, 'about what you've been up to.'

The boy began to protest, but she stifled his complaint with a dismissive wave of her hand.

'Hear me out. If I wanted to go to the Peelers, I would have done it already. Now, here's how I see it. I think, Charlie, that, a while back, you started going through your master's papers when he was "indisposed" or out of the office. Perhaps you were just curious; perhaps you were looking for something, I don't know. I think you found some of those drawers hadn't been opened for years. You thought it was a terrible shame, all that old paper going to waste.'

Charlie Grubb looked distinctly shame-faced, but said nothing.

'So, by-and-by, you took a good pile of it and hawked that old paper round Leather Lane and thereabouts. It's on your way home, isn't it? You said you had it as perks, and a couple of shops took it off your hands, no questions, because it was cheap as anything.'

Charlie Grubb shrugged, avoiding her gaze.

'But then something happened. Maybe that old drawer needed opening again; and perhaps those scraps of paper weren't so unimportant after all. So your master set out to get them back, and keep it dark; he didn't want anyone to know what had happened. So he made up a ridiculous story about a bet – went round trying to buy up every article in a certain cheesemonger's and a certain butcher's. One obliged; one didn't. Am I right so far, Charlie?'

'That's a good story, if it suits you,' muttered the boy.

'Isn't it?' said Mrs. Tanner. 'But what I don't quite understand is how a gang of Lambeth roughs got dragged into it.'

Charlie Grubb shrugged.

'You see, I know a thing or two about your pals;

none of it that appealing. Now, why does a respectable solicitor use boys like that? That's what I don't twig, Charlie; and, for that matter, why would a junior clerk keep company with them, either? And, while I'm at it, why would your Mr. Wilmot keep you on? Or doesn't he know nothing about it? Are your pals just helping you to put things right?'

'I don't know why you're asking me,' said the boy.

'Because whatever I say *is* just a story, until you tell me otherwise,' said Mrs. Tanner. 'And because I don't think you're as bad as all that.'

'How do you mean?'

'If you were, you wouldn't have shouted out when your pal Cranks tried to dash my brains out with that tile.'

The boy shrugged again.

'Well, if you won't talk, then I suppose I'll have to ask your old man. What's he like, your Mr. Wilmot?'

'Don't!' exclaimed the boy, abruptly turning to face his interlocutor.

'Why shouldn't I? Are you in enough trouble already, is that it?'

Charlie Grubb looked particularly flustered.

'Why do you have to stick your beak in, anyway?!' he shouted, standing up. There were almost tears in his eyes. 'It's no bleedin' business of yours, is it?'

'Do you think it's right, then,' she replied calmly, 'what your pals have done? Those rumours about horse-meat nearly got George Sanders killed. And I didn't come out of it much better, either.'

'That ain't my look-out, is it?'

Sarah Tanner sighed. 'Look, if you are in trouble, Charlie, I might be able to help. You only have to tell me what's going on.'

'I don't need your help,' said the boy. 'I don't need help from no-one.'

'Then I'll have to talk to Mr. Wilmot, won't I?'

'Go on then, see if I care! You can go to hell!'

Charlie Grubb spat on the ground and stalked off, towards the northern part of the Green. Sarah Tanner, for her part, frowned, but let him go, watching him disappear from view amongst the passers-by. She put the eels to one side – for there was something a little too salty about them for her liking – got up from the step, and, with a sigh, turned back in the direction of Leather Lane.

'I've been thinking, missus,' said Ralph Grundy, some hours later, as he helped his employer edge the New Dining and Coffee Rooms' shutters into place. 'It don't quite make sense to me.'

'What?' replied Mrs. Tanner.

'I mean, the boy sold the paper, that's plain enough. But why should his master keep it quiet? He could have the boy before a magistrate, soon as he liked. And why use this gang of boys to get the stuff back?'

'I can guess at the former,' she replied, slotting the final bolt into place. 'A lawyer is paid to keep things discreet, to keep secrets; it would not impress Mr. Wilmot's clients very favourably if his name appeared in the "Police" column of *The Times*.'

'Ah, but he could still dismiss the boy, couldn't he?' said the old man.

'You might think so.'

'And what about your friend Cranks and his little gang?' continued Ralph.

'Odd company for a respectable solicitor, certainly.'

'So you think he might not be so straight as all that?'

'At present, Ralph, the only thing I know for certain is that Mr. Wilmot drinks to excess in the afternoon. In that, he's probably no worse than half his profession. Maybe he knows nothing about what's been going on – except . . . who went round to York's and bought all his cheeses? It wasn't one of Cranks's little cronies.'

'But I expect you'll make inquiries about Wilmot?'

'I already have done,' she replied, as her interlocutor slipped back inside the shop, grabbed his hat and coat, and returned outside. 'And I will judge for myself tomorrow, when I see him.'

'Fair enough,' returned the old man, but in rather gloomy tones.

'Is there something wrong?' she asked.

'If I didn't know better, missus,' replied Ralph, 'I'd swear, you go looking for trouble.'

'I didn't go looking for Master Cranks.'

'No, that's true enough. But no-one asked you to play detective again neither. You should open an Inquiry Office. Give what's his name – Field – a run for his money.'

Sarah Tanner smiled. 'I just don't like people interfering with my affairs.'

'But you're happy enough to interfere with theirs? I'm just saying, missus, don't get mixed up in something that needn't concern you. Remember what happened last time.'

'Good night, Ralph.'

'Aye, well, I know how much heed you pays to my advice, missus, don't you fret.'

And, with those words, Ralph Grundy put on his hat with an emphatic tug at the brim, and walked off towards his lodgings.

Mrs. Tanner, meanwhile, went back indoors, and locked the shop. Upon retiring upstairs, she was not entirely surprised – for it was not unusual – to find Norah Smallwood still awake and dressed, loitering on the landing by her bedroom door.

'What was old bag-o'-bones going on about?' asked Norah.

'He thinks I should drop this solicitor business.'

'Maybe you should,' said Norah.

'Do I get a lecture from both of you? Is that it?'

'No,' said Norah, 'wouldn't be my place, would it? I was just going to ask if you'd sent a letter back yet.'

'A letter back?'

'To *you-know-who*.'

'If you mean Arthur, then I can tell you that I haven't, and I don't intend to. Lord! I wouldn't have told you anything about it, if I knew you'd harp on so!'

'Only it's a bit peculiar you're troubling yourself over all this, but when someone particular – who was very particular – asks you for help . . .'

'Norah, I have not given a thought to Arthur DeSalle for God knows how long. Now, if you please . . .'

'I know,' replied Norah Smallwood, sullenly. '"Go to bed." I'm only saying.'

'You needn't say anything at all,' said Mrs. Tanner, firmly. 'And even if you don't want any sleep tonight, I do.'

⁓

Sarah Tanner sat at her dressing-table by the light of her oil-lamp, turned down so that Norah Smallwood might not notice its light beneath her bedoom door. Before her lay Arthur DeSalle's letter, a blank sheet of paper, a pen and ink.

She wrote her name. Then her address. Then she began with 'Dear Mr. DeSalle'.

After five minutes of sitting, staring at the blank sheet, she put down her pen.

CHAPTER EIGHT

——

It was half-past nine on the following morning when Sarah Tanner walked up to the door of Dovey's Chambers. Dressed in honest black, she rang the same bell as she had done the previous day. She did not hear it ring, since any sound from within was drowned out by the passing of a drayman's waggon. Nonetheless, the door eventually opened, and she found herself once more at the mercy of the same dour functionary who had greeted her upon her first visit.

'I have an appointment with Mr. Wilmot,' she said, without waiting for preliminaries.

'Follow me,' he replied, apparently quite grateful to be spared the onerous duty of conversation. She did as instructed. As they reached the top landing, however, the man stopped abruptly.

'Looks like you'll have to wait, ma'am,' he said drily, then turned and began to traipse back down the stairs.

The cause was the figure of Mr. Biggs – the elder of the two clerks – standing in his coat, outside his own office door, with his hat in hand. Mr. Biggs bowed politely.

'I'm sorry, ma'am. I'm afraid my master is a little

delayed this morning and so we are not yet able to receive you. I did, however, inform him of your visit yesterday.'

'Thank you for that, in any case.'

'He's normally regular as clockwork, ma'am,' said the clerk, with an insistence which somehow made his listener doubt his veracity. 'Perhaps if you were to come back in an hour or so?'

'Oh, I'd prefer to wait, Mr. Biggs, if I may.'

'As you like, ma'am,' replied the clerk, obligingly enough, though he shuffled rather awkwardly from one foot to the other as he spoke. Mrs. Tanner wondered how often he had to contrive an excuse for his master.

'Is your young colleague not present either?' she asked.

'My colleague?' said Mr. Biggs, plainly a little surprised at the question. 'No, ma'am, I can't say he is.'

She nodded. Any further conversation was interrupted by footsteps upon the stairs, and the presence of a gentleman whom she took to be Mr. Wilmot, if only from the slightly hunched and nervous posture of supplication which his clerk immediately adopted.

Mr. Wilmot himself was a tall, thin-faced man of some sixty or so years, with a balding head, distinguished by two unappealing tufts of thin grey hair about his ears. If he had a deep affection for liquor, Mrs. Tanner decided, it was not the sort that provoked merriment and gave rise to red-cheeked jollity; rather, it was the sort that encouraged a poisonous, livid pallor in the complexion, and a face that would be more suited to an undertaker.

'Good morning, sir. This is the lady I was telling

you about, sir,' said Biggs hurriedly, by way of introduction, 'Mrs. Tanner.'

Sarah Tanner inclined her head. Mr. Wilmot, in turn, gave a slight bow, yet seemed to gaze past her into the middle distance. There was a distinct aroma of alcohol that clung to the solicitor's dowdy black suit, and loitered on his breath.

'I understand there is some confidential matter we must discuss, ma'am,' said Mr. Wilmot, with little sign of interest.

'If you can spare me a few minutes of your time, sir.'

'Naturally, ma'am,' replied the solicitor. 'One moment.'

It took more than a moment for the lawyer to unlock the door, as his hands seemed determined to fumble with the key. Nonetheless, Mr. Wilmot then walked briskly into his outer office, ignoring any politeness due to his visitor, who was escorted inside by the young clerk.

'Grubb is late?' said Mr. Wilmot, barely pausing in his tracks.

'Yes, sir,' replied the clerk.

'Unfortunate. Well, Mrs. Tanner,' continued the lawyer, 'I suppose you had better speak to me, if you must. If you'd care to step inside my office?'

She nodded, and stepped inside the solicitor's inner sanctum, as he held the door open.

It was a large room, in proportion to the outer chamber, with two identical sashes upon the right-hand side, begrimed with the dust and soot of the street below. It differed, however, in several ways: it smelt decidedly more strongly of tobacco and spirits; it boasted shelves of legal volumes, filling an entire wall, with fine gilt titles etched into their spines; there was a grandfather clock in one corner; a heavy Turkey carpet covering most of the floor; and last, but most importantly, a substantial pedestal desk of dark mahogany.

Sarah Tanner, however, noticed hardly any of these details, except for the desk. For, slumped upon its surface was the body of Mr. Wilmot's junior clerk, Charlie Grubb, his face turned to one side; his hands were spread in front of him, his lifeless eyes staring at the wall.

It was quite clear that the boy was dead: his skin was white and bloodless as marble. The green leather inlay of the desk-top, meanwhile, was stained rusty brown, pooled about the spot where his neck had been sliced open with a sharp blade – the same bloodied razor that lay beside his hand.

'Good God!' exclaimed the lawyer.

She looked at Wilmot. His shock seemed as real as her own; he stood quite rooted to the spot. It was only when he recollected the presence of his visitor that he seemed to recover his senses.

'Please, ma'am, for pity's sake, come away,' said Mr. Wilmot, ushering her back into the ante-chamber.

She followed without demur, not looking back. Wilmot closed the office door firmly behind him.

'What are we to do?' said Wilmot, though he addressed no-one in particular.

Mrs. Tanner hardly heard him.

'Whatever is it, sir?' asked the lawyer's clerk.

'Grubb has done away with himself – and the young fool has done it in my office!'

What was it he said?

'We must call the police, sir,' said Biggs.

That was it.

It's no bleedin' business of yours, is it?

The boy had told her, but she had not listened.

Ralph and Norah had said much the same.

And now the boy was dead.

CHAPTER NINE

Sarah Tanner watched the detective – an inspector by the name of Burton – as he wandered around the outer office, having completed his study of the inner chamber and the body of the deceased clerk. The policeman was a man of average height, in an ordinary tweed suit, his appearance distinguished by a fulsome head of ginger hair, and a rather unruly beard, which, at intervals, he had a tendency to stroke methodically with his hand. Unfortunately, if his intention was to convey mental absorption, the effort failed: to the casual onlooker, it seemed more like a nervous tic. Indeed, there was something rather aimless in his inspection of every nook and corner of the room. Mrs. Tanner could not help but wonder whether Scotland Yard happened to have its best men occupied elsewhere. If so, she was grateful for it: for there were at least two serving members of the Detective Branch with whom she already had a passing acquaintance; an acquaintance which she was in no great hurry to renew.

At length the policeman gave up upon his surroundings, and walked over to where Mrs. Tanner was seated, sipping from a glass of hastily procured brandy, intended to calm her nerves.

'A dreadful affair, ma'am,' intoned the detective.

'Awful,' added Mr. Wilmot, who stood upon the opposite side of the room, his head turned away, looking through the window at the street below.

'Quite,' replied Mrs. Tanner.

'You came to see Mr. Wilmot on some private matter, I gather?'

Mrs. Tanner weighed her options, looking at the solicitor. But Mr. Wilmot did not turn his face towards her.

'Yes,' she replied. 'A difficult and confidential matter – a relative whose will . . .'

'You need not explain, ma'am,' said Burton, graciously. 'I have no wish to pry, I am sure. Indeed, I believe I shall ask the coroner if you might be spared the inquest; I cannot see any need to burden you with further distress, given the circumstances; it all seems quite straightforward.'

'Straightforward, sir?'

'Well, yes, ma'am,' replied the inspector, puzzled by the tone of interrogation in Mrs. Tanner's voice. 'The unfortunate youth left a note upon the desk. It seems quite clear he killed himself in a fit of despair.'

'A note? What did it say?'

'I hardly think you need trouble yourself—'

'If the poor boy gave any explanation or excuse for his horrible deed, sir,' said Mrs. Tanner, firmly, 'then I should imagine that I have the misfortune to be the party most entitled to hear it.'

'Well,' said Burton, a little taken aback, 'if you wish it, ma'am.' He took a piece of folded paper from his pocket. 'He had little to say for himself, I'm afraid,' continued the policeman. '"Sir, please forgive me for what I have done. I meant no harm by it; and did not profit much."'

'Whatever had he done?' she asked, looking carefully at the solicitor – but Mr. Wilmot's gaze remained resolutely directed to the street.

'That I can't say at present, ma'am,' replied the detective. 'Something will turn up, I am sure. Do you keep cash upon the premises, sir?'

Mr. Wilmot looked up. 'No, Inspector, I can't say that I do.'

'Well,' continued Burton, regardless, 'it's generally some form of thieving with these boys. I expect his conscience got the better of him in the end.'

'A boy does not cut his own throat with an attack of conscience,' said Mrs. Tanner.

'Well, of course, I expect his mind was disturbed as well, ma'am,' added Burton, his tone somewhat patronising. 'That stands to reason.'

'I expect it does,' she replied, all the while watching Charlie Grubb's employer.

But the solicitor's blank expression gave nothing away.

An hour after her departure from Dovey's Chambers, Sarah Tanner sat in the tap-room of the Bottle of Hay, nursing a restorative gin-and-bitters. It was an old-fashioned public-house, lit by oil-lamps at night, but rather dingy and dusty by day. Any hint of sunlight only served to throw into relief the treacly rings of porter stains upon the pewter-covered bar, and the miserly amount of sawdust allotted to the stone-flagged floor. No more than a minute or two's walk from the New Dining and Coffee Rooms, it was widely considered the best public on the Lane, and it was the one such establishment which Mrs. Tanner patronised, albeit but rarely. She was accompanied by Ralph

Grundy, who sat beside her, a glass of fourpenny ale in front of him. The old man, having heard his employer's account of the morning, sighed deeply and took a long drain of his liquor.

'A regular bad do, missus, and no mistake,' opined Ralph.

Sarah Tanner looked the old man in the eye. 'I killed him, Ralph.'

'Hold up, missus,' said Ralph, spluttering into his beer. 'Let's not have nonsense like that.'

'It wasn't my hand on the blade,' she continued, 'but it might as well have been.'

'It's not your fault if the boy was a bad lot.'

'You don't understand, Ralph. It was just curiosity – I wanted to know what he was up to. I threatened to tell Wilmot about the papers; I could have just let it be and the wretched boy would still be alive.'

'Aye,' said Ralph, 'well, maybe you could, but that ain't neither here nor there. You didn't make the lad do nothing; sounds to me like he weren't in his right mind – to do something like that.' The old man took another gulp of his drink. 'Anyhow, I suppose we'd better be getting back. I wouldn't leave madam on her own too long, not if I were you.'

Sarah Tanner smiled, albeit half-heartedly. 'Norah will cope, I imagine. I thought you had a little more faith in her these days. Besides, you haven't heard the worst of it.'

'What?' asked the old man, bemused.

'I don't think that he killed himself; not for one minute.'

Ralph Grundy raised his eye-brows. 'Now, missus, I must be getting addled in my old age, because you just told me—'

'Nervous young men don't cut their own throats,

Ralph – not with one clean stroke, anyway – and that's what I saw – one *very* clean stroke. And why was he in the office, for pity's sake? Why there, of all places? What kind of apology was that for his master?'

'I couldn't say,' replied the old man. 'Men do all sorts of things when their heads ain't screwed on tight.'

'Men, possibly. He was only a boy. Besides, there's two things that's puzzled me,' continued Mrs. Tanner. 'Charlie Grubb got hold of some papers he shouldn't have done, and sold them for waste – that seems plain enough. But why would anyone go to such lengths to get them back? And if the boy's master is behind all this, why keep Charlie Grubb as his clerk – after he'd already robbed him? You said as much yourself, yesterday.'

'I did, missus. It sounds like you've got an answer and all.'

'The only one that makes sense – that Wilmot didn't – perhaps still doesn't – have a clue what Charlie got up to. If he's dead drunk often enough, it's quite possible.'

Ralph shook his head. 'I must be addled, missus, because I don't follow. Who else would know that the boy had gone and sold these precious papers in the first place – especially if his nibs didn't even know himself? And who else would be so bleedin' desperate to get hold of them again?'

Sarah Tanner shrugged. 'I can make a guess. It's a wild guess, but all the same. What if – apart from Charlie pilfering paper on his own account – someone else has been dipping in and out of old Wilmot's office when he was too far gone to notice – or, at least, got Charlie doing it for him? He didn't strike me as being that bold or that sharp; too nervous to be a decent thief; but if someone else was involved, someone who put him up to it . . . someone who might be annoyed that he'd gone and sold certain articles for his own profit.'

Ralph nodded his head. 'Ah, I see now, missus. You think it was Cranks who set him up to do it?'

'No, it's hardly in young Cranks's line, Ralph. A mutual friend, though; that might make some sense – a villain all right. Perhaps the same gentleman who visited George Sanders and offered to buy all his meat. There's always secrets in a lawyer's office; and there's some who'll pay good money to get hold of them. Then, let's say, this gentleman hears from Charlie that I'm going to tell the whole thing about the paper – his own stupid little effort at thieving – to Wilmot. Who knows? The police might even get involved . . .'

'And that's why you're blaming yourself, is it?'

'I think Charlie went off somewhere after I saw him yesterday. I think he told someone about what I said. And I think that's the someone who killed him – they knew Wilmot would find out that he'd lost . . . well, Lord knows what . . . much better to cut your losses, blame it on a dead boy; a petty thief; that way no-one asks further questions.'

'Hold up – weren't the door locked?'

'It was. I heard Burton say there was a key in the boy's pocket, too; one that he shouldn't have got his hands on in the first place. But he's a fool if he thinks that means suicide. If Grubb could get hold of one key, then getting another copied wouldn't be too hard.'

'It sounds a bit fanciful to me, missus,' said the old man, after a little reflection.

'There was nothing fanciful about what I saw today, Ralph.'

'You know, as much as anything, I think you enjoy playing detective, missus. I'll swear it.'

Sarah Tanner shook her head. 'It's not that straightforward. If I'm right, then that boy's death wasn't simply just murder.'

'What then?'

'At best, it was a warning; to stop me interfering in whatever game's going on at Wilmot's.'

'And at worst?' said the old man.

'I can expect the same.'

It was one o'clock in the afternoon when Sarah Tanner returned to the New Dining and Coffee Rooms, much to Norah Smallwood's consternation, who complained bitterly that she was 'put upon enough'. Sarah Tanner's reply was cut short, however, by the sight of a customer in the last of the shop's booths. With a curt exchange of words, she dismissed Norah to the kitchen, left Ralph Grundy at the counter, and walked over.

'Sarah, my dear, lovely as ever,' said Charles Merryweather, rising from the bench at the table with a melodramatic flourish of his hand. 'I have come to grace your delightful little eating-house with my presence.'

'Charlie,' she replied, glancing at the empty table. 'Will you take something? A coffee?'

Mr. Merryweather visibly flinched. 'My constitution, my dear – so delicate – quite forbids it.'

'I wasn't expecting to see you.'

'My dear Sarah, you send me a note, I comply instantly; it is my nature – I cannot help it. I am the most obliging creature in the world.'

'I was expecting another letter.'

'Some things are worth bringing in person, my dear. You see, I have made inquiries, as you requested.'

'Go on, then.'

Charles Merryweather smiled. 'Your Mr. Wilmot: he is a respectable man of the law; given to drink in recent years, but nothing else known to his detriment.'

'What about his clients?'

'Ah, well, that is the thing. Very well-to-do, my dear; gentry and even aristocracy. Wilmot's is an old family concern, long-established bonds of trust, *et cetera*, *et cetera*. I gather he has no need for new clients; he rests upon his laurels. Now, I have a list here, that may interest you.'

'A list?'

'Of the respectable families who place their trust in Mr. Wilmot.'

Sarah Tanner took the proferred piece of paper. She instantly knew exactly why Charles Merryweather had come to observe her reaction to his news: the third name upon the list.

DeSalle.

CHAPTER TEN

The coroner's inquest into the death of Charles Grubb was reported in *The Times* some two days later. The 'rash and horrid act' was considered by the jury to be the melancholy end of an unfortunate young man, whilst overwhelmed by temporary insanity. Mr. James Wilmot, his employer of some six months, declared the boy to have been satisfactory in carrying out his duties; moreover, he could not, he affirmed, attribute any particular misdemeanour to the callow youth, and believed the boy's last missive to be the ramblings of a disordered intelligence, most likely fixated upon some trifling peccadillo. The boy had no family: his landlady, one Margaret Maggs (widow), of Plumber's Place, Clerkenwell, spoke for his general good character, and stated that the young man had been 'agitated in his spirits' upon the day of his death. In short, a verdict of suicide was swiftly returned.

Sarah Tanner put down the paper.

'Not to your liking, missus?' said Ralph Grundy, who stood upon the other side of the coffee-house's counter.

'Wilmot said nothing at the inquest,' she replied. 'Either he's a fool or a liar. He must have discovered there are things missing!'

'Maybe he wants to keep it quiet, like you said; won't do his trade any good if word gets out.'

'Maybe.'

'Well, there's an end to it,' said the waiter.

'I cannot get the boy from my mind that easily.'

The old man fell silent for a few moments, then finally spoke.

'I once had a boy that age,' said Ralph, 'though it were a few year ago now. Well, at least, he belonged to my missus.'

'Really? I didn't know you were married, Ralph.'

'Never was, not regular, at the altar, anyhow,' continued the old man. 'It weren't a good match, neither; but I made the best of it and did my damnedest for that boy, even though he weren't my own flesh and blood. But he were a bad'un; and you can't do nothing for them that won't help themselves.'

'What are you suggesting I do, then?'

'All I'm saying is that it's far too late for Charlie Grubb, missus. He didn't thank you for your trouble when he was alive, neither; so what good is worrying on it?'

Sarah Tanner looked back at the old man. 'What happened to your step-son?'

'I don't know all the particulars,' said Ralph Grundy tersely. 'Last I heard he was in Portland, hard labour.'

Mrs. Tanner looked back at the old man quizzically; but, as he seemed disinclined to say more, she let the matter rest and returned to her own thoughts. 'It's still my doing, Ralph – I could have left him alone.'

'Maybe it is, but you can't put it right, missus – not for that boy. You say you should have left it alone – well, there's your lesson!'

Sarah Tanner shook her head. 'No – it's not that simple. Watch the shop.'

'Where are you going?'

'To ask a few questions.'

Ralph Grundy raised his eyes heavenwards.

———

Plumber's Place was a narrow court not five minutes' walk from Clerkenwell Green. There were several signs chalked above doors offering the luxury of 'dry lodgings' but it did not take Mrs. Tanner long to make inquiries and locate the residence of Margaret Maggs, Charlie Grubb's erstwhile landlady. Situated at the end of a row of narrow tenements, the house had a neglected air, with a front step indistinguishable from the muddy pavement around it, and a front door which lay ajar, having shifted arthritically in its hinges at some point in the distant past, doomed never to return to a wholly vertical condition.

Mrs. Maggs, it turned out, held a permanent levée in the large ground-floor room which served as kitchen, dining-room and lounge for her impecunious lodgers. Furnished in a spartan fashion, the room nonetheless boasted two substantial tiled fire-places, one with a cooking-stove and one with merely a small handful of burning coals, above which a boiling copper was suspended. Three tenants were present in the somewhat smoky room – all about forty years of age, rather shabby in appearance – seated at a large deal table provided for their convenience, engaged in a game of cards. The lady herself, meanwhile, sat to one side, beside the fire, with an air of general superintendence. She was a large woman – or, at least, the bulky chocolate-coloured crinoline which she wore did nothing to contradict the evidence of her face, her features being plump, rosy, and rather complacent.

'Mrs. Maggs?' inquired Sarah Tanner.

'I am, my dear,' said Mrs. Maggs, looking at the new arrival with a rather questioning stare, as if to say 'And who might you be?'

'Might I have a word with you in private?'

'In private?' said Mrs. Maggs. 'Why, whatever for? You know, my dear – perhaps I should say it plain – I don't take ladies; we keep a very respectable house for gentlemen.'

'No, I don't need a room,' persisted Mrs. Tanner. 'I wanted to speak with you about one of your lodgers . . . Charlie Grubb.'

'Ah! Poor Charlie!' said the landlady, as if struck by a sudden revelation as to her visitor's intentions. 'Now that's a sad tale, ain't it, gentlemen?' (The gentlemen in question each offered a half-hearted grunt of assent.) 'Well, now I understand you, ma'am. But owing to circumstances of the tragedy and all, and with poor Charlie having been behind in his rent—'

'It's only reasonable,' apostrophised one of the respectable gentlemen.

'It is, sir, you are quite right,' continued Mrs. Maggs, building steam. 'Owing to them facts, I'm charging a shilling.'

'A shilling?'

'Why, to see the room, of course – the very room where he spent his last night upon this earth . . . before the melancholy incident. People have such an interest in a suicide! It's a curious old world, ain't it, ma'am?'

Marvelling inwardly at the commercial acumen of her host, Sarah Tanner considered the proposition.

'Sixpence?'

'Done,' said Mrs. Maggs with a smile – though she did not stir from her chair until the coin was produced.

The room itself proved to be situated upon the top floor of the house. As accommodation, it had little to commend it. A wooden wash-stand, wardrobe and desk were the only appointed luxuries, in addition to a low bed. The view through the single small casement was of the roof-tops of neighbouring manufactories; there was a hint of damp in one corner.

Mrs. Tanner opened the wardrobe, but found it empty.

'I had to clear out his things,' said Mrs. Maggs, noting her visitor's disappointment. 'Expecting another tenant tonight.'

'Did you keep them? Or did you sell them?'

Mrs. Maggs flinched a little at the blunt question but, perhaps in the hope of a further gratuity, restrained herself from any hasty riposte. 'They were collected, as it happens, by Mr. Wilmot – the boy's master. Such a pleasant gentleman! What did he say? He'd keep them "in trust" in case there was any family we didn't know of, what turned up. And he's paid for a chapel burial. Wouldn't dream of letting him go out on the parish, he said. Now, that is proper consideration, ain't it, ma'am?'

'I suppose so. Did you know the boy well?'

'Stayed with us two year,' said the landlady, proudly. 'Came to me an orphan; cholera took his father and mother both. You know, he called me Mother Maggs. Ain't that remarkable?'

'Quite,' replied Mrs. Tanner with little feeling. 'Do you know why he . . . ?' she asked the landlady.

'Committed the act? No, I can't say I do – though he was in a queer state when I saw him that night. Something preying on his mind – well, I suppose *that* stands to reason.'

'He was not in any trouble, then?'

'Well, I'll say this,' said the landlady, adopting a rather confidential tone. 'I didn't say nothing at the coroner's – 'cos I don't care to speak ill of the dead – but there was one or two gentlemen who pestered him, who'd come hanging about the house.'

'Gentlemen?'

'I can't say no more. The sort that takes particular interest in young boys, if you catch my meaning. I'd send 'em packing.'

In truth, Sarah Tanner was a little surprised. 'You mean an immoral interest?'

'It don't do to dwell on it – it don't matter now, does it? He was a good boy, Charlie – that's how we remember him here. We just pray he finds forgiveness from his Maker.'

Mrs. Tanner nodded. But she was distracted by a square of folded coloured paper that poked from beneath a leg of the wash-stand, presumably to keep it in balance on the rather uneven floorboards. Without seeking the landlady's permission, she bent down and pulled it loose, unfolding it. It was an advertisement, displaying a variety of entertainments in pictorial form – from acrobatics to fireworks, from a scene of couples gaily dancing in a moonlit grove to astonishing feats of equestrianism. Its provenance was plain, boldly proclaimed in large block capitals across the topmost portion of the page: VAUXHALL GARDENS.

'Ah!' said Mrs. Maggs, adopting a tone of affection that bordered on sincerity. 'He collected them bills, did Charlie. Loved reading through them, telling me all about them. He was proper educated; used to come and sit downstairs and read to me – all sorts of things. Poor boy! He loved the Gardens too. Especially the balloons; loved to watch the Nassau go up at night. He'd have been there every night of the week, if he could have. Not that it's like what it was in the old days, not when I was a girl; now, that was a sight!'

'Is Vauxhall where he met those men you spoke of?'

'Likely as not,' conceded Mrs. Maggs. 'Well, I suppose if that's all . . .'

'I suppose it is,' replied Mrs. Tanner, ignoring the hopeful expression which flitted across Mrs. Maggs' face, and striding purposefully towards the door. 'Thank you.'

Mrs. Tanner descended the stairs. The landlady, meanwhile, was left standing in the room, open-mouthed.

'Sixpence and nothing more to show!' she muttered. 'Why, it's insulting the dead!'

———

That very evening, Sarah Tanner began a letter in the comfort of her bedroom, whilst the noise of the bustling coffee-shop could still be heard below. She had come to a resolution about Arthur DeSalle; besides, she told herself, there was no reason why she might not kill two birds with one stone.

When she had finished, she read it through to herself:

> The New Dining and Coffee Rooms
> Leather Lane,
> Holborn
> 7th May

Dear Mr. DeSalle,

I hope this letter finds you well. Do you still wish to meet with me?

If so, you will find me at the Grove, Vauxhall Gardens, tomorrow night at eight.

Yours sincerely,

S.

She hesitated, then placed it in an envelope. The letter was brief enough to be a telegram; the tone cold enough to be that of a mere acquaintance.

'I suppose that will do,' she said to herself.

She began to write out the address.

CHAPTER ELEVEN

The following evening, a few minutes past eight o'clock, an ageing hackney cab drove over the iron spans of Vauxhall Bridge. The bridge's gas-lamps, placed upon the parapet on either side of the road, cast but little light into the cab's interior. But Norah Smallwood's face was still quite visible, pressed eagerly against the carriage's glass window.

'Norah!' exclaimed Sarah Tanner, seated beside her. 'Must you do that?'

'Must I?' said Norah, not altering her posture. 'How often do I get a ride in a cab? I might as well enjoy it!'

Norah squinted into the darkness, even though there was little to be seen. Beneath the bridge, the undulating silt waters of the river were barely visible, concealed by the shadowy hulks of coal barges, moored two deep against the Lambeth shore.

'I don't know why you brought us, anyhow,' continued Norah, 'if I ain't enough of a lady for you.'

'You're no sort of a lady at all,' countered Mrs. Tanner. 'But I thought you might like a chance to see Vauxhall – every year they say it will close for good and get flattened by speculators. Besides, I may need a chaperon.'

'What do you reckon you'll find out, anyhow?'

'Someone is sure to know Grubb or our friend Cranks – apparently they both have – had – a fondness for the place.'

'And maybe your Arthur will be waiting for you,' said Norah, pointedly.

'He can do as he likes,' said Mrs. Tanner, brusquely. 'It is up to him. We are here now, in any case.'

The cue for arrival was the cab's passage beneath the grimy viaduct carrying the South Western Railway, located almost directly in front of the Gardens. It was hard to believe that the district had once been famous for its rustic charm. Nonetheless, amidst the crowded streets of Lambeth and the tall chimneys of the nearby river-side factories, beside the railway line, the oasis of Vauxhall had somehow been miraculously preserved, behind its brick walls, hidden from the world.

Sarah Tanner paid the cabman and pulled down the modest spotted veil which fitted her bonnet – for she had concluded that a degree of fashionable discretion might be wise. There was no queue at the pay-place, an illuminated toll-booth, with an iron turnstile beside it. Consequently, at the sacrifice of five shillings, two tickets for the night's entertainments were procured.

The entrance itself did not lead directly into the Gardens, but rather into a long, ill-lit passage, that opened into a gloomy outdoor path. The arrangement was a deliberate one, however, for, just as Norah Smallwood concluded that the astonishing effects of Vauxhall-by-night were much exaggerated, they turned a corner.

One end of the South Walk lay immediately before them: a seemingly endless grand avenue, laid with gravel, lined on each side by great elms, from which hung row upon row of coloured lamps – red, green and blue, strung artfully from branch to branch. To one side lay a semi-circle of supper-boxes, constructed in the Classical fashion, as if a section of the Roman Colosseum had been transported to the metropolis; and there sat a handful of the Gardens' visitors, waited upon by red-coated attendants, scurrying back and forth from some unseen spring, whose product seemed to be not mineral waters but either rack punch or bottled stout. Upon the other side, a Grecian temple in miniature, which seemed to serve no purpose in particular, save to provide a home for statuary of similar style.

'What do you make of it?' said Mrs. Tanner.

Norah stood open-mouthed. In truth, when she had heard of the Gardens and their lamp-lit groves, she had pictured something more modest in scale. As she peered down the grand walk, she noticed for the first time the great triumphal arch, a couple of hundred yards distant, worthy of a Roman general.

'I ain't never seen nothing like it. Who pays for all those lights?!'

'The tickets aren't cheap,' replied Mrs. Tanner. 'I'd heard it had gone to ruin this last year or two but I think the rumours were exaggerated. Come on – and you don't have to gawp so.'

She led the way along a narrow path. Ducking under a small brick archway, following the sound of distant music, they came at length to a rectangular clearing amidst the greenery, surrounded by covered colonnades, thronging with visitors. The music was louder and more distinct. For the 'Grove' was the centre of the Gardens, and at its heart was the famous orchestra – a two-tier Gothic construction tipped with spires and ornament – housing a great organ and raised stage, upon which a dozen musicians sat, racing through a fast polka, whilst numerous couples danced gaily below.

'Where do we start then?' said Norah, surveying the people upon the dancing platform with a rather envious expression.

'I suppose we talk to the waiters, the bar-maids – anyone who might know Charlie Grubb—'

She was about to go on, when another voice interrupted.

'Sarah? It is you, isn't it?'

Sarah Tanner turned and found herself facing Arthur DeSalle.

She looked at him closely without lifting her veil. It was a year since they had last met and little had changed: dressed in an impeccable silk suit, he retained his boyish, but handsome features. Only his eyes somehow seemed a little older and troubled by care.

'Good evening,' she replied.

'And Miss Smallwood, if I am not mistaken. I trust you are well?'

Norah struggled to find a suitable reply. In the end, she muttered something inaudible and managed something resembling a rather nervous curtsey, which occasioned a wry smile from her employer.

'You'll forgive me,' continued DeSalle, addressing Sarah Tanner once more, in a tone of mild surprise. 'I had expected you to be alone.'

'I cannot imagine why,' she replied. 'We are hardly on terms of intimacy – not these days. Besides – coming to Vauxhall, unaccompanied – whatever would people say?'

'I see. Well, I have a supper-box,' he went on, 'if you would care to join me?'

85

Mrs. Tanner glanced at Norah, purposefully taking her arm, pre-empting any similar offer from DeSalle. 'I should think we would both be delighted.'

It was a short walk to the box, situated upon the far side of the Grove. It was little more than a wood-built alcove facing towards the orchestra, indented side by side within a row of identical bays, like cells in a hive, each containing a bench and table for the use of visitors. A cold collation of ham sandwiches and lobster salad was already laid out, together with a jug of water and another of punch.

'I was not expecting supper,' she said. 'Were you, Norah?'

Norah shook her head.

'I thought I had better make the best of it,' said Arthur DeSalle. 'Forgive me, Sarah, but I must say, it is a peculiar place to meet. I confess, I am unlikely to stumble across any of my acquaintances here, but all the same.'

'I have my reasons. Besides, it was a peculiar letter.'

'Yes, well, again, forgive me, might we not speak in private?'

'Norah is familiar with all my affairs, I am sure.'

'But not with mine.'

'You told me you require my help, Arthur, not vice versa.'

Arthur DeSalle took a deep breath, as if restraining his emotions.

'Miss Smallwood,' he said, 'I wonder if you might excuse us, just for a few minutes.'

Norah hurriedly nodded. 'I'll go and talk to some people, missus, like you said.'

'There is no need—' said Mrs. Tanner.

Norah Smallwood interrupted her employer. 'No, missus, I reckon there is.'

And with that, before another word could be spoken, Norah Smallwood was gone.

Arthur DeSalle sighed, placing his hat on the bench beside him.

'Poor girl,' he said, after a stifling pause. 'She is no fool. She knows that you only brought her here to embarrass me.'

'Well, then, Norah has her uses. I must tell Ralph; he still swears quite the opposite.'

'Sarah, I did not think you would be so cold.'

Mrs. Tanner adjusted her shawl, leant forward and picked up a glass of punch from the table.

'I am warm enough. I did not think you would actually marry her. But you did.'

'Arabella? Ah, I see. That is it.'

I trust your wife is in good health.'

'She is well, thank you.'

'Very well, then,' said Mrs. Tanner. 'We are done with polite questions. Now perhaps you can tell me what you want from me?'

'Sarah, was I ever like this when you came to me? After all that has happened, after the months we have spent apart, I had thought we might remain friends.'

There was something in the rebuke – in the mildness of Arthur DeSalle's tone, even when provoked – that made Sarah Tanner pause. When she spoke again, her voice was somewhat softer.

'We are, I suppose. That is why I'm here. Tell me, then, what is this "delicate situation" you're so troubled by?'

'You will hear me out?'

'Of course.'

'It is no small matter,' said DeSalle. 'I fear my mother has been the victim of some dreadful kind of fraud or imposition.'

'Your mother?'

'Let me begin at the beginning. I do not suppose you are aware that two months ago, my father was a victim of apoplexy? It has rendered him paralysed; he has lost his speech and, most likely, his mind in the bargain.'

'Good Lord – I'm sorry.'

Arthur DeSalle shook his head. 'He is not a young man; it could be borne by the family – if . . . no, I am getting ahead of myself . . .' He paused, composing himself. 'We were all much distressed, of course. But my mother was utterly prostrated. She wept for days on end; and she has struggled to reconcile herself to the change in him. Indeed, for a week or more, I thought she would not recover.'

'What about your father? Is there no hope for him? Will his condition improve?'

'The doctors say not. He can eat and sleep; there is nothing more; he is reduced to the condition of a helpless infant – it is quite pitiable. But my mother *did* regain her senses; and she hired a "sick-nurse", upon the recommendation of Lady Pennethorpe.'

'Ah, I gather the nurse is the difficulty,' said Sarah.

'I met the girl three weeks ago. I had expected, well, a respectable, domesticated creature. Instead, she is a young woman, rather abrupt in her manners, with an insolent look about her. To my mind, the care she provides for my father seems most perfunctory – his valet already caters for his every need – and I cannot conceive why she is required.'

'A bad choice, then? But I cannot see why you need my assistance.'

'I did not say anything to my mother – not at first. It was employing the girl that seemed to raise her spirits; I feared lowering them again. But then I saw the girl again, last week, quite by chance.'

'By chance?'

'I was coming back from the Opera along the Haymarket – Rossini. It had gone eleven o'clock. She was entering a night-house near St. James's Square . . . the sort of place only frequented by ballet-girls and whores.'

Sarah Tanner smiled. 'And so, naturally, you thought of me.'

'Sarah, please . . . it is no laughing matter.'

'If you had such doubts as to her character, surely you spoke to your mother?'

'Of course; I went to her and told her the next morning – in the most delicate terms possible – that I had seen the girl on the streets, entering a house from which no woman's reputation could emerge intact.'

'What did she do?'

'She said she would talk to the girl.'

'Talk to her?' said Sarah Tanner. 'Not dismiss her?'

'She talked to her: in private, not in my hearing. She wrote the next day to assure me that I – her own flesh and blood! – had been mistaken; that it must have been another girl.'

'You could not be mistaken?'

'No! I know the evidence of my own eyes.'

'But you did not go after her that night – when you saw her?'

'It was a private house – I could hardly burst in and demand to interview the woman. Besides, I was in a cab and had Arabella with me.'

'I see.'

'Sarah, please, do not be like that – you are the only one who can help me.'

'To do what, precisely?'

'Find out what the girl is up to; to obtain some

definite proof of her true character. She seems to have my mother completely in her spell; it is not like her at all.'

'Why not the police?'

'No, with my father's condition and my mother . . . no, I do not trust some plodding Peeler with my family's good name.'

'But you would trust me?'

'Yes, in fact, I would, if you gave me your word that the matter would be kept in confidence. I would back you against any policeman. If the woman is unfit for her position, if there is some kind of fraud, you can find her out. You know that world well enough. And, of course, I could pay for any expense incurred.'

'You assume, Arthur, that I have nothing better to do with my time than solve your family difficulties?'

'I assume nothing – but I do presume to ask.'

She thought the matter through.

'Very well,' she said, after a long interval. 'I will do it. But first I think I had best tell you a story in return. It may concern you.'

'A story?'

'Yes. It starts with a plate of beef hash . . .'

CHAPTER TWELVE

Arthur DeSalle took a sip of punch, having listened intently to Sarah Tanner's account of the persecution of George Sanders and the demise of Charlie Grubb.

'So that is why we are in Vauxhall?'

'It seemed a reasonable place regardless; as you say, you are hardly likely to meet an acquaintance. The place is mostly full of clerks and tradesmen nowadays. Would your wife object, if she knew you were here?'

'I trust you won't inform her of it.'

'That is hardly likely,' replied Mrs. Tanner. 'We do not move in the same circles.'

'Very droll.'

'So you cannot tell me anything about Mr. Wilmot?'

DeSalle shrugged. 'He is my father's lawyer; I know nothing to be said against his character.'

'Do you know that he drinks?'

'No, I do not; but I should not think it would bother my father overmuch: he has never lived along temperance lines himself, to say the least. Why do you ask?'

'I am not sure what his role is in all this. It is interesting that he is paying for the boy's funeral; and he has kept the theft quiet.'

'You said yourself – if anything confidential has

been stolen, he will not want to announce the fact. As for the burial, it seems a simple act of generosity.'

'I merely wondered if he had a fondness for boys, as well as liquor. If what his landlady told me is true, it might explain how Charlie Grubb got his job.'

'I am pleased to say I have no reason to suspect him of any such thing!'

Sarah Tanner shrugged. 'With luck, Wilmot's peccadillos are not your affair.'

'How do you mean?'

'Mr. Wilmot acts for several families. There is no reason why this business should relate to your father.'

'Sarah, you make me uneasy. What if this business with my mother and what has happened at Wilmot's *are* connected? What could it mean?'

'I cannot say. All the more reason that I find out what is going on.'

'And you think you may be in danger yourself?'

'Possibly. Arthur, I fear I am not much of a detective. You should, I suppose, at least tell me the name of the nurse.'

'Smith – Helena Smith, I believe, is the full name. I have it from my father's valet, the man I mentioned to you; he is a good fellow. I can rely on him, at least – I have asked him to keep a careful eye upon the girl.'

'Does she live in?'

'No, thank the Lord! She is only there during the day.'

'But you do not know, I suppose, where she lives?'

'I am afraid not.'

Sarah Tanner sighed. Her attention was distracted, however, by the re-appearance of Norah Smallwood, who walked eagerly towards the box.

'Did you find anything out, Norah?'

'Nothing, missus – I asked, honest. Except one thing . . .'

'What?'

'I heard a fellow say there's fireworks from the "Monster Dragon Tower" in ten minutes. It sounds prime, don't it? Shall we have a look at it – I mean, seeing as how we're here?'

Norah's employer smiled. 'It was not quite what I had in mind – still, I promised you a night at Vauxhall. Will you join us, Mr. DeSalle?'

It was Arthur DeSalle's turn to hesitate.

'Very well,' he said, at last.

———

In Leather Lane, Ralph Grundy looked mournfully round the New Dining and Coffee Rooms. In one booth sat a credit draper – his own description; a tallyman to anyone else – who, having failed to interest the waiter in a satin waistcoat he had to hand, 'never worn but once, and on good terms', had retired to his seat and nursed a cup of coffee for a good hour. In another sat a pair of costers engaged in a learned discussion of the respective merits of mules and donkeys, both displaying the stubbornness associated with their favoured beasts of burden. There was no-one sitting at the counter and, if truth be told, Ralph was rather bored. His mood was lifted, however, by the arrival of Joe Drummond. A burly coster in his early fifties, Mr. Drummond was one of the local market men for whom the old man had a modicum of respect – not least because it was the very same Joe Drummond who, the previous year, had rescued Sarah Tanner from the awful inferno that had engulfed her premises. It was for this very reason that, upon the re-opening of the coffee-house, the coster had been granted an unlimited supply of restorative mocha, gratis, for the rest of his natural days. And it was to Joe Drummond's great credit – or so Ralph Grundy saw it – that he did not avail himself of the privilege more than once or twice a day, generally in the quiet of an evening.

'Keeping well?' said the coster.

'Well enough,' replied the waiter, placing a mug of coffee before him, 'for an old man, leastways. Not that there's a soul here to notice, even if I weren't.'

'Left on your own? Your missus taken the gal out?'

'You wouldn't believe it if I told you . . .'

Joe Drummond raised his eye-brows rather non-committally; he was familiar with Ralph Grundy's gripes, on a variety of topics.

'Gallivanting at Vauxhall,' continued Ralph, 'when there's me here toiling and a'moiling on her behalf without a kind word to show for it.'

Joe Drummond raised his eye-brows higher, possibly in surprise at the revelation of Sarah Tanner's base ingratitude; or possibly to indicate that he did not share the old man's estimation of the work involved in the coffee-house line – at least, in comparison with the coster trade.

'I expect you'd a'gone with 'em, given half a chance, eh, old chap?' said Mr. Drummond, after a medita-tive sip of his drink. 'Shown 'em a fancy jig or two?'

The waiter, however, did not immediately reply.

'Did you hear that?' he said, after a moment's pause.

'Hear what?'

Ralph frowned. 'Anyhow, you wouldn't catch me down Vauxhall if you paid me ten pound – a load of fools freezing themselves to death in the . . . Here! Now, what's that?'

Joe Drummond shrugged, oblivious to the mysterious

cause of the waiter's distraction. 'Lost me, old fellow. What is it?'

Ralph Grundy, however, came out from behind the counter.

'Floorboards! Will you watch the cash-box for us?'

'As you like,' said Joe Drummond, perplexed.

'Thank'ee,' muttered the old man, as he walked towards the back of the room, in a rather agitated manner. And, as he went, he grabbed a lit candle from one of the empty booths in one hand, and a dirty knife, from the pile of plates that lay ready for washing-up, in the other.

'Is there something up, old chap?' said Joe Drummond. But, by the time he spoke, the waiter had already disappeared up the stairs.

Ralph Grundy walked cautiously up to the narrow landing that led to the rooms of Sarah Tanner and her tenant. The candle shed only a faint aura of light, but it was sufficient to see two things. First, that the door to Norah Smallwood's bedroom was open, with the hint of a breeze that set the candle's flame flickering. Second, that someone – an indistinct shadowy someone – was in Mrs. Tanner's room, rummaging through her dresser.

'Here!' exclaimed Ralph. 'You come out of there! I warn you!'

The figure turned, pulling one of the drawers with such force that it tumbled to the floor.

'Here now,' said Jem Cranks, 'I was only thinking I was wanting a glim. Pass us that light, old man, and I can see what I'm about!'

⬥

Norah Smallwood looked up at the Monster Dragon Tower with a species of awe writ across her face.

95

To her employer, the tower was merely the Gardens' old firework platform, some eighty feet high of scaffold, decorated with pasteboard and cheap fretwork in an oriental style; to Norah, on the other hand, the structure and its garish painted backdrop seemed exquisitely exotic. It was, without a doubt, the latter view which held sway with the crowd. For, with every burst of gunpowder, with every explosive shower of colour, they let out a collective gasp of excitement, as the Chinese scene before them, painted on the surrounding backdrop, was vividly illuminated.

'I remember taking you to the fireworks at Cremorne,' whispered Arthur DeSalle to Sarah Tanner.

'That was a long time ago—'

Her response was cut short, as she looked around the audience standing before the platform. For, loitering by the edge of the crowd, she saw a boy talking to a young man dressed in brown tweed. She did not know the latter, but recognised the dark-haired boy immediately – the same insolent youth who had spoken to her in Brooke's Market. The young man drew back from the firework ground, and began to saunter off along one of the illuminated walks. The boy, in turn, seemed to wait a short time, then walked off in the same direction.

'What is it?' asked DeSalle.

'I thought I recognised someone. Will you keep an eye on Norah?'

'It is one of those wretched boys, isn't it? The ones you came to find? There is no need for any pretence. I saw him too.'

'I just want to see what he's up to,' said Mrs. Tanner, peering into the distance.

'Then I should come with you.'

'Arthur, I can look after myself; he is only a boy.

I do not want to draw his attention. Norah, on the other hand . . .'

'You were happy to let her wander about not ten minutes ago.'

'She was safe enough in the Grove – but if the whole gang of them is roaming about . . . I do not care to expose her to more danger; not again. Look at her, for pity's sake – she is little more than a child.'

Arthur DeSalle glanced at Norah Smallwood. There was, indeed, something rather innocent in the joy with which she gazed at the bursts of pyrotechnic colour that filled the sky.

'Had it not occurred to you, Sarah, that you might have done better not to bring—'

But Arthur DeSalle stopped in mid-sentence. For, when he turned back to look at Mrs. Tanner, he found that she had already vanished from his sight.

—◆—

Jem Cranks walked out from the bedroom in a leisurely fashion, eyeing up Ralph Grundy, who stood opposite.

'You're a game'un, old'un,' said Cranks, 'waving that pig-tickler about like you mean it, an' all.'

'I know your game all right,' said Ralph, though any assurance in his voice was rather undermined by a slight tremor in his hand, as he held the table knife.

'Do you now? Well then, you can just tell us where your missus keeps the letters, and we'll be on the square and best of pals.'

'I ain't no pal of yours,' said Ralph, 'and I'll thank you to come downstairs, careful-like.'

Jem Cranks shrugged, and sauntered towards the waiter. But as Ralph Grundy stepped back to let the boy past him on to the stairs, Cranks twisted his body round, kicking the old man's legs out from under him, whilst grabbing his wrist in a vice-like grip, far too fast for Ralph Grundy to react. The knife dropped from his fingers, only to fall into Jem Cranks's dexterous hand; the candle tumbled to the floor, the flame spluttering out as it fell. And, by the time the old man had recovered his senses, he found that the boy was behind him, one arm locked around his throat, the other holding the blade.

'I reckon you're the one as ought to be more careful, old'un,' whispered Cranks in Ralph Grundy's ear, brandishing the knife close to the waiter's face. 'Waving an article like this about. A party could have an accident. Now, like I said, where's your missus keep 'em?'

'Whatever it is, she wouldn't be fool enough to keep 'em here, would she?' said Ralph, half choking, as the boy tightened his arm.

'Where, then?'

'I don't know,' exclaimed the old man. 'And I wouldn't tell you nothing if I did!'

'Wouldn't you just?' said Jem Cranks. 'My! Well, ain't that something! I only wish it weren't so damned dark, then I could see this chiv proper . . . feels like a rusty old article to me; bet it wouldn't cut a slice of Vauxhall ham. What do you reckon, old'un? Shall I give it a trial?'

And, with those words, Cranks pressed the flat of the blade against Ralph Grundy's cheek.

CHAPTER THIRTEEN

Sarah Tanner walked cautiously along the winding path. There was no illumination but the pin-prick lights of the stars above, and the thunderous flashes of the firework display, barrages that came and went in a second, casting hasty shadows, granting brief glimpses of the way ahead.

She had followed the boy easily enough but only until he veered into the forest of secluded trees and shrubbery that lay at the northern boundary of the Gardens. The track was a narrow one, bereft of lamps, most likely intended for the small army of gardeners who maintained Vauxhall's lush greenery in the hours of daylight.

And now she had utterly lost sight of her quarry.

She halted, at a fork in the path, uncertain whether to abandon the effort. Everything seemed to have narrowed; her clothing was catching upon the nearby bushes; and she was conscious that, once the fireworks stopped, anyone might hear her, moving awkwardly through the foliage.

Then she heard voices. They could not be too far distant; she was quite sure of it. One was raised in anger; the other quieter, pleading. Taking up her skirt, she hesitantly manoeuvred past a thick clump of bushes, peering into the blackness, trying to follow the sound of the argument.

She saw nothing until another flash blazed across the night sky.

In a clearing of sorts, a hundred yards distant, were two figures: the young man and the boy she had seen a few minutes earlier. At first, in the brief flash of light, she mistook their attitude for an embrace. But, even in the darkness that followed, she soon realised that one was wrestling the other, scrambling about on the muddy ground.

It was a desperate struggle. The young man was taller, the boy seemed more violent and determined. It was the latter who settled the contest: with an ungentlemanly kick, which left his opponent doubled over, an agonised yelp escaping from his lips. The boy, in turn, stood up straight and aimed a second blow at his prostrate opponent for good measure.

'That'll learn you some manners, eh?' said the boy. 'Always best to pay up, straight off.'

And, with a brisk step, the boy stalked off into the night.

Sarah Tanner was simply thankful that he did not come in her direction. The man in the clearing, meanwhile, was still alive, if not in the best condition: she could hear his wheezing breath and a choking guttural cough, as he pulled himself upright. She realised that she had but one opportunity to speak to him. Cautiously, she stepped forward.

'Sir?'

The man all but jumped out of his skin. It seemed to take a moment for him to recover the power of speech.

'Good God! What right have you creeping upon a fellow like that?!'

'I am sorry, I did not mean to unnerve you,' she replied, stepping closer. Even in the darkness, she could still make out a trickle of blood that disfigured the young man's face.

'Leave me be,' muttered the young man, pulling a handkerchief from his coat to wipe his mouth. 'I have no need of you.'

Mrs. Tanner knew what the young man thought of her; what any man would think of any woman who walked alone through the most secluded parts of Vauxhall by night.

'I said be off!' he repeated, angrily. 'Or should I call a constable?'

'I should think you might call for one yourself – the boy cannot have gone far.'

'The boy?'

'I saw him attack you. Why did he follow you?'

'Why? I do not know,' replied the young man, hastily. She noticed, as he spoke, that he was hurriedly adjusting the buttons of his clothing about the waist. 'I stepped off the path to make water and . . . Good Lord! I do not have to explain myself to some bloody whore! There is nothing for you in this quarter, rest assured.'

'You mistake me, sir,' she replied emphatically, 'though I don't blame you for it. But if that boy has robbed you—'

The young man shook his head, and violently pushed past his interrogator.

'Damn your interference!' he exclaimed, striding off back through the bushes. 'Damn you to hell!'

Sarah Tanner stood still, marshalling her thoughts. There seemed little point in following the young man. At length, she turned and headed in the direction which his persecutor had taken. She could soon make out the coloured lamps of one of the Gardens' principal avenues; the boy clearly knew the Gardens well: it was a swift short cut.

It was just as she set foot upon the gravel walk, however, that she heard the sound of footsteps behind her. She spun round, only to find herself face to face, once more, with Arthur DeSalle.

'Sarah! There you are! Where the devil did you get to?'

'I told you not to follow, Arthur,' she replied, although, despite herself, she felt relieved. 'And where, may I ask, is Norah?'

'Never mind the girl – I paid a waiter to take her back to the Grove. Whatever became of you? I have been up and down this wretched lane twice over! I thought the young brute had . . . well, I don't know what I thought!'

She shook her head. 'It wasn't me that he was after, rest assured.'

'How do you mean?'

'Can't you guess?' she said.

'I am afraid I cannot.'

'You saw them at the fireworks, just as I did. It's an old game; a lay best worked by young boys. You pick a gentleman, get him talking – doesn't have to be about anything in particular – so that people see you together. You walk along a while, until your man's in a quiet spot, answering a call of nature, then you demand money.'

'On what grounds?'

'Don't be a fool, Arthur. Sometimes I think you haven't lived at all. You tell your man he obviously has a fancy for boys; talk a bit about magistrates and immoral purposes. It works wonders in most cases.'

102

'The boy you followed – that is what he was up to?'

Sarah Tanner shrugged. 'That is my guess. There was a fight; I didn't see the beginning of it. Of course, come to think of it, his trousers . . . he *said* he was relieving himself but—'

'Sarah, please!'

'Arthur – don't be such a prude. You asked me to explain it, after all. The lay works both ways – if your man *does* have a taste for that lark, well, so much the better. He's twice as likely to pay up. This one got into a scrap about it, though, so I've no idea . . . but that's the game, I'll swear it.'

'You think this . . . this revolting trick is how these boys make their living?'

'Who knows? Perhaps it's just a pastime; a quick couple of bob. But if that was Charlie Grubb's work at Vauxhall, I doubt we'll find anyone willing to talk about it.'

'I can't believe it bears any relation to my father; of that much I am certain.'

'Why? Because he is a peer of the realm? You'd be surprised, Arthur. I've known boys who work that trade and—'

'Please, don't be ridiculous. Really, Sarah, must you be so disgusting? I can only think you try to provoke me.'

'Am I ridiculous or disgusting?' said Sarah Tanner, archly. 'Perhaps you should make up your mind before you engage my services.'

'Sarah, please,' said Arthur DeSalle, with a sigh, reaching forward and taking her hand. 'There is no need to twist my meaning. You know my opinion of you full well. I swear, when I lost you the first time, I could not bear it. When I thought that you were in danger just now . . . well, it seemed an eternity until I found you here.'

As he spoke, Arthur DeSalle looked earnestly into his former lover's eyes. There was something in his gaze that made Sarah Tanner relent; something that made her stomach flutter; and, for a second, she almost forgot everything that had passed between them. DeSalle himself seem to notice her hesitation and, in the glow of the lamps, he inclined her head, as if to kiss her.

'Sarah, you know that I—'

She turned away hurriedly, pulling her hand free.

'Some things stay lost, Arthur. I've offered you my help – I owe you that much, after what you did for me and Norah – that's all. Now let's find her and we'll go. I've had enough of Vauxhall. Besides, Ralph will be wondering where we've got to.'

<hr>

'Well, what do you have to say now, old'un?' said Jem Cranks, pushing the flat of the knife deep into Ralph Grundy's cheek. 'I reckon you could do with a good shave. Can't swear I won't give you the odd nick, mind. I ain't much of a barber, see?'

'What do you want from us?' gasped Ralph.

'Lor! I thought I'd said it plain enough!' exclaimed the boy. 'I want them letters; and if you can't oblige, I'll have to persuade you otherwise, won't I?'

'I told you, I don't know nothing about it,' said Ralph, straining against the boy's grip. 'And the missus wouldn't leave nothing lying about for the likes of you to swipe it.'

'Oh, she's wide awake! Just! You don't have to tell me, old'un – I've seen her. But that don't get you out of it, not likely. Where's she gone and hidden 'em?'

'These letters – what good are they to you, anyhow?' groaned Ralph.

'Let's just say I'm obliging an old acquaintance and leave it at that, eh?' said the boy.

Jem Cranks grinned, but his efforts at interrogation were interrupted by the sound of heavy boots on the narrow stairs, heralding the appearance of Joe Drummond, who took a moment to assess the scene before him, peering at the darkened landing.

'Who's this then?' said Cranks, his customary self-assurance a little diminished by the presence of the coster, a man twice his size.

'Never mind that,' said Drummond. 'Your game's up. I'd hook it, if I were you.'

'Would you now? And, if I was you, I wouldn't go interfering in what don't concern you,' said Cranks, maintaining his hold on Ralph Grundy's neck, brandishing the knife in front of him.

'Don't it, though?' said the coster. 'Maybe it don't; but that didn't stop me sending my lad for the Peelers when this old fool went chasing after burglars. And he'll be back here afore long, I reckon; in company.'

'You're lying,' said Jem Cranks.

Joe Drummond shrugged, and casually pulled out a pocket-knife from his trousers, flicking open the blade.

'What you doing?' said Cranks. 'You just watch it—'

'Well, fair's fair, ain't it?' said the coster. 'I mean, if you're wanting to make a match of it, I ain't unwilling. Only I reckon I keep this here blade a damned sight sharper than Mrs. Tanner keeps her cutlery.'

Jem Cranks said nothing, but suddenly pushed Ralph Grundy, sending him flying towards the coster.

There was little the old man could do to stop himself tumbling forward. Joe Drummond, in turn, instinctively dropped his knife and grabbed hold of the waiter as he fell. By the time Ralph Grundy had found his feet, Jem Cranks had vanished, having dashed into the back bedroom, and jumped out through its open window.

Ralph breathed a sigh of relief, rubbing his neck with his hand.

'I'm in your debt, Joe Drummond,' he said at last.

'Aye, well, never mind that,' said the coster. 'Weren't he a treasure! What's he want here?'

'How much did you hear?' asked Ralph.

Joe Drummond scratched his chin. 'Something about letters and all. I suppose it's all down to your missus, ain't it?'

'It ain't her doing, but she don't know when to leave well alone,' said Ralph Grundy, glumly, 'that's her trouble. Did you send for the Peelers?'

'Not likely,' said Joe Drummond with a grin. 'But the young devil, he didn't know that, eh?'

CHAPTER FOURTEEN

———

Later that same night, having returned from Vauxhall, Sarah Tanner stood by the wall of Norah Smallwood's bedroom, as Joe Drummond hammered at a wooden board which had been placed right across the back-window. Once the board was nailed tight, only a small part of the lower half of the sash was visible, a gap too narrow for even the most youthful of burglars. The coster wiped his brow with the back of his hand and put down his mallet.

'It's good of you, Joe,' said Mrs. Tanner, as she stepped up and drew the curtains, concealing his work.

'It's no trouble, missus. I've had that bit of wood lying around for years; came off my old barrow. Not much of a view for your Norah, mind.'

'She'll manage. If she must stay here, at least I can see to it that she's safe.'

'You'd better just hope there ain't another fire,' added the coster, 'God forbid. Not that anyone would have got out that window without breaking their necks, anyhow – exceptin' your young pal.'

'He seems to have a head for heights, I'll give him that,' replied Mrs. Tanner. 'Thank you again, Joe, especially for Ralph's sake – I don't know what that boy's capable of.'

Joe Drummond blushed. 'No trouble, missus, honest.'

'All the same – Mrs. Hinchley will do you a proper feast next time you're in.'

'Well, that's uncommon kind,' said the coster with a shy grin, as he picked up his tools. 'I reckon I'll say good night, then, and I'll see the old'un to his lodgings on the way.'

'Good night,' said Mrs. Tanner, remaining in the room, as Joe Drummond left, alone with her thoughts.

A minute or two later, however, Norah Smallwood appeared at the door.

'Is he done, then?'

'Yes, he's done.'

'Good thing I ain't over-fond of fresh air, eh?' said Norah, pulling back the curtains and surveying the work.

'None of it's a good thing,' sighed Mrs. Tanner, musing. 'I shouldn't have let it get this far; Ralph could have been killed – and for what? My own wretched curiosity. I shouldn't have agreed to help Arthur, either.'

'I bet regular detectives have half-a-dozen cases on the go at once.'

'More than likely, but they probably don't keep a coffee-house. Besides, I'm no detective.'

'Your Arthur reckons you are, though, don't he?' said Norah. 'Unless, of course, it's just an excuse and he still . . .'

'Still what?'

'You know,' said Norah, coyly, rather enjoying her employer's embarrassment. 'Harbours sentiments.'

'"Harbours sentiments"!' exclaimed Mrs. Tanner, her frown becoming a smile. 'My! Where did that spring from?'

'I overheard some gent talking in the Gardens.'

'Well, I don't much care what he harbours. I'm just doing him a favour – because of what he did for us when you were . . . well, never mind that.'

Norah Smallwood's face, in turn, suddenly grew more serious. She looked once more at the window.

'Missus,' she said, her voice tentative, 'do you think I could kip with you tonight? I won't take up any room, honest.'

'We should be safe enough now, you know. Downstairs is locked and shuttered. No-one can get in.'

Norah shrugged, disappointment etched on her face. Her employer reluctantly relented.

'Very well, just one night. And you had better not snore.'

―――――

If Norah Smallwood did not actually snore, there was nonetheless a slight rasp to her breathing that, once noticed, was quite impossible to ignore. Sarah Tanner, therefore, slept uneasily and, a little after two o'clock, found herself wide awake, quite uncertain in her own mind whether she had, in fact, slept at all.

Unable to remain still, she crept cautiously out of bed. Suppressing her growing irritation, she put on her night-gown and walked over to the window, drawing back the curtain a fraction and gazing out into the night. She had no particular purpose in mind and the nocturnal street was all but deserted. Nonetheless, to her surprise, there was a solitary figure, standing no more than thirty yards distant, loitering on the corner of Back Hill. The dim glow of the lamp was no great assistance – for the figure had his jacket collar turned up and a cap pulled down low over his forehead. And yet, by his height and build – even the cut of his clothes – she was sure of his identity.

Jem Cranks.

She looked back at Norah, finding her still fast asleep. She stealthily opened her wardrobe and retrieved her day-dress; then, carefully, she stepped back to her dresser by the window and knelt down beside it, tugging lightly at one of the floorboards.

Norah Smallwood shifted in her sleep at the noise, but her eyes remained closed.

———

Jem Cranks leant casually against the brick wall, beneath the glimmering yellow flame of the gas. His head turned towards the front of the New Dining and Coffee Rooms, he toyed with a ha'penny, flipping it into the air with his thumb and forefinger, and catching it in his palm, whilst affecting not to look at the coin's progress. As an old man stumbled past – a tatty-looking gentleman, loudly cursing himself, the world and the cobbles – the boy gave up on the coin and followed him with his gaze, much as a somnolent cat might observe a mouse. But, if he was tempted by the old man's pockets, he had no time to accomplish his purpose.

'Looking for me, are you?'

Cranks spun round. Sarah Tanner stood but a few feet behind him.

'Lor!' he exclaimed. 'You've done it again, missus! I never heard a bleedin' thing! You *were* a prig an' all – stands to reason. A good'un too! It ain't a regular woman what can creep up on us like that! How did you manage it?'

'There's a back door to the shop; I'd thought you would know that, of all people.'

'And you went all the way round the houses and back? Blow me!' said Cranks, with a grin. 'Well, I'm honoured, missus – honest!'

'Enough. I'm tired of your little games, Master Cranks,' said Mrs. Tanner, wearily. 'Very tired.'

Jem Cranks visibly bridled at the appellation of 'Master', but maintained his customary grin. 'No need to be insulting a fellow, missus. I ain't done you no harm, have I now?'

'By my reckoning, you nearly ruined my business, burgled my home, and threatened violence to an old man who I happen to consider a friend. If that is "no harm", I'd hate to be your enemy.'

'Well,' said the boy, 'that ain't nothing that can't be put right. I didn't take nothing, did I? And the old fellow – well, he's all right, ain't he?'

'What do you want from me?' persisted Mrs. Tanner.

'I want them letters, missus – you know that. The old'un weren't too sure if you had them; but I figure there ain't many so wide-awake to this sort of game as you – I reckon you got 'em off the butcher, by hook or by crook. Besides, if you don't have them, why have you been troublin' yourself to make calls on a certain party by Gray's Inn? So I says to myself, "Jem – you pay a visit to that Mrs. Tanner and see if she'll come to terms."'

'"Come to terms"?'

'Ten guineas, missus. If you hand them over sharpish.'

'You've never seen ten guineas in your life,' she replied. 'Who's paying?'

'That ain't your affair,' said the boy, defensively. 'Well, will you do it? Ten shiners ain't nothing.'

Sarah Tanner sighed. 'I believe, if it meant I would

111

see the last of you, I'd give you those letters right now.'

'Well then, that's settled,' replied the boy.

'Except for one small point – I don't have them.'

Jem Cranks scowled. 'But you said—'

'I never said anything. Lord knows, I have wasted enough time on this nonsense. I was just curious as to what was going on: that's why I went to Wilmot's. Listen to me – I will make *you* an offer. I don't have your blessed letters and I want no part of this wretched intrigue of yours, whatever it may be. If you leave me and mine out of it, you have my word that I won't interfere in it again.'

'Is that so!' exclaimed Cranks. 'You're slippier than an eel, missus! Now, how do I know that's the God's honest truth?'

'You have my word on it.'

Cranks laughed.

'Well,' he said, deftly picking something from inside his jacket, 'words are well and good, eh? But how can a fellow be sure?'

Sarah Tanner observed the boy's hand. The glint of a knife blade was visible beneath the gas-light.

'And what do you intend to do with that?'

'Nothing, missus,' replied the boy, 'exceptin' maybe you and me can talk about them letters a bit more, and I can make certain – one way or another.'

'I think not,' replied Mrs. Tanner.

'No?' said the boy, amused. 'Why's that?'

'Because I happen to have a pistol in my hand that can put a bullet straight through your wretched hide; and every step you take closer makes me desperately inclined to use it.'

Jem Cranks stopped in his tracks – for, as Mrs.

Tanner removed her hand from her pocket, the muzzle of a small pistol became visible.

'Now, listen to me,' she continued. 'I don't know quite what you're up to; it has come to a point that I don't even much care. I assume you're done with George Sanders; and, I swear, I have nothing for you. Let us leave it at that. Now, hook it, before I put a hole in you.'

Jem Cranks tilted his head, as if to indicate that he didn't think much of the threat. Nonetheless, he turned about and began to walk away with deliberate slowness.

'Charlie said you were trouble, missus. He was a fool but he were right.'

'Charlie?' said Sarah Tanner. 'You mean that night, don't you? I'll bet he went to you, after I talked to him on Clerkenwell Green. He told you I was going to speak to Wilmot. That upset things, didn't it? Your little pal was all nerves, wasn't he?'

'He weren't much of a pal. More an acquaintance.'

'He wasn't steady; you could see that. He might not have kept his mouth shut. Is that why you killed him? Because it was you, wasn't it? That's why the door was locked; you didn't even need to use it. You cut his throat, just to stop him talking. Then you climbed out of that window.'

Jem Cranks turned his head back to look at Mrs. Tanner, a smile on his lips.

'Look here, missus,' said Cranks, seemingly disregarding the accusation. 'If you're telling the truth about them letters, then we'll call it a truce between you and me – word of honour. But if not . . .'

'What?'

''Pon my life, you'd better watch your neck an' all.'

And with those words, Jem Cranks grinned and

turned the corner on to Leather Lane. Sarah Tanner followed cautiously in his footsteps, but, by the time she reached the same spot, the boy had vanished from view.

'Word of honour!' she muttered to herself. 'Heaven help me.'

CHAPTER FIFTEEN

If anything, Jem Cranks's declaration of a 'truce' left Sarah Tanner more uneasy than before. However, when there was no sign of the boy the following day, or the day after, nor any other sort of trouble, she concluded that she might fulfil her promise to Arthur DeSalle.

In consequence, a little after six o'clock in the evening, she quit the New Dining and Coffee Rooms and walked down Liquorpond Street, past Meux's brewery, towards Gray's Inn Lane. Wearing her plain dress and woollen shawl, she kept a wary eye on the nearby alleys, until she came to the corner of Holborn. A trio of cabs were at their stand, awaiting hire, tended by a single elderly water-man. His principal role was not so much the care of the horses, nor the cleanliness of the vehicles – though a bucket was kept near at hand, as a token of his occupation – but rather the regular supply of tobacco and porter to the cabmen. After a brief consultation, the old man divined which driver was least attached to his pipe and pint. Mrs. Tanner then stepped inside the waiting hackney, and settled back in her seat, as the cabman raised the reins and bid his horses a laconic 'off'.

The cab sped quickly along Holborn and Oxford

Street, and it was no more than ten minutes before it turned off the main thoroughfare, into the aristocratic purlieus of Mayfair, and finally into Berkeley Square. The driver raised the trap in the cab's roof and inclined his head towards his passenger.

'Anywhere in particular?'

There was a distinct hint of sarcasm in his voice, above and beyond the phlegmatic drollery typical of his occupation. It was clear that he was dubious as to what business an unassuming female – and one from the vicinity of Leather Lane, at that – might have in the heart of the West End. In fact, if the cabman imagined anything, he pictured his fare engaging in an illicit romantic tryst with an impressionable young coachman or junior footman; and, if so, he rather wondered whether he could really expect a full shilling for his trouble.

'The house third along, but stop opposite, just there,' replied Mrs. Tanner, pointing to the boundary of the great railinged garden, almost a park in miniature, which formed the centre of the square.

'Opposite the house?' said the cabman, querulously.

'And there's something for your trouble,' she continued, passing him a pair of coins. 'And a good deal more to come, if you wait and say nothing.'

'I can't hang about for ever.'

'An half-hour, an hour at most. I'll pay three bob – six if it's the hour.'

'And what if someone comes? What if a copper comes round, eh?'

'Just say that your passenger felt faint; and she had to sit still a while.'

The cabman cast a skeptical glance in his passenger's direction – but he closed the trap all the same.

Mrs. Tanner adjusted the window blind of the cab,

so that she could gaze at the house opposite without being observed. The home of Lord DeSalle, though immaculate in its white stucco, was not the grandest in the square. Rather narrow, it was part of a terrace in the fashion of the previous century. Nonetheless, it bore the distinguishing features of a well-appointed residence, not least its own gas-light, suspended above the front steps by an elaborate ironwork arch, springing up from the house's protective railings. There were grand sash windows too, double the height of those in any suburban home, hinting at sumptuous chambers within. She pondered Arthur DeSalle's description of the nurse, supplied as they left Vauxhall. She half hoped that he had been mistaken in seeing her in the Haymarket. For, seated in the cab, as the night air became colder, her own affairs suddenly seemed quite complicated enough.

It was a full hour later, just as darkness descended and heavy damask curtains were drawn shut in the upper windows, that a solitary female ascended from the house's basement steps up to the street. She was dressed in the plain fashion of a servant, with a brown bonnet and black cloak. There was no doubting her identity since she quit the house at the hour predicted by Arthur DeSalle, when any regular servant would be fully occupied indoors. Sarah Tanner peered at her face, as the sick-nurse walked briskly towards the north of the square. She was thin, no more than twenty-five years of age, with a pale complexion, and thick jet-black hair, that escaped from her head-gear and trailed around her shoulders. There was nothing peculiar about her demeanour; and, though she pulled the hood of the cloak around her face, as if to conceal herself from the world, Sarah Tanner had to concede that there was a chill in the air, and that she herself

117

would have done much the same. She rapped on the cab roof.

'Follow that woman, but keep your distance,' she said to the cabman, as he opened the trap.

'Follow her? Who do you think you are?'

'Here's three bob, on account – now, if you want the rest, follow her. Go slow; stop now and then; let others pass you by. If she goes down the back-streets, then I will pay you and get out.'

The cabman puffed vigorously at his pipe, but, glancing at the coins, gave way.

There was, as it turned out, no question of Sarah Tanner quitting the cab prematurely. For the nurse took a straightforward route through Mayfair, passing by the corner of Grosvenor Square and along Duke Street, crossing the great mercantile avenue of Oxford Street, and continuing northwards. At length, however, she turned left and then paused outside the doors of a rather grand building, part of a row of similar properties raised a little above the street, boasting a flight of tall stone steps leading to a pair of impressive double doors, illuminated by twin lamps. Removing her bonnet, the nurse walked hurriedly up the steps and went inside.

'That will do,' said Mrs. Tanner. 'Stop here.'

'What do you want with her, anyway? She after your sweetheart or somethin'?' said the cabman, as Sarah Tanner stepped out on to the pavement.

'Something like that.'

The cabman shrugged and, jangling the coins into his coat pocket, muttering something about 'more money than sense', he tapped his horses with the whip, setting them off at a trot, leaving his passenger on the street corner. Mrs. Tanner, for her part, followed the nurse's footsteps to the front of the building. There was, she noticed, a brass-plate attached to the frame of the door, which read *Marylebone Literary and Scientific Institute*.

Perplexed, she ascended the steps and cautiously pushed open the doors. They led into an open atrium, mimicking the lobby of a superior hotel or gentlemen's club, with a floor of black-and-white-tiled marble and the musty scent of old leather in the air, hinting at the proximity of the Institute's library. The atrium was quite empty, but for a single individual. Behind a desk placed by the door, sat a whiskered gentleman, engaged in an official capacity, who eyed the new arrival with a rather reproving gaze.

'No solitary females for the lecture,' said the clerk, with a rather heavy emphasis on the word 'solitary', 'if you please. Members can introduce ladies; that's all.'

Mrs. Tanner looked at the materials on the desk; in particular, there was a guest-book, pen and ink; and a long list of names recently inscribed on the open page.

'Forgive me, sir, I'm accompanying Miss Smith – she just came in, I think. I had to pay for our cab, you see.'

'Is that so?' said the clerk. She could tell there was some hesitation in his mind.

'Quite. I trust we are not too late?'

The guardian of the atrium pursed his lips, but relented. 'I'll have to charge you the regular shilling, mind; and put you at the back; the theatre's quite full.'

'Of course. Perhaps a gentleman may oblige with a seat.'

'Hmm,' replied the clerk, with a tone that gave the distinct impression that his interlocutor was – he believed – not worthy of such consideration.

It took a minute or two more for the formalities to be completed, as the clerk seeming to glory in his own sluggishness. A shilling was presented; a receipt written out by hand; an entry in the Institute's guest-book. All the while, Mrs. Tanner scoured the atrium for some indication of the nature of the occasion; and why Lord DeSalle's nurse might have preferential treatment on the point of admitting unaccompanied females. The nurse's dress was no better than her own apparel. Nor, she reasoned, was it likely she could assume superior manners, if Arthur DeSalle's description was any guide. But no clue was to be found.

At last, with officialdom satisfied, she was directed down a corridor that led to the lecture theatre.

She slipped inside, just as applause echoed throughout the building. The lecture room was an amphitheatre in miniature, ornamented with Grecian columns supporting a small balcony above, laid out in descending semi-circular tiers of wooden seats, with a central podium and lectern below. She gathered from the applause that the podium had been recently vacated. The audience, meanwhile, remained in their seats. They appeared, in large part, to be respectable members of the middle class and their wives, with a few artisans sprinkled amongst the crowd, easily distinguished by the fidgety manner in which they tugged at tight shirt-collars, normally reserved for Sunday service. She looked around hurriedly for a glimpse of Helena Smith, but the nurse was nowhere to be seen.

'Would you like a seat, missus?' said a man who sat near to the door, a possessor of one of the unfortunate collars.

Sarah Tanner did not demur and took the proffered chair; not least because a printed programme lay on the floor beside it. Barely stopping to thank her bene-factor, she picked up the paper and read its contents.

MESMERISM – THE NEW SCIENCE. The MARYLEBONE LITERARY and SCIENTIFIC INSTITUTE, 17 Edward-street, Portman-square. Tuesday 10th May and Wednesday 11th May. At the above Institution, Prof. FELTON and Dr. STEAD will give a LECTURE upon the medicinal and curative value of animo-magnetic phenomena, phreno-magnetism, and the origin and principles of ELECTRO-BIOLOGY. Accompanying the lecture, a series of EXTRAORDINARY EXPERI-MENTS . . .

Mrs. Tanner stopped reading the notice, for a hush had descended over the room, as a man ascended the podium and began to speak.

'Thank you, ladies and gentleman. Thank you. Now, Professor Felton has graciously condescended to intro-duce to us his esteemed colleague, Dr. Stead. The doctor will now conduct a series of experiments upon a female subject.'

A ripple of applause and excitement ran through the room, as a man strode up to the podium and, beside him, a young woman was led to a cushioned seat, brought forward by gentlemen of the Institute.

The nurse.

Helena Smith.

CHAPTER SIXTEEN

The nurse sat quite motionless on the chair, still wearing her plain uniform. Nonetheless, there was something sufficiently animated and self-conscious in the manner in which she demurely bowed her head, as the man began to speak, as to suggest that she had not yet been magnetised. The speaker himself was of modest height, with a neatly trimmed moustache, almost Continental in fashion, and a short tapering beard. There was nothing extraordinary in his dress, which ran to a black suit, burgundy waistcoat, and an impressive watch-chain, the heavy gold left dangling in a great loop. Nor was there anything terribly peculiar in his voice, with the trivial exception that it was tinged with a northern accent, and sufficiently voluble to fill the small theatre. Yet he did seem to have a natural self-confidence, as if addressing an audience of two hundred was much the same as addressing an acquaintance in the street. As his speech commenced, Sarah Tanner wondered to herself whether he had any experience upon the stage.

'Ladies and gentlemen,' he began, 'may I first thank the Institute for hosting this evening's experiment. It signifies – to this, your humble servant, at least – that the spirit of honest scientific inquiry is not dead in our great capital; nor, indeed, in the minds of its most enlightened citizens.'

A predictable ripple of applause.

'Professor Felton has already outlined the conclusions which his study of animo-magnetic phenomena have revealed; and I must say there is no individual in this great kingdom – nor, indeed, upon the European or American Continents – who is a greater authority on this extraordinary and wondrous new science. It ill-behoves me, therefore, to present any species of abstract argument; it would be quite otiose and redundant. I am, I freely confess, a mere neophyte in the field; whereas the Professor, upon whose wisdom and guidance I frequently rely, is a veritable sage.'

A further ripple of applause. A round-faced grey-haired gentleman in the front row, the man in question, half rose from his chair and bowed, in a rather restrained fashion, to the audience.

'I will say only this,' continued Dr. Stead, waiting for the applause to fade, 'that those who blithely say of the science that "there is nothing in it!" – and I will speak bluntly now, as it my wont – are either fools or knaves. Proofs have been offered again and again; such proofs as you will see this evening – nay, and stronger ones besides. Of course, those who *have* championed the science – and its material benefits and advantages to health – have been derided and traduced, in a manner that ought to shame any right-feeling individual. But, like the camomile plant, ladies and gentlemen, the practice and study of mesmerism and electro-biology flourishes all the more for being trodden down; and I hope to provide you, this very evening, with adequate testimony to its effects!'

A rather excited murmur in the crowd. Sarah

Tanner's gaze wandered back to the mesmerist's subject, who appeared the epitome of calm reserve.

'I admit, I myself was once of a skeptical disposition,' Dr. Stead expounded. 'There is no shame in that. A skeptical mind is a rational mind. Indeed, it is little more than a year since I was introduced to Professor Felton, and I said to him plainly, "Sir, I no more believe that mesmerism" – of which I then had no experience whatsoever – "I no more believe it is an auxiliary to the healing science, than I believe in the man in the moon." At the time, my dear friends, I suffered from a paralysis of the hand, induced by an unfortunate fall from my horse. And so, I said to Professor Felton, again quite plain – he must forgive me repeating it before such an august company – "I will make trial of your mesmeric arts, sir. And if you can relieve my suffering, I will eat my hat." Relieve my suffering? Did he proceed to do just that? Why, here is the proof!'

Dr. Stead raised his arm in a dramatic gesture. spreading his fingers wide and then forming a fist.

Polite applause.

'Humbug,' muttered Sarah Tanner to herself.

'This success, which seemed prodigious to your humble servant, was a mere trifle to Professor Felton. I began, nonetheless, to inquire into the science of animal magnetism; to make my own small trials. I found that I myself – like any individual with a firm intellect and will – could direct and animate the mesmeric fluid in certain subjects. Indeed, I'll wager that a dozen men – aye, even a rare female – are sitting in this theatre who could do the very same, did they but know it. You will see, therefore, that I claim no great distinction for myself in standing before you tonight. Rather, I seek to aid a worthy cause; to assist my esteemed friend, Felton; and bring before the public another instance of the many proofs to which I have already alluded.'

Dr. Stead took a breath, and walked over to where the sick-nurse had remained seated.

'Now, my friends, allow me to introduce Miss Smith' – the nurse looked up and acknowledged the lecturer – 'who has kindly deigned to aid us in this experiment. She is a respectable young woman; a sick-nurse by profession, with whose family and circumstances I am personally acquainted. Will you say a few words, Miss Smith – to assure those present that you are in good health?'

'I am quite well, thank you kindly, sir,' replied the nurse.

'And you are content to assist in this demonstration?'

'Oh yes, sir,' said the nurse, enthusiastically.

'And why is that, may I ask?'

'Well, sir, after all you and the Professor have done for me, I'm ever so happy to oblige you.'

'And will you tell our good friends here tonight what *was* done?'

'I was cured of my fits, sir,' said the nurse.

'Quite so,' intoned Mr. Stead. 'Indeed, Miss Smith came to my consulting-room complaining of fits; nervous seizures which could utterly prostrate her for days at a time. I applied the principles of mesmeric science and, within a week, her condition had abated. She remains possessed of nerves which are uniquely sensitive to my agency. In consequence, my friends, she is the ideal mesmeric patient. Now, first I must ask for complete silence to prevail in the room . . .'

Dr. Stead paused rather theatrically, as if waiting for someone to deny him said condition.

'Excellent. And now, so as not to try your patience

further, I will begin to prevail upon Miss Smith's senses. Again, I must ask for silence, so that I may assert my agency with full vigour.'

Sarah Tanner sighed wearily, causing a respectable-looking man and woman seated in front of her to turn round and stare, in a fashion not so much mesmeric, as openly hostile. She smiled in polite apology, but it was only the fact that they might miss the experiment that made them turn back.

Stead began by kneeling down in front of his subject, trapping the nurse's feet between his knees. Taking off his gloves with the ostentation of a concert pianist, he took Helena Smith's right hand and turned it palm upwards, resting on her lap; then covered it with his own left hand, fingers splayed out. His right hand, he placed on the woman's temple, fixing her head in position, his eyes looking into hers.

He said nothing; did nothing; but the room remained in perfect, almost breathless silence. Indeed, it was not simply the mesmerist's gaze that was fixed: every last soul in the lecture theatre watched the nurse's pale features with high expectations writ large upon their faces.

Seconds passed into minutes; the mesmerist and his subject forming an utterly still *tableau vivant*. Then, just as a cough was heard in the far reaches of the theatre, there was a distinct spasm visible in the woman's throat and her eyelids began to rapidly twitch and quiver. Seconds later, Helena Smith's eyes closed; her head lolled to one side; and her left arm, previously on her lap beside the hand in Stead's grip, fell limp against the side of the chair.

The more susceptible female members of the audience gasped. Dr. Stead, in turn, nodded knowingly, and slowly released the woman's right hand, with the

utmost fastidiousness, as if fearing a sudden movement might somehow do her an injury. Then, with
similar gentleness, he rose to his feet, took hold of
her head and held it straight, muttered a single word,
and let go – leaving her sitting bolt upright, albeit
with eyes shut.

'A simple procedure, ladies and gentlemen,' said
Stead, in a voice that somehow contrived to sound
whispered and confidential, yet still filled the room.
'The mesmeric fluid is invisible; intangible; and yet this
marvellous liquid – this aether – this current – call it
what you will – pervades this room; it permeates into
our very bodies and our nerves, and we must store it
up. In some cases, the fluid is in balance with the
constitution; in others, not least those who labour under
a weakness of nerves, a surfeit of fluid may be utilised
to bolster the system. And we believe it is this introduction of a superfluity of vital force, as the Professor
has explained, that overwhelms the earthly senses, and
produces the great effects familiar to the students of
mesmerism.'

Stead paused.

Was it Sarah Tanner's imagination, or had the gas
in the room been turned down?

'Very well,' continued the doctor. 'It is easy enough
to talk of "effects". Professor Felton has mentioned
the prodigious faculties of perception with which the
magnetised subject may be endowed. Does Miss Smith
possess such faculties? Indeed, is she magnetised? Can
the New Science be subjected to proof? We must begin
our trial.'

Another rather theatrical pause.

'The first test of the magnetic state being induced
is complete insensibility to the world, with the
subject's earthly senses disconnected from the body.

We must, therefore, if we are to approach the subject scientifically, discover whether Miss Smith is in such a condition.'

Stead walked over to a table adjoining the podium, turning his back on his subject. In front of him, laid out on a green baize cloth, sat three glasses of colourless liquid, each covered with a cloth.

'Now, would a gentleman care to step forward and assist in the experiment?'

There was a slight lull in proceedings, then several gentlemen from the front of the audience offered their services. One was selected, a thin man in his forties, with rather prodigious whiskers, and directed to stand upon the opposite side of the table.

'Now, sir,' said Dr. Stead, 'you see before you three glasses, do you not?'

'I do, indeed.'

'May I ask that you taste the first one, here? It is quite harmless, you have my word.'

The mesmerist pointed out the glass in question. The gentleman, in turn, removed the cloth and took a rather cautious sip.

'What is it, sir?'

'Well, I don't know – sugared water?'

'Quite. Now, the next glass, if you will.'

The gentleman again did as instructed.

'What does it contain?'

'I should say tonic water,' replied the gentleman.

'True. Now, the final glass – but, please wait, my dear sir. Merely remove the cloth and place it beneath your nose.'

The gentleman raised the glass to his face; as it came near, however, he let out a choking cough and placed it firmly back upon the table.

'Too close, my dear sir. I do apologise. But you

will concede that it is a solution of ammonia, I trust?'

'Surely.'

'Very good. Then the test may begin. In short, I first wish to demonstrate what the Professor has called "community of sensation" – the peculiar dislocation of the physical senses, such that they are not simply disconnected from the body, but transferred, in sympathy, from subject to operator. Sir, you will concede that Miss Smith's eyes are shut, and that, with my own body thus situated, she cannot see the table.'

'Again, I cannot deny it,' replied the gentleman.

'Then please hand me a glass of your own choosing.'

The gentleman glanced back at the table. Then, carefully, he selected a glass and passed it to the mesmerist's outstretched hand.

Stead slowly raised the glass towards his lips, but a rasping cough escaped from the woman seated behind him.

'Lor!' exclaimed Helena Smith. 'Don't that sting!'

Small exclamations of amusement and astonishment echoed around the theatre. Stead merely smiled.

'Was it the ammonia, my dear sir?'

'Yes, indeed,' said the gentleman.

'And I gave Miss Smith no indication of the contents? I restrained myself from any cough or splutter, did I not?'

The gentleman nodded.

'Very well. Let us try the experiment again. Pick a glass, sir. It may be the same glass, it may be different; it matters not.'

The gentleman frowned, and selected a glass for the second time. Stead slowly moved it to his lips, and took a sip. The nurse, eyes still shut, licked her lips and swallowed at precisely the same moment.

129

'What do you make of that, Miss Smith?'

'Sweet, sir,' said the woman, thoughtfully. 'Like lemonade.'

The mesmerist smiled once more. 'Is she correct, my dear, sir?'

'The sugared water – yes, it is indeed.'

A smattering of applause from the audience. Dr. Stead effected a humble bow.

'Thank you, ladies and gentlemen. Sir – you have my thanks, and I beg you to resume your seat. Now, I come to a second test. We have shown dislocation of the senses, but not the physical insensibility which invariably accompanies that condition. Now, I must ask the ladies in the hall to render me their forgiveness, in anticipation of what I am about to do; please bear in mind the scientific and experimental purpose of my actions, and judge me solely upon my good intentions and the effect produced.'

And, with those words, the mesmerist strode briskly to the opposite side of the podium, behind his entranced subject, reached inside his jacket, and pulled out a silver-barrelled pistol – which he aimed squarely at the nurse's head.

CHAPTER SEVENTEEN

Stead pulled the trigger.

The explosive crack of the pistol being fired echoed around the theatre. It was accompanied by screams from several female members of the audience, and astonished exclamations from a number of men, many of whom rose to their feet. There was no smoke, however, and the first voice to be heard above the general confusion was that of the mesmerist himself.

'Ladies and gentlemen – please! If you will resume your seats, you will be able to ascertain that Miss Smith is quite unharmed. The pistol was capped, but not loaded.'

The mesmerist spoke with such calm authority that, in a matter of seconds, the audience seemed to gather its collective wits, and do as instructed. Stead, meanwhile, continued with his explanation, unfazed by the shocked expressions of some of his listeners and the relieved laughter of others.

'You will perceive that Miss Smith is unharmed and, indeed, has remained utterly insensible throughout. Now, I apologise for such a theatrical display. Nonetheless, the opponents of mesmerism credit the likes of Miss Smith with every form of imposture, and, thus, such things become necessary. Gentlemen, ask yourselves this: could your wives or daughters undergo such a trial – mere inches from the firing of a weapon – and remain utterly still, even if they anticipated its discharge? It is merely one test, I grant you. But I have no great love for pricking the arms of a young woman with pins, or poking lit matches about her eyes, or wheeling out galvanic apparatus – such torturous proofs have been given before now, on numerous subjects, and I do not see the need to repeat them here.'

Sarah Tanner frowned. Helena Smith had not moved a muscle. The audience, meanwhile, though a little disturbed and restless, was clearly eager to see what might come after such a demonstration.

'Very well. We have dealt with the disconnection of the senses; we have seen insensibility. These are the states which accompany the mesmerised subject. But I have made claims for Miss Smith's faculties of perception in the mesmeric state – the condition of lucidity to which my learnt colleague animadverted, commonly called clairvoyance. Now, I propose to put *that* to the test.'

Mrs. Tanner sighed once more. The man who had vacated his seat for her leant forward.

'Is there something wrong, missus?'

'Only that I've seen the same cheap tricks done a hundred times by run-of-the-mill hucksters,' she replied, 'just without the pretence of it being "science".'

The man raised his eye-brows, but said nothing. The mesmerist, on the other hand, continued unabated.

'You will see that I am tying a blindfold about Miss Smith's eyes. It matters not – she cannot see with her natural senses – but, my dear friends, I wish there to be no possibility of trickery, no matter how remote. Now, the first principle of clairvoyance is merely the faculty of vision being loosed from the body. Again – may I have a volunteer? He need not come forward – merely stand up and make himself known.'

Several men instantly complied. Stead selected one, directing the others to sit down.

'Now, sir – if you please, take something from your own possessions about your person, and hold it out in front of you.'

The man reflected on it, then removed a jewelled tie-pin from his cravat and held it out in his upturned palm.

'What do you see, Miss Smith?'

The sick-nurse leant forward a tiny degree, as if concentrating.

'A pin. Lor! You silly man – your neckerchief's all loose!'

A roar of laughter echoed about the room and the man in question positively blushed.

'Thank you, sir – please do sit down. You must forgive Miss Smith . . . the mesmeric influence is liable to unbalance certain faculties; some consider it akin to intoxication in that regard. Consequently, she may say things for which we cannot hold her proper self accountable.'

More amiable laughter from the crowd.

'Now, the second principle of clairvoyance, my dear friends, is that which allows sight to wander great distances – to places never visited by the subject. Perhaps I might turn to our respected hosts, the governors of this august institution' – here the mesmerist gestured to the front row of seats – 'and ask one of them to assist in proceedings?'

Again, the request produced several volunteers.

Dr. Stead, however, demurred from picking anyone himself – 'for fear of an imposture' – and waited until a grey-haired, distinguished-looking gentleman in his sixties was selected by common consent.

'Sir – am I correct in saying that you have never invited Miss Smith to your home?'

Again, laughter. Perhaps too much: for the governor in question did not smile, but rather seemed to take offence at the suggestion.

'Please, sir,' continued Stead hurriedly, 'forgive me. I only mean to say that there is no possibility that Miss Smith, or indeed myself, have visited your home?'

'None,' said the governor, with rather icy emphasis.

'Of course. Then perhaps you might invite her to walk through it – ask her to describe its contents?'

The governor gave out a rather disparaging snort, but nonetheless complied.

'Very well, Miss. Will you visit me at my house?'

'Of course, sir,' replied Miss Smith.

'Where shall you find it?'

'In Park Lane, sir. I'm standing outside.'

'I see. Well, can you go inside?'

'Yes, sir. I'm in a splendid hall, with a marble table between two pillars on one side, and a great flight of stairs, on the other.'

The governor raised his eye-brows, as if to concede that this much was correct.

'Well, then, go up to the drawing-room. What do you see now?'

'Some pictures, sir. Seven, large ones, of the countryside.'

'Really? Are there windows?'

'Three at the bottom of the room.'

'And what about the curtains?' said the governor, with a note of surprise quite obvious in his voice.

'They're red, sir, with gold trim.'

'I see,' said the governor, pausing. 'And what colour is the carpet?'

Helena Smith frowned. 'There ain't no carpet, sir, begging your pardon – it's boards.'

'Good Lord! The girl is right to the very letter! But I will swear – she has never set foot in my house!'

A murmur of approbation ran through the audience, followed by a smattering of applause.

'Thank you, my friends, again, thank you,' said Dr. Stead, with a smile. 'Now – lest we fatigue our subject – we come to the final demonstration I should like to place before your attention – that of the third principle of clairvoyance, where sight travels into the mists of futurity. It is, of course, the most inspiring of the attested effects which may be produced by the agency of magnetism. I believe it is the eye of the spirit opened into that realm that will be ours after death; and I do not ask our subject to make such a journey lightly. Nonetheless, if any party here tonight should like to question Miss Smith in respect of the future, please make yourself known. Perhaps – forgive me – a lady might grace us with a question?'

The theatre fell quite silent and, for a few seconds, it seemed like the mesmerist's audience had lost their nerve. At last, however, a woman rose hesitantly to her feet, followed by half-a-dozen more.

'Miss Smith, what does the future hold for me?' asked a well-spoken, matronly woman not far from the podium.

The sick-nurse frowned. 'I see an elderly woman. A sick relative . . .'

'I have an aunt who is very ill.'

The sick-nurse nodded her head. 'She will let go of

135

this life; I see her leaving – she will be smiling – smiling at you.'

Sarah Tanner sighed once more, and carefully rose from her seat, turning her back on the stage.

'You may have your chair back, sir,' she said, in a whisper, to the man who had vacated his seat. 'I've seen enough.'

'Don't you believe in it, missus?' said the man, as another woman spoke to Helena Smith.

'Not a jot,' said Mrs. Tanner. 'Nor any other cheap gipsy trick.'

'But that fellow's house?'

'How many governors are there?' said Mrs. Tanner. 'Anyone could find out such details from a man's servants.'

The man, a mechanic or artisan of some sort, looked a little deflated.

'Why don't you try her out, missus?' he urged.

'You try her, sir, if you are so keen.'

The man grinned and seemed to take the proposal as a challenge. Urging his interlocutor to remain a few moments, he began to wave his hand in the air.

'Yes, sir?' said the mesmerist, who could not fail to observe the movement. 'Do you have a question?'

'There's a lady here who wants to know what sort of fellow she'll marry.'

A laugh from the crowd. Then silence.

'Ah,' said Dr. Stead, with a rather patronising tilt of the head, 'there cannot be any mesmeric sympathy between Miss Smith and the lady, if that party will not speak herself.'

Sarah Tanner merely shook her head and turned away; she had no great desire to play along with the game. She consoled herself that the gas at the back of the room had grown so dim, she could hardly be seen by the audience, let alone the man on stage.

Helena Smith, however, spoke, quite firmly.

'It won't be the fellow what she wants.'

A ripple of laughter; another woman rose to speak.

Sarah Tanner quit the lecture theatre. As she walked along the corridor that led back to the atrium, she was certain the woman's remark was a joke; designed, by a conscious mind, to startle and amuse a crowd of willing dupes.

She knew it.

And yet, strangely, she suddenly felt quite unnerved.

CHAPTER EIGHTEEN

It was nine o'clock when the crowd of lecture-goers began to emerge from the Marylebone Literary and Scientific Institute. The display of mesmeric effects had been concluded by a further speech from Professor Felton; testimonials as to the efficacy of the science, provided by members of the audience; and a grand reception in an adjoining room – disappointingly teetotal – at which Professor Felton had given another brief address. Dr. Stead had then attested once more to the Professor's achievements and Helena Smith had been paraded around the assembled crowd, introduced to the Institute's dignitaries in a manner worthy of visiting royalty.

Sarah Tanner had left the building a good hour earlier. In fact, she had quit the lecture theatre with every intention of returning home and simply directing Arthur DeSalle to attend the next evening's performance, if he would know something about the character of his father's sick-nurse. But, even as she walked away, she found herself wondering whether, despite her skepticism, there was not something unusual about the equanimity with which Helena Smith went through her paces; if merely attending a mesmeric display – even as subject – would be considered grounds for the nurse's dismissal; and if, all in all, she should let the matter rest so easily. Consequently, after some debate with herself, she had turned back and resolved to wait in a dimly lit spot by the corner of a mews, a few yards from the Institute, a location that rendered her all but invisible to passers-by. It was from this hiding-place that she watched the audience leave.

For the most part, they quit the building animated and in high spirits. The well-to-do dispersed into a row of waiting carriages, ordered well in advance. Some improvident souls went in search of a cab; the remainder, the humbler working men and their wives, the lower order of clerks, walked in the direction of Oxford Street or Paddington, with brisk determined step, as if to imply that they were simply taking the night air. It was only when the crowds had dissipated, however, that she was rewarded by the appearance of the three individuals in whom she had an interest: the two adherents of magnetism and their female subject. The men, deep in conversation, left the building together, with Miss Smith trailing meekly behind. Slipping back into the shadows, she strained to hear their voices. It was the older man – Professor Felton – who spoke first.

'I must thank you again for your assistance, sir. And you, Miss Smith. Your presence is invaluable on these occasions.'

Miss Smith said nothing; or, if she spoke, her remark was inaudible.

'I declare it a bullseye, sir!' exclaimed Dr. Stead, cheerily. 'A palpable bullseye for the New Science. You floored them with your speech, sir—'

'You flatter me, Doctor.'

'Not a whit, my dear Felton. You floored them; prostrated their collective intellect. I – and dear Miss

Smith – merely provided the *coup de grâce*, as our foreign cousins so eloquently put it.'

The Professor smiled, rather shyly accepting the extravagant praise.

'And you are quite certain, Miss Smith,' said the Professor, 'that I cannot provide some small reward for your co-operation?'

The sick-nurse shook her head.

'Miss Smith won't hear of it, sir,' said Stead on her behalf. 'She has no interest in personal gain. Indeed, if it were not an indelicate subject, I would bring that very point to the attention of the public – another proof, my dear sir! Another proof!'

'Miss Smith need hardly prove herself to me, sir. I do not question her talents. Very well – I will bid you both good night. This is my cab, I believe. We shall meet again at the usual time, I trust?'

'Indeed. Good night, my dear Felton.'

The older man nodded, and climbed into the hackney that had pulled up by the kerb as the two men spoke. As the cab pulled off, Dr. Stead turned to his erstwhile subject.

'Shall I walk you to the bridge, my dear?'

Again, the answer was inaudible to Sarah Tanner. But the sick-nurse took Stead's arm without complaint, and together they began to walk away.

Mrs. Tanner followed.

⁓

The walk down to the Thames took Stead and the nurse back through the streets of Mayfair, down to Piccadilly and the Haymarket, then finally towards Charing Cross and Hungerford Market. There, hidden behind the market's empty stone basilica – its shops long since closed for the night – lay the steps leading to Hungerford Bridge, and the toll-box where a ha'penny was demanded of anyone crossing the river.

Sarah Tanner heard nothing of the conversation that passed between the couple as they traversed the city; they had exchanged few words, and those that had passed between them were in quiet, restrained tones. But the market's stone colonnades afforded an opportunity to draw closer unobserved, as they stopped at the turnstile. If, however, she had expected to overhear some revelation, she was disappointed. Nothing was said beyond the commonplace, as Stead paid the toll on the nurse's behalf, and bid her good-bye.

Mrs. Tanner pondered whether she should follow him back through the market. But he was too quick and, even if she could manage it, there was but one imputation that could be laid upon a solitary female following a gentleman in the vicinity of the Strand – one which might draw the attention of the police. Instead, she walked up to the toll, paid her coin, and set off in pursuit of Helena Smith.

The suspension bridge itself was a peculiar sight, even in the hours of darkness, its twin Italianate towers rising midway between the Westminster and Surrey shore, as if defending some forgotten outpost of Venice or Naples. Between the great chains that supported the spans, the figure of the sick-nurse suddenly seemed terribly small and distant, and Mrs. Tanner hurried to keep up with her. At length, Miss Smith reached the far side, passed the toll-box, and descended to the streets below, beside the hulking walls of the riverside manufactories and the great chimney of the Lion Brewery. A couple of drunks made a half-hearted effort to stop her progress, but she brushed past them with ease – so forcefully, in fact, that it did not even occur to them to interfere with the woman who dogged her steps. It was only when she had walked another half-mile or so, past the warehouses and works, down to the more populous Waterloo Road, that Helena Smith slowed her pace, and finally stopped.

At first, Sarah Tanner assumed it was the coffee-stall, situated on the corner of the New Cut, that had caught her attention. The Cut was a market street far longer and wider than Leather Lane, with a busy night-time trade, and the stall was correspondingly magnificent: its sign illuminated by half-a-dozen lamps; a wide tarpaulin draped from scaffolding to protect customers from the elements; and a brass urn of giant proportions, pristine and polished. But the sick-nurse had come to a halt with peculiar abruptness, as a look of agitation flashed across her face. She directed her steps not towards the proprietor of the stall, but rather towards a small crowd of his patrons, coffee-mugs in hand, who seemed to have gathered in a merry semi-circle about an unseen attraction – one that caused them to whoop and jeer at intervals.

Sarah Tanner drew nearer until she could make out the source of the crowd's rather cynical amusement and cat-calls. It was not uncommon for a street performer of one kind or another to set out to entertain such an audience, but the man who stood before them appeared quite ridiculous. He was a haggard-looking individual in his late forties, dressed as an acrobat, but in a fashion that was so shabby that it made a mockery of his wearing the gaily-coloured costume. His tight-fitting stockings of elastic cotton had shrunk, and split round the ankles; his short span-gled drawers of red velvet were patched with rags; his jersey had transmuted from purest white to a murky laundry grey. His clothes alone would have provoked some merriment, but his voice was guttural and

142

slurred, in a manner that marked him out as a confirmed drunkard.

'Now then,' he barked to the crowd, bending down to pick up some items from beneath his feet, 'ladies and gentlemen all, you have seen me tumble, ain't you? Well, now observe the original performance – from the man who taught Ramo Samee the tricks of the trade – as he takes these here commonplace objects and makes 'em perform rapid revolutions in the air, the like of which you ain't never seen afore!'

The commonplace objects in question were a trio of potatoes, from a sack that lay upon the ground. Without further ado, the down-at-heel acrobat began to juggle, throwing them up with an uncertain wobble of his hands, and a tense, aggravated expression that presaged disaster. A couple of the lookers-on applauded; a couple booed, protesting they had seen better, many a time. But then one of the potatoes broke from its appointed orbit and came down with an audible thump, landing squarely on the acrobat's forehead, leaving him visibly stunned, tottering to one side, as the remaining two vegetables slipped through his fingers.

The crowd erupted into laughter.

The acrobat, however, far from being disheartened, suddenly grinned.

'You likes that, do you?' he said, bending down to select three more potatoes. 'How's this for a trick, then?'

And with those words, he launched them high into the air, and positioned himself directly below, such that, one by one, each crashed down upon his head in quick succession, causing him to stagger uncertainly from one side to another.

Sarah Tanner watched the peculiar spectacle; if she

felt any sentiment, it was not amusement but pity. The sick-nurse, on the other hand, wore an expression approaching contempt.

'There! I ain't dead yet! Now, I've got two big'uns here,' said the acrobat, recovering his balance and pointing at the bag. 'Who'll chuck me tuppence into the ring? Tuppence, and up they goes!'

A brown copper flew through the air: striking the acrobat on the forehead, leaving a bloody scratch.

'There – that suit you?' exclaimed a young man, much amused with himself. Several uncharitable members of the crowd laughed along with him. As the missile hit its mark, however, Helena Smith grew visibly agitated. Striding forward, she grabbed the acrobat by the arm and tried to pull him away by force.

'Come away!' she said.

'Away?' said the acrobat. 'I ain't hardly started!'

'You're making a fool of yourself, and me and all.'

'Oh, is that right, young miss?' he replied, angrily. 'Is that so? Well, listen here, you don't talk to your father like that! Do you hear me? Or I'll dish it out warm, mark my words! Do you hear me, eh?'

Some of the audience turned away; whether through embarrassment, or over-familiarity with the scene enacted before them, Sarah Tanner could not tell.

'Go on then,' said Helena Smith, goading her drunken parent. 'Go on – you just try it.'

Angered by the reply and true to his word, the acrobat lunged violently at his daughter, aiming to hit her square across the face with the back of his hand. But the nurse easily dodged his blow, which threw him so off-balance, that he fell backwards on to the pavement.

Helena Smith said nothing. A quick contemptuous

glance was all she bestowed on the man lying prone on the ground, before she stalked off in the direction of the market.

Her father, however, seemed to undergo a transformation, even as his daughter vanished from sight. All the anger in his face ebbed away, his mouth gaping open in a pathetic rictus. Struggling to his feet, he scrambled after her, pushing through the crowd, calling her name.

Before she knew it, Sarah Tanner realised it was too late to follow: they had both disappeared amidst the nocturnal bargain-hunters thronging the Cut.

'Pathetic,' muttered the young man who had thrown the coin, addressing the man beside him. 'I'd cut him loose, if I was her. Same every bloody week when the beer dries up.'

'Do you know the man?' asked Sarah Tanner.

'Know him, missus?' said the young man. 'He's a regular on this pitch, he is, ain't he, Phil?'

'Used to do a proper turn at Vauxhall, I heard,' replied the second man, 'but he took to drink.'

'Everyone hereabouts knows Bob Cranks, all right,' continued the first young man, 'More's the pity – you've seen the way he treats his girl, eh?'

Sarah Tanner looked back at the young man.

'Did you say "Cranks"?'

'Aye – that's his name. You a friend of the family?'

'No,' said Mrs. Tanner emphatically. 'Not at all.'

CHAPTER NINETEEN

The following evening, a smart black brougham, with blinds drawn, stopped upon the corner of Gray's Inn Lane. It came to a halt beside a veiled woman, who stood waiting. The door opened; a few brief words were exchanged and she stepped hurriedly inside.

'I'm sorry we cannot meet more openly,' said Arthur DeSalle, as Sarah Tanner sat down beside him. 'I should not like anyone to, well, think badly of you.'

'I know your position in life, Arthur, and you know mine. Leave it at that. If anyone mistakes me for a common whore, I suppose I can bear it. I've been called worse. In any case, I should have thought you would be at the Professor's lecture.'

'The lecture? Good Lord, no. The description in your letter was quite sufficient. I have no desire to see the wretched entertainment for myself; not least when the creature on show is also charged with the care of my father.'

'Have you spoken to your mother?'

'Not yet,' replied DeSalle. 'I intend to do so tomorrow. As it happens, I think I've already found enough to have Miss Smith dismissed.'

'Really? So you did not need my help?'

'Possibly not. Do you recall I mentioned my father's valet – a fellow by the name of Winters? A good man. He promised to watch the girl – at least, watch for anything untoward. He sent me a note this afternoon. You may as well read it for yourself.'

Mrs. Tanner took the piece of paper which Arthur DeSalle retrieved from his jacket, and read it beneath the light of the small lamp fixed to the carriage roof.

Berkeley Square
11th May

Sir,

I trust you are in good health.

You asked me to favour you with any observations about Miss Smith and her doings in this house. I hope you will accept my assurance that I take no pleasure in acting the part of a spy. Indeed, had I not already formed an unfavourable impression of the young woman's character, despite Her Ladyship's placing trust in her, and were not the health and well-being of my master at stake, I hope I would not have considered embarking on such a course. You must forgive my impertinence in putting such sentiments on paper; but I should not like you, nor the family, to think the less of me, for what I have done *at your behest*.

I should begin by saying plainly that there has been, to my knowledge, no *particular* harm done by Miss Smith. Nor, however, can I see much good. Her attendance upon His Lordship seems, to my mind, to be one consisting of small attentions, paid quite sparingly. Occasionally, a pillow is straightened; a damp cloth may be applied to his face; a mouthful of food put to his lips. These are all things which we might have done ourselves and which, in large part, I continue to do for His Lordship.

There is one point alone upon which Miss Smith has always seemed quite determined. Twice a day, she brings two bottles of water (I am sure it is only water, for I have tasted it myself) up to His Lordship's room, and stays with him for an hour, with instructions that she should not be disturbed. (The bottles themselves are delivered to the house upon her special request.) When the hour is done, the bottles are empty, having been used to fill a small punch-bowl which she has placed in the room.

At first I thought that Miss Smith made some preparation for His Lordship's benefit. I know that some females have a fondness for manufacturing toilet-waters, and I did not think much of her guarding her secrets. I soon realised, however, that the water was not used for such a purpose: nothing about His Lordship's person indicated it; there was never a fragance upon him or in the room; and the bowl, which we emptied upon Miss Smith's behalf, was always full to the brim – and always of plain water.

Sir, this puzzled me greatly. Moreover, after you and I spoke, it began to trouble me. I decided yesterday to put the woman, and her odd arrangements, to the test.

It is only because I took your words to heart, sir, that I took steps; and I hope you will not consider it improper, under the circumstances in which I was placed, by your particular interest in Miss Smith's morals and character.

I may as well confess it straight out. I secreted myself in His Lordship's dressing-room, just before the very hour at which Miss Smith was accustomed to make use of her bottles of water. I situated myself such that I could see through the French screen which separates the rooms; and I watched the whole spectacle from start to finish.

Miss Smith came in at her usual time. She took the water and filled the bowl with it. This much I had expected. But she then sat facing His Lordship in his bath-chair, placed the bowl between them, and took His Lordship's hands and placed them in the bowl together with her own, an inch or two apart – not washing them, mind you, but merely letting them rest there. Then she began to speak to him in a most impertinent fashion – not least addressing His Lordship as 'Billy'. I almost broke forth from my hiding-place when I heard this, to hear a mere girl taking such liberties with a gentleman. It went on for almost an hour, with Miss Smith talking utter nonsense, and making free and familiar with His Lordship's name like she had every right to it.

Now, sir, I am not surprised the woman practises this 'water-cure' in secrecy. I may not understand the fashion of the times, but I call it rank quackery of the first order. Indeed, I would have gone directly to Her Ladyship, if the circumstances of this revelation did not cast the possibility of unfortunate doubts laid against my own character.

I trust, however, sir, that you will be satisfied with the veracity of this account; and that something may be done that will put matters to rights.

Your father has always been good to me, and I fear he is being terribly ill-used.

Yours,
G. Winters

'What do you make of that?' said DeSalle. 'He's a reliable old fellow; he would not invent it.'

'I have a fair idea,' replied Mrs. Tanner.

'As do I,' continued DeSalle, 'although it would not have occurred to me, I suspect, had I not received your letter the same day – it made me recall an article I read some years ago. The girl has had the water "magnetised" by this Professor, has she not?'

'And twice a day she conveys a healing current through the "fluid",' said Mrs. Tanner. 'I think it shows admirable dedication to her work.'

'Good God – please do not tell me you believe in this magnetic tomfoolery, Sarah?'

'Not for a second. But it appears that she does, which rather surprises me.'

'How so?'

'The tricks I saw at the "lecture" were just that, Arthur. I've seen them at a dozen fairgrounds. Memorising details; clues in the way things are said or done; peering through a blindfold – it is not terribly difficult. But apparently she has a genuine belief that she is doing your father some good – otherwise, why carry out this strange charade with the water?'

'I do not care what the blasted woman believes,' said DeSalle. 'I will not have her left alone with my father, to practise her . . . well, damn me, the thing is almost pagan!'

'Are you going to tell your mother all of this? What about your loyal Mr. Winters? I think he fears for his place.'

'I have thought of that. I will enter the room un-announced myself, during one of these performances; my mother needn't know that he had any part in it.'

'A reasonable plan,' said Mrs. Tanner. 'Only I am not sure it will solve the problem.'

'Whyever not?' said DeSalle.

'I didn't tell you everything in my letter. You see, I followed your Miss Smith home. She lives in the New Cut, with her father. A man by the name of Cranks.'

'Cranks?' said Arthur DeSalle, as the significance of the name took a moment to come to mind. 'The same as the boy who was plaguing you?'

'The same as the boy who's threatened me and Ralph with a blade; the same as the boy that I reckon killed Wilmot's clerk. He could even be her brother.'

'Good Lord! You think he killed the clerk? I mean, you are certain of it? You should go to the police, surely?'

'The police don't think very highly of me, Arthur, in case you've forgotten. Besides, I have no proof; and the boy is dangerous; I have no wish to make myself a target.'

'For pity's sake, Sarah, what on earth am I to make of this? You think the girl might be in league with this youth – with a cold-blooded murderer? To what end?'

'I have no idea,' replied Mrs. Tanner, candidly. 'Tell me, did your father place any letters in Wilmot's hands? Something that might be valuable?'

'Why do you ask?'

'I spoke to the boy two days ago. He gave this much away – that he was looking for some letters. Willing to pay for them, too. Can you think of anything?'

'I am not so privy to my father's affairs, Sarah. And he is in no position to make them known to me now.'

Arthur DeSalle paused, as if the thought of his father's condition temporarily overwhelmed him.

'What should I do?' he said at last.

'Have your mother dismiss Miss Smith – that's a fair start. I suppose you might visit Wilmot – ask him about these letters . . . or, at least, drop a few hints.'

'Is Wilmot a party to . . . well, whatever is going on? What about these so-called "Professors" of magnetism?'

'I wish I knew. I have heard of Felton – or, at least, his lectures are always advertised in the papers; they have been for some years. I've never heard of Stead. Perhaps Wilmot may give something away; tell me what he says.'

'Of course.'

Mrs. Tanner fell silent.

'What is it?' asked DeSalle.

'When I saw the boy, I promised him I would not interfere in his business. It might be better I hadn't told you about any of it.'

'I am grateful you did. Besides, you said he is a murderer. An out-and-out villain.'

'Most likely.'

'Then you owe him nothing. Some promises are made to be broken.'

True enough, thought Sarah Tanner to herself, as a bitter memory came back to her unbidden. *You'd know*.

But she bit her tongue and said nothing.

CHAPTER TWENTY

The following afternoon, the scarlet frock-coat of a postman was seen on Leather Lane, in the vicinity of the New Dining and Coffee Rooms. Although Norah Smallwood did her level best to intercept the letter as it arrived, she was beaten to the door by her employer. The hand of Arthur DeSalle on the envelope, however, was quite unmistakeable. In consequence, it was with a very knowing look from the waitress that Sarah Tanner ascended the stairs to her room, closed the door, and read the contents.

> The Reform Club,
> Pall Mall,
> 12th May

Dear Sarah,

I had hoped to write with better news. Indeed, I readily admit that I had expected that, in unmasking Miss Smith's dubious pretensions to 'magnetic powers', I would undo whatever mischief she might have already wrought, or have planned. Nothing, however, could be further from the truth. If my family is a victim of some plot by Miss Smith, or the boy Cranks, or some other party, I have been utterly ineffectual in stifling it.

Where to begin? I paid a call upon my mother at eleven this morning. I invented a pretext upon which I could pass my father's sick-room (a book I wished to borrow from his library) and, as we planned, I interrupted Miss Smith in her peculiar labours, precisely as Winters described them. Moreover, standing by the door, I even overheard her address my father as 'Billy'! She withdrew her hands from the bowl, upon the moment that I entered, and made a pretence of washing them. I demanded to know what she meant by speaking to my father in such an impertinent manner; but I was met by mute insolence. Naturally, I went directly to my mother, promising the woman that she would be summarily dismissed for her pains.

I found my mother in the drawing-room. Never have I had a more unprofitable or unedifying conversation.

I spoke to her first about Miss Smith's engagement at the Institute. She said, to my utter astonishment, that she knew of it; that I had no right to interfere with Miss Smith's activities outside her hours of employment; and that she did not think it discreditable to her character, if she *played a small part in the advancement of scientific knowledge*!

Second, I told her of the water and the magnetic experiment that I had just seen performed in my father's sick-room. My mother told me that *she herself* had encouraged Miss Smith to make these trials; and that she had enjoined secrecy, in case of talk amongst the servants. I questioned the propriety and wisdom of any activity one felt obliged to conceal from one's own household; but she would not listen to reason.

Finally, when I spoke of the familiar and coarse tone in which Miss Smith addressed my father, she simply said I was *not to mind such idle talk*.

I checked my temper; I could easily have quit the house there and then.

It transpired, as we talked further, that Miss Smith was hired by my mother solely because of her 'talents' in the mesmeric sphere, since my mother rather considers herself a 'convert' to the 'New Science'. Lady Pennethorpe apparently credits the girl with easing her gout and that is how she came to hear of her. Never was a more baleful influence exercised! Miss Smith herself is employed under the general supervision of Dr. Stead, the very man you saw at the Institute. Moreover, I gather that it is that self-same worthy individual to whom my father's care is now entrusted. Our own doctor – a man who has served the family for over thirty years – banished from the sick-room!

I tried every reasoned argument to sway her but to no avail. My mother has become convinced of the merits of mesmerism and of the restorative powers of Miss Smith, though I see no evidence whatsoever for the latter, and little for the former. To my mind, my father's unfortunate condition seems unchanged, in every respect. In addition, my mother talked of Dr. Stead with a zealous, unchecked enthusiasm that quite disturbed me. If I did not know better, I should think the man had 'mesmerised' her himself – certainly he could find no better apologist!

What was I to do? I held my tongue and left the house; I could do naught else.

Of course, under other circumstances, was I not already cognisant of your discovery concerning Miss Smith's parentage, I might have thought that my mother, depressed in spirits, had merely fallen prey to one of the peculiar crazes which distinguish our modern age. Doctors of mesmerism; professors of phrenology; peddlers of patent cures: all such fellows can turn a woman's credulity to their pecuniary advantage. Yet my mother seemed simultaneously quite sane, and utterly beyond reason; I could not and cannot explain it, even upon long reflection.

Following your advice, I next resolved to visit Wilmot, and without delay. I hope you will not think me foolish to act so hastily.

I found him in his office. There was, indeed, an atmosphere of liquor and much of the place appeared to be in disorder, with documents strewn wildly about his desk. He could not, however, refuse me admittance.

I talked briefly about my father's condition and the question of power of attorney, which may soon be required – a point I had been meaning to raise with him regardless. In fairness, the man gave a good account of himself; he was not so drunk as *that*. Then I asked him about the letters. Rather, I should say, I asked if there were any letters that my father had entrusted to his safe-keeping; I said that we thought my father had indicated as much in a brief spell of lucidity (would that he were capable of doing so!). I believe I made it sound convincing enough. Indeed, I am quite sure of it.

For the fellow froze.

He recovered his composure; he replied that there were various documents, some being letters, which he held in trust for my father. That he could not vouchsafe their contents, even to me, without breaking the bonds of professional integrity, *et cetera*. I let the matter rest at that; I had nothing more that I might ask of him. Yet I am certain that I touched a nerve.

Sarah, what am I to do? There is something amiss here. Yet I cannot go against my mother's express wishes; and I have no explanation as to these 'letters' which appear to be at the root of the business with Wilmot.

What is your advice? I fear I am in dire need of your counsel.

Yours,
    Arthur DeSalle

Sarah Tanner put down the letter with a despairing sigh.

Her advice?

She had no idea whatsoever.

⸻

'You know my advice, missus,' said Ralph Grundy, tidying up the empty coffee-house's little booths, as the hour drew close to midnight, 'though you don't like to hear it.'

'"Best leave well alone."'

'There you go.'

'I am asking for your help, Ralph, not a moral,' said Sarah Tanner. 'You've a sharp enough mind.'

The old man shook his head, but nonetheless seemed pleased with the compliment.

'Well,' muttered Ralph, 'how do you reckon it stands at present?'

'Well, I think some letters belonging to Lord DeSalle have been lost from Wilmot's office; and there's someone who wants them back; someone who had Charlie Grubb killed to keep the whole thing quiet.'

'Sounds likely enough,' replied the waiter. 'And what about this "Smith" girl?'

'It can't be coincidence that she's looking after Arthur's father. But why? That's what I can't fathom. If Arthur's right, and it is some kind of wretched conspiracy – well, I have no idea to what end. Who gains by it? It is the same with these "letters" – I don't even know their contents. Tell me, Ralph, what would a proper detective do?'

'From what I know about it,' said the old man, 'a Scotland Yard man does three things: asks a few questions, lurks about, and hopes something turns up. Only you ain't in a position to go demanding anything of nobody, missus; and you can hang about Berkeley Square all you like, but you ain't never going to get inside that house. And, as for something turning up, I've a feeling it'll be a turn for the worse. I can't see your Miss Smith being too talkative neither. And what about your pal Cranks? As soon as he hears you're sniffing about again, he'll be back. And I ain't over-fond of his company.'

'Nor I,' replied Mrs. Tanner. 'But I made Arthur a promise.'

Ralph Grundy adopted a rather world-weary

expression. 'It ain't my place to say it, missus, but I'll come out with it anyhow. It won't matter what you do, your Mr. DeSalle, he won't be getting shut of his wife in a hurry.'

'Ralph! Don't be ridiculous.'

'Ridiculous, is it? I've seen your face when those letters of his turn up; lights up like a lamp. It ain't worth risking your neck – nor mine, neither, come to that – just because you're still sweet on him.'

'It's not your place,' said Sarah Tanner, frowning, 'you're right on that score.'

The old man shrugged. 'Said as much, didn't I?'

Mrs. Tanner fell silent. As the waiter finished his chores for the evening, however, she spoke up again.

'I'm sorry, Ralph. I didn't mean to be harsh.'

'No, missus.'

'Just tell me one thing – if I left you in charge of the shop – the whole thing, mind you – for a few days, would you do it?'

'I reckon,' replied the old man, albeit without much certainty in his voice.

'And if I wasn't here, you could stop the night, and keep an eye on Norah?'

'If I had to, I suppose.'

'Good,' she said, with a smile playing about her lips. 'Because you've given me an idea.'

⁓

The next day, Arthur DeSalle looked at the letter, sitting in the pigeon-hole reserved for his personal correspondence at the Reform Club. It was a female hand, which he recognised as Sarah Tanner's. Placing it in his pocket, he waited until he found a quiet armchair in the corner of the smoking-room, opened the envelope and read the contents.

Fortunately it was a gloomy, dimly lit corner. For, if anyone had been looking at Arthur DeSalle as he read, they would have seen a rather shocked expression flit across his face.

CHAPTER TWENTY-ONE

At mid-day on the following Monday, a peculiar sight was seen on Leather Lane. Sarah Tanner, proprietress of the New Dining and Coffee Rooms, was observed leaving her establishment, together with a small trunk, and getting into a hackney. A few of the meaner-spirited females, who watched Mrs. Tanner's comings and goings, wondered whether she might be quitting for good – ahead of a bailiff or police constable. One even went so far as to mutter something about horse-meat. Joe Drummond, however, having a general interest in the subject, ventured to inquire within, and was informed by Ralph Grundy that Mrs. Tanner had been called away to a dying relative, somewhere in the north of the country, would be travelling by train, and was likely to be absent for a week or more.

Which was, of course, utterly untrue.

The hackney, in fact, pursued a pre-determined course westwards, along Oxford Street, turning south into Mayfair, and finally stopping a short distance from Grosvenor Square, outside Mivart's Hotel, ranked as one of the first-class London establishments. There, the trunk was unloaded and Mrs. Tanner, dressed in a rather superior silk, descended from the cab and followed her luggage inside.

—

Not long after her arrival, Sarah Tanner left her suite and found a quiet corner in the hotel's coffee-room, where she could sit and observe the comings and goings of the hotel's guests. She waited patiently as a white-aproned waiter laid out the requisite silver-ware for taking tea and she showed no surprise when, a few minutes later, the same waiter showed Arthur DeSalle to her table.

'Mr. DeSalle, how charming to see you again.'

'The pleasure is mine, ma'am,' he replied, albeit with a degree of hesitation. 'I trust you had a pleasant journey.'

'Indeed. Please, won't you have a seat?'

Arthur DeSalle sat down, looking somewhat anxiously in the direction of the departing waiter.

'Arthur! I swear,' said Sarah Tanner, *sotto voce*, 'you look like you expect to be arrested at any moment.'

'You know full well, Sarah, that I am not accustomed to such deception.'

'I know nothing of the sort; you are just out of practice. Besides, it is Mrs. Richmond, now, if you please. People *will* talk, if you are not more careful.'

'That is precisely my concern. If Arabella were to hear that I was conducting some sort of illicit liaison in broad daylight—'

'I thought you had told her?'

'Of course – that I had promised to pay a call upon the friendless, widowed cousin of an old acquaintance. I said nothing of your age or . . .'

'Or what?'

162

'Beauty.'

Despite herself, Sarah Tanner blushed. 'I see. And what of the acquaintance?'

'Earl Stanhope is in India; I have written to him. He is a good fellow; he won't gainsay me.'

'Then I am perfectly respectable; a harmless female, obliged to spend a few days in the metropolis. You have nothing to fear, unless you plan to make love to me over your cup of tea.'

'Nothing to fear?' said DeSalle, skeptically. 'When meeting a solitary woman at Mivart's? When her rooms and every article in her wardrobe have been paid for at my behest!'

'I hardly think we need mention that detail. Besides, you used an intermediary, did you not? The principal point to recall is that I am in London to meet with lawyers, in order to receive a bequest from a relative.'

'I know the story you concocted, Sarah. You do not have to drill me on it.'

'Doesn't it answer well enough?' asked Mrs. Tanner. 'A widow on the brink of a fortune is as good a bait as any.'

'I suppose I should just consider myself fortunate that Arabella is not at home.'

'Really?'

'She has gone to visit her mother in Surrey.'

'Without her husband? You've not been married a year.'

'I accompanied her there, of course. You know there is no great intimacy between us, Sarah. Besides, this business with my father makes it necessary that I remain in town.'

'Then, as I say, there is nothing to worry about.'

Arthur DeSalle shook his head. 'No, I should never have agreed to this mad scheme in the first place.'

'It is a little late for that. If we think Miss Smith is a fraud—'

'Do you doubt it?'

'I mean above and beyond her "powers". If she has another motive for acting as your father's nurse, then it is either with the connivance of her employer or without. For my part, I suspect that Dr. Stead is, at best, a charlatan. I think it would be as well to find out, don't you? If he is innocent of any wrongdoing – well, who knows, *he* may wish to dismiss the girl.'

'That is all well and good,' said DeSalle. 'But I never expected that I should have to introduce you to my mother!'

'You will be introducing "Mrs. Richmond", if that is any consolation. And your mother may reveal some clue that may help unravel this mystery. Unless, of course, you think she will be sullied by my mere presence.'

'Sarah, if she discovers who you are,' said DeSalle, 'or what you once were to me, I cannot conceive of the consequences.'

Sarah Tanner sighed. 'I have no intention of mentioning either point. You asked for my help; if you prefer to go to the police, then by all means put an end to this now.'

'And make my mother a laughing stock? A victim of some "mesmeric" fraud? No, I will not have it.'

'Then we are agreed?'

Reluctantly, Desalle assented.

'I am putting my faith in you, Sarah. I hope I am doing the right thing.'

'I will do my best. Will you have some tea? It might steady your nerves. Now, remind me, at what hour did we agree I should call?'

That same day, at four o'clock precisely, Mrs. Sarah Richmond – or, at least, a woman answering to that name – arrived in Berkeley Square. Dressed in cream barège, wrapped in a knee-length talma mantle, she gave every indication of being a well-bred woman of fashion, from the dozen flounces of her skirt to the draped pagoda sleeves, and hair neatly dressed in weaved bandeaux, just visible beneath her bonnet. Having rung the bell, and presented a card, she was conducted to the first-floor drawing-room. There, before a white marble fire-place, Italian in style, carved in intricate floral designs, stood Arthur DeSalle in his best morning-suit, his hands clasped rather too tightly behind his back. To his right, seated in a high-backed armchair, sat a woman whom Sarah Tanner knew must be the Viscountess DeSalle. She possessed only the slightest likeness to her son, but there was something refined, elegant and commanding in her features, that made the conclusion inescapable.

'This is Mrs. Richmond, Mama,' said Arthur DeSalle, rather hastily, as if to check any uncertainty upon the subject.

'My Lady,' said Mrs. Tanner, with a curtsey.

'I trust you are well, Mrs. Richmond.'

'Yes, thank you, ma'am. Your Ladyship is very kind.'

'My son has just been speaking of you. We are happy to make your acquaintance. You are a relation of Earl Stanhope's, I understand. A very agreeable young man. Does he thrive in India?'

'I believe so, ma'am. In truth, our only connexion has been through correspondence – although he has shown me great kindness.'

'Please, Mrs. Richmond, take a seat,' said Lady DeSalle, graciously. 'I trust you will take tea? Arthur, will you ring the bell?'

Arthur DeSalle obliged, but, rather than take a seat himself, coughed rather nervously.

'I'm afraid, Mrs. Richmond – if you will forgive me – I have an engagement elsewhere that I cannot break. I had not realised the hour. I wish I could remain a little longer in your company.'

'Of course, sir.'

Arthur DeSalle nodded, bid his mother good-bye, and left the room. If his mother thought his departure a little abrupt, she refused to show it.

'I gather you are new to London, Mrs. Richmond?' said Lady DeSalle, as a maid arrived bearing a tea-service no less handsome than that of Mivart's Hotel.

'Yes, I am. I have always had a horror of the place. It is so vast and bustling and noisy; I cannot comprehend it.'

'I much prefer the country myself,' replied Lady DeSalle, with a lofty certainty of tone that rather hinted that anyone suggesting otherwise would be little short of lunatic. 'But the demands of Society are such that one must keep a house in town.'

Mrs. Tanner smiled in polite agreement. If her own experience of Society had taught her anything, it was the requisite amount of deference to be applied to the aristocracy.

'I understand you are a widow, Mrs. Richmond?'

'Two years now,' replied Mrs. Tanner.

'I am sorry for your loss. And Arthur tells me you were obliged to travel to London alone?'

'Yes, ma'am, only with my maid. We live in a remote part of the country in Northumberland, and my husband, God rest his soul, lived a very quiet life, with only a handful of acquaintances and few friends. I am obliged, on occasion, to fall back upon my own resources.'

'How exceedingly trying,' said Lady DeSalle, taking a sip of tea.

Sarah Tanner paused for thought. She resolved to seize the opportunity, even though she might offend her hostess.

'I trust Lord DeSalle is in good health, ma'am?' she said.

Lady DeSalle's studied impassive countenance seemed, if only for an instant, to display a tremor of emotion.

'I'm afraid my husband is not at all well, Mrs. Richmond; quite the contrary.'

'I'm sorry, ma'am. I do hope I haven't distressed you.'

'There is no need for an apology,' said Lady DeSalle, her brisk tone returning. 'You were not to know of my husband's illness.'

'I trust he will recover, ma'am.'

'We hope for the best,' replied Lady DeSalle. 'He is in a somewhat debilitated condition but we pray daily for his recovery.'

'If I may be so bold, ma'am,' said Sarah Tanner, with deliberate timidity, 'in my experience, there is much to be said for sea-water. I am afflicted by certain ailments myself, and I find it most efficacious.'

'I am sure, in some trivial circumstances, Mrs. Richmond, bathing is quite appropriate,' said Lady DeSalle, with polite condescension, 'but not in this instance.'

Sarah Tanner nodded, attempting to look suitably apologetic. She had a feeling that more might be accomplished by silence; there was something in Lady DeSalle's voice that suggested a desire to confide in – or, at least, educate – her guest.

'Have you heard, in Northumberland, of the New Science, Mrs. Richmond?'

'Ma'am?'

'The application of the principles of animal magnetism to the healing art,' said Lady DeSalle.

'Mesmerism? I have heard of it, ma'am,' she said, cautiously, 'though I know little about it.'

'I can tell from your reticence, Mrs. Richmond, that you have heard nothing in its favour. Magnetism has been much traduced in recent years. Nonetheless, you may take my assurance that one may gain a good deal more benefit from the judicious application of magnetic influence, by a medical man who is a skilled practitioner of the art, than a month's submersion in salt-water.'

'You believe in the practice, ma'am?'

'My dear Mrs. Richmond, from what I have seen and heard, with my own eyes and ears, I believe in it wholeheartedly.'

'Your Ladyship,' replied Mrs. Tanner, as if struck by a sudden thought, 'I do not suppose that you know of any such gentleman in London – a respectable medical man, I mean – whom I might consult, during my visit? Forgive me – I do not mean to impose . . .'

'Why, of course, my dear,' said Lady DeSalle, visibly pleased, despite her composed manner, to have made such an impression. 'I can recommend an excellent man. His name is Dr. Stead. I have consulted him myself. I will give you his card.'

'Your Ladyship is really too considerate,' said Sarah Tanner, suppressing the slight smile which formed upon her lips. 'I could not ask for more.'

CHAPTER TWENTY-TWO

The practice, and London residence, of Dr. John Stead was in a good position at the end of Upper Wimpole Street, Marylebone. One of a long terrace of identical homes, constructed in the time of the Prince Regent, built after the fashion of the period, it possessed iron railings, stone steps, and a facing of white stucco, etched into faux monumental blocks, which served to conceal plainer, less substantial walls of yellow London brick – walls which, unadorned, would never have been deemed suitable for such a respectable district.

To Dr. Stead's left lived a retired surgeon; to his right, a dentist; and dotted all along the street were men who made a living from the ills of others. For the district had the reputation of being something of a medical *quartier*, a self-perpetuating fame which obliged the best physicians from every corner of the capital, if not the country, to take rooms within its boundaries, whether in Harley Street, Wimpole Street, or the surrounding environs. It was, therefore, no surprise to Sarah Tanner to discover that Helena Smith's employer, as a doctor to the aristocracy, could be found in Marylebone. Indeed, it would have been peculiar to find him anywhere else. And yet, even as the maid-servant who accompanied her pulled the door-bell, she could not shake the first impression she had formed at the mesmerist's lecture; namely that Dr. John Stead was nothing but a fraud.

The door was answered by a bewigged footman, who received them into the hall. Sarah Tanner let her maid remove her mantle and take her gloves. Had the footman been more alert, he might have noticed that the maid – who bore an uncanny resemblance to the waitress of a certain Leather Lane coffee-house – did so rather clumsily and winked at her employer in the process: a form of communication not normally reserved for mistress and servant. But the footman was an elderly individual, with poor eye-sight and little curiosity, who had little interest in Norah Smallwood's true character. Instead, he merely guided the two women into the doctor's empty waiting-room, which, in an entirely private residence, would have served as a dining-room or front-parlour. In this instance, however, the handsome, lofty chamber was given over to a surfeit of comfortably padded chairs and settees, enough to accommodate some twenty or so patients, with only a small sideboard, a pair of landscape pictures and a cheerful fire in the grate, to offer a semblance of domesticity.

'I will tell the doctor you are here, ma'am,' said the footman, with a bow. Turning on his heels, he quit the room via a green baize door, that led into another chamber at the back of the house.

'And what on earth was *that*?' said Sarah Tanner, in a whisper, imitating Norah Smallwood's wink.

'I didn't mean nothing,' said Norah. 'It just struck me – me, a lady's maid!'

'He might have seen you.'

'No, he wouldn't,' said Norah, defensively.

Sarah Tanner sighed. 'I should have hired a girl from the hotel.'

'Oh, no, missus,' protested Norah, 'don't say that. I wouldn't have missed this for the world! Here, what do you think he's going to do to you?'

'Whatever it is,' replied Mrs. Tanner, 'just hold your tongue and do nothing.'

'I can manage that,' replied Norah.

'I wish I was so sure.'

The green baize door opened once more.

'Please come through, ma'am,' said the footman. 'The doctor is expecting you.'

The doctor's consulting-room was little different from any regular drawing-room, with furniture of sturdy mahogany and heavy curtains of crimson damask, partially drawn, so as to exclude any source of distraction. The only clue to Dr. Stead's occupation was a porcelain bust which sat upon the mantel-piece, the skull divided into phrenological portions. The man himself rose from his desk as his guests entered the room. Mrs. Tanner noticed the same conspicuous watch-chain she had seen at the Marylebone Institute, hanging down from his plump waist. For although the doctor was not fat, he had a round face and a look of well-padded comfort about him, suggestive of hearty breakfasts and substantial dinners.

'Please, ma'am, do take a seat,' said Dr. Stead, addressing Mrs. Tanner, before turning to Norah Smallwood, appraising both women with a quick glance. 'And you, my dear.'

'Thank you, sir.'

'First, ma'am,' continued the doctor, 'may I apologise for keeping you waiting. I have only just finished my morning levée; I take a few patients gratuitously in the early hours – it takes up a good deal of my time.'

171

'It was but a moment, sir,' replied Mrs. Tanner. 'Think nothing of it.'

'Thank you, ma'am. Most kind. I would, of course, happily have paid a call upon you at home.'

'As you know, I am only temporarily resident in the capital. Mivart's is a very decent hotel, but I prefer to be discreet in such matters; I trust it is not an inconvenience?'

'Not at all, my dear lady. Not at all! I hope Lady DeSalle is in good health?'

'I cannot claim an intimate acquaintance with Her Ladyship, sir, but I found her well. It is my cousin, Earl Stanhope, that is a friend of the family, but Her Ladyship was good enough to give me your card. Indeed, she said you are amongst the best physicians in the capital.'

'Her Ladyship is far too kind,' replied Stead. 'She has acquainted you, perhaps, with the principles upon which I practise?'

'If you mean the application of mesmerism, sir, then, yes, she has indeed. However, when I read your card, I realised that I was already aware of your abilities.'

'Really?' said the doctor. 'And how did that come about, ma'am?'

'I was amongst an audience for your lecture at the Marylebone Institute only last week.'

'Ah! Ma'am! I see you already have formed an interest in the New Science; that explains a good deal. I trust you will not think me an incorrigible reprobate, if I correct you upon one point. The honour of giving the lecture must be accorded to my mentor, Professor Felton. I am, at best, the Professor's apprentice. I was merely present to provide an object lesson.'

'A remarkable demonstration, though.'

'A commonplace example, ma'am, rest assured. The girl in question is particularly sensitive to my influence; and, if I may advert to the medical aspect, it was a simple matter to cure her of her fits; merely a restoration of the magnetic equilibrium.'

'Tell me, does she come from a good home?' asked Mrs. Tanner. 'I was struck by how calm and self-possessed she appeared.'

'A poor, but respectable upbringing, ma'am. I have known the family for some years, and her condition was a sore trial to them. Once one thoroughly understands magnetic principles, however, these things are swiftly resolved by a medical man; I have dealt with all manner of feminine nervous complaints in the same manner. Perhaps, ma'am, if you can advise me of your symptoms?'

Norah Smallwood glanced slightly nervously at her mistress.

'It is, unfortunately, a question of general fatigue,' replied Mrs. Tanner. 'A weariness that, on occasion, quite overwhelms me. I have seen several medical men, and most have recommended salt-water.'

'To no effect?'

'Precisely.'

Dr. Stead clasped his hands together, sitting forward in his chair.

'That, ma'am, does not surprise me. Bathing is of limited value in such cases. And you have not subjected yourself to magnetic influence?'

'No, sir, not as yet,' said Mrs. Tanner, timidly. 'I have attended several lectures and learnt a good deal. Would you say it is dangerous?'

'Only to inexperienced dabblers in the art, ma'am; there is some small danger if a subject cannot be wakened. But you need not worry on that score. I flatter myself that I possess sufficient knowledge. I could begin a course of treatment today, in this very room, if you are willing and prove a suitable subject.'

'Is not everyone suitable?'

'It is merely a question of time. The transfer of magnetic fluid, the creation of a sympathy between operator and subject, all depends on the patient's particular constitution.'

Sarah Tanner smiled demurely.

'Very well, sir. I am willing to put your powers to the test.'

'This very day?' said the doctor.

'Indeed, sir, if you can spare me your time.'

'Any acquaintance of Lady DeSalle is worthy of my undivided attention,' said the doctor, graciously.

'Then how shall we begin? I know you will require absolute silence. Is it best that I dismiss my maid?'

Sarah Tanner looked at the doctor closely as she spoke; for she chose the question quite deliberately. The doctor's reply, however, was immediate and decisive.

'I fear that would place us both in an invidious position, ma'am. It is incumbent upon humble practitioners such as myself to remain beyond reproach. Unfortunately, there are still those who consider the practice of mesmerism a cloak for outrages upon female virtue. If the girl merely remains present, quiet and composed, that will suffice.'

'Of course,' replied Mrs. Tanner. 'Forgive me.'

Dr. Stead smiled a consoling smile.

'Well then, ma'am, if you are willing, let us see what can be achieved.'

The curtains were drawn and a solitary lamp lit. In the flickering light, Norah Smallwood looked on as

174

the mesmerist positioned his new subject, telling Mrs. Tanner to remain seated in the high-backed walnut chair, but to turn ninety degrees, so that she sat sideways, with no support for her back. He then took his own chair and sat down facing her.

'Now, ma'am, if you would be so good as to place your hand outstretched, palm upwards, so that it may become a conduit for the magnetic influence, which I will bring to bear.'

Mrs. Tanner complied. Dr. Stead, in turn, placed his left hand atop his subject's, his fingers curled as if clutching an invisible ball.

'And now, I shall place my right hand upon your forehead.'

Norah watched her mistress, who remained unmoved, as the mesmerist spread his fingers across her temples.

'Now, ma'am, I beg you,' said Stead, leaning forward, so that his face was mere inches from his subject's, 'you must do nothing but look directly into my eyes. It is imperative that your gaze does not waver. Do you understand?'

'Indeed.'

'Very well.'

The darkened room fell silent as Norah Smallwood watched the peculiar spectacle play out before her. The mesmerist, hunched forward, grasping his subject, might have seemed comical in striking such a theatrical posture; but there was something horribly intense in his expression, combined with the silent submission of his subject, that gradually filled her with a peculiar sense of dread. As the minutes passed, and both Stead and Mrs. Tanner remained unmoving, she began to wonder if her employer was genuinely paralysed by the power of the doctor's eyes. Every few seconds, she looked at the carriage clock that sat on the mantelpiece opposite, but its hands seemed quite frozen. At length, her own mind began to wander; she fancied the only sound in the room was that of her own heartbeat.

Then, suddenly, it happened; she had not imagined it could happen, but it did.

The muscles in Sarah Tanner's neck seemed to twitch; her eyes rolled heavenwards, as her eyelids drooped shut and her head lolled forward, though her body remained perfectly upright.

The anxious, surprised expression on Norah's face did not escape her host, who, relaxing his posture slightly, had turned to look in her direction. There was, it must be admitted, a look of some satisfaction upon his face.

'Do not be alarmed, my dear; your mistress is in good hands. Now I can begin to treat her.'

Norah Smallwood nodded, dumb-struck. Dr. Stead, meanwhile, gently removed his hands from his subject and began to clench and unclench both his fists, as if flicking invisible sparks from his fingertips. Then, without stopping the odd spasmodic gestures, he moved his arms from the top of Sarah Tanner's shoulders to her feet, in slow sweeping passes. Norah counted two dozen, before he stood and removed himself to crouch behind Mrs. Tanner's back, repeating the same procedure from the nape of her neck to the base of her spine, again and again. It resembled the preamble to some strange conjuring trick; or simply the actions of a madman. And yet the doctor seemed utterly in earnest.

Norah looked back at the clock; ten minutes had passed.

'There!' said the doctor triumphantly, although

Norah could see no particular reason for the exclamation. 'Now, we must bring your mistress back, eh?'

'If you please, sir.'

Dr. Stead chuckled. 'It is easily accomplished, my dear, rest assured.'

He positioned himself once again upon the chair in front of Mrs. Tanner and began making the magnetic passes in reverse, from her feet to her forehead, as if pulling at countless unseen strings.

A minute passed; and another.

Then Sarah Tanner opened her eyes.

~

'You were an excellent subject, ma'am,' said Dr. Stead, as he accompanied his patient to the door. 'I believe you will feel the benefit of our trial with immediate effect; but for the process to be truly efficacious, I would recommend regular treatment, supplemented by the taking of magnetised water.'

'Indeed,' said Mrs. Tanner, 'I do feel lifted in spirits. I am, however, only in London whilst I resolve the matter of a bequest from a relative; I cannot linger in the capital too long.'

'Of course. Yet, I fear there are few truly effective practitioners in the more remote parts of the country. I am myself in the process of establishing an infirmary so that, in combination with Professor Felton, I may provide treatment in superior accommodation for provincial patients, and for those in need of daily attendance. Perhaps you might care for me to send you particulars?'

'By all means, write to me at Mivart's,' replied Mrs. Tanner, as the footman opened the front door. 'Tell me, sir – I have read that the extraordinary ascendancy of the magnetiser over his subject is indicative of the operator's moral and intellectual superiority. I am curious, do you subscribe to that doctrine?'

'It would be indelicate of me, as a gentleman, to answer in the affirmative, ma'am, so I will beg your leave to remain silent,' said the doctor, with a profoundly humble bow.

'Good day, sir.'

'Good day.'

A carriage stood ready outside the doctor's residence. Norah Smallwood held open the door for her mistress, then swiftly followed her inside. The waitress-cum-maid-servant could only contain herself a few seconds, however, before speaking in awed tones.

'Missus! Tell us! What was it like?'

'What was it like?'

'When he mesmerised you!'

Sarah Tanner smiled. 'Norah, you are a remarkably trusting creature. You should know better.'

'What?' exclaimed Norah. 'No! It was all a dodge? Never!'

'The man's talent is for making money out of willing victims, nothing more. I merely played my part.'

'Didn't you just! Lor! It gave me goose-flesh! You should be in Drury Lane, missus! Why didn't you say something, then?'

'What good would that do? "Sir, you are a fraud!" It would not help one jot. Now, at least, we know he is complicit in concealing Miss Smith's origins – "poor but respectable" indeed! And we know how he makes his money: "magnetising" women and "magnetising" mineral waters! The only question is whether he is simply fleecing Arthur's mother in the same manner as his other patients, or if there is more to it. That's what I cannot understand – *she* does not strike me as a fool, not by any means.'

'You don't think he knew you were kidding him?'

Sarah Tanner smiled. 'I think Dr. Stead was far too busy being my moral and intellectual superior to notice.'

CHAPTER TWENTY-THREE

The following morning, a hackney rattled briskly over Waterloo Bridge. Inside sat Sarah Tanner, and, upon the seat opposite, Arthur DeSalle. The former wore a day-dress of black cotton, a plain and practical outfit that might suit a poor woman in mourning, or any female of limited income and little imagination. It was, decidedly, not a dress that might be worn at Mivart's Hotel or in Berkeley Square. Her companion, likewise, was dressed in a suit of distinctly shiny black cloth that bore no resemblance to his accustomed fine silk, and a shirt and collar that seemed to cause him to flinch whenever he moved his neck.

'I swear, Sarah,' exclaimed DeSalle, as the cab began to slow, 'I do believe that half your schemes are designed with my particular discomfort in mind.'

'It was the best I could find, you have my word,' replied Mrs. Tanner, with a hint of amusement in her voice. 'You can hardly turn up in Lambeth in something that cost twenty guineas. And you have the look of an honest man; who else could I ask? A solitary woman would not be taken seriously.'

'I am still not quite certain what you hope to accomplish.'

'Dr. Stead is something of a fraud – I have found

that much out for myself. In that regard, he may be much the same as every professed "mesmerist" in the capital. But the fact that he is preying upon your mother's credulity may not help you get rid of him. If she has such confidence in his abilities . . . well, I doubt my word alone will sway her. And, unfortunately, he is not the sort of wily debauchee one reads about in the penny press: he had every chance when I offered to dismiss Norah. Whatever he uses his "powers" for, it does not seem to be that.'

'Thank God!'

'But he has lied about Miss Smith and her family. I want to know what they say about him. There is something there, I'm sure of it.'

'You think you can win this man Cranks's confidence? What if the boy should appear?'

'We had better hope he does not.'

Arthur DeSalle said nothing in reply, as the cab pulled to a halt on the Waterloo Road, a short walk from the New Cut and the same coffee-stall to which Sarah Tanner had followed Helena Smith.

'Now, remember,' said Mrs. Tanner in a whisper, as she quit the hansom and let DeSalle pay the driver, 'do try and look pious.'

And with those words, she took a small black leather-bound Bible from her pocket, and clutched it earnestly between both hands.

———

Locating Bob Cranks was, as Sarah Tanner had suspected, a simple matter of visiting various low publics in the vicinity of the New Cut. She was also quite correct in her assumption that sombre dress, a Bible, and the occasional dropping of pamphlets belonging to the New Protestant Truth Society (mysteriously removed *en masse* from outside the Society's offices that very morning) all combined to ensure that their presence, though not especially welcome, went unquestioned, even in the worst beer-shops.

At last, however, she saw the man himself. He was seated alone in a corner of the tap-room of a rather gloomy house that went by the name of the Black Bull, dedicated to serving customers from the New Cut Market. Dressed in a threadbare fustian suit, rather than his professional attire, he cut a less farcical figure than he had by the Waterloo Road coffee-stall; but there was the same look of despair in his countenance, as he contemplated the dregs of porter in the pint-pot that lay before him.

'That is the man.'

'He looks like a confirmed drunkard. It will not work.'

'Really, Arthur,' whispered Mrs. Tanner, 'you should have more faith. Follow my example; and remember everything I told you.'

Arthur DeSalle's reply was stifled as, with a nod to the barman, his companion began to move around the dozen or so tables.

'Forgive me – I am soliciting your aid, gentlemen, for the Samaritan Guild for Distressed Entertainers and their Families. I wondered if you would care to . . . No? I am sorry to have troubled you.'

Arthur DeSalle hesitantly followed suit, ignoring the rather unenthusiastic response of several of the men present. At last, Mrs. Tanner worked her way to Bob Cranks's table.

'I ain't got nothing to spare,' said Cranks, before Sarah Tanner had chance to utter a word. 'I don't bother the Almighty over much, and He don't bother much with me – not least, as far as I can make out.'

182

'It is a worthy cause,' persisted Sarah Tanner, with calm perseverance. 'We are a new Society whose mission is to provide aid and succour to those who have provided wholesome public amusement and entertainment in their working life, who have given joy to others – and, one might almost say, a glimpse of the joy to come.'

'Don't you Heaven-and-Earth me, missus,' muttered Cranks, with a distinct slurring of his speech. 'From the sound of it, you should be sending something my way, not taking it out of my pocket!'

'I don't follow you,' said Mrs. Tanner, with deliberate naïveté.

'Well, ain't I one of them creatures you're talking of?' said Mr. Cranks, rather puffing up with a drunk's pride. 'Ain't I just! If anyone brought amusement, ma'am, it was me – Cranks! "Expert Tumbler and Posture Master"! One time, I played Astley's, Vauxhall and Cremorne – all in one night! If the rheumatics hadn't put paid to it, ma'am, you'd know my name well enough – you mark my words!'

'Well, then you would be eligible for tickets, my man, there is no question of it,' said Arthur DeSalle. 'A decent meal once a week.'

'Would I now?' said the erstwhile acrobat, a somewhat beery suspicion entering his voice. 'Well, I don't need charity slops from some district visitor neither, since you ask. I can still feed myself; I ain't that desperate.'

Sarah Tanner smiled sweetly. 'I commend your natural pride, sir, but do not let it overcome your best interests. The Guild is even endeavouring to place some worthy individuals, who come to our attention, in newly built alms-houses; and to supply small pensions to those in difficulty.'

Bob Cranks raised his eye-brows. 'Is it now?'

'We did not mean to disturb you,' said Mrs. Tanner, making to move away. 'I see the barman would like us to take our leave.'

'Hold on now, hold on,' said Bob Cranks hurriedly. 'I have to think of my family, missus. Sit down here. Tell us more about it. What's a fellow have to do, to earn one of these pensions?'

'Well, you would have to prove what you have told us, for a start,' said Arthur DeSalle. 'I mean to say, about your career upon the stage.'

Bob Cranks downed the remainder of his porter, and stood up from his seat.

'You come with me, sir. I'll prove it all right – just you come home with me!'

⚊

Bob Cranks's lodgings lay in a narrow lane, just off the New Cut, within a few paces from the market. Known by the name of Windmill Court, the place had a distinct odour of rotten cabbage, and a trio of ancient properties, so deeply grimed in fallen soot that they appeared to have been painted black. The acrobat possessed a pair of rooms upon the ground floor of one of the buildings. The bedroom lay at the rear, concealed by a makeshift curtain; the sitting-room, meanwhile, boasted an ill-fitting blind covering the solitary window, disjointed uneven floorboards, and walls that, in several places, were damp to the touch. Even the hearth-stone was chipped and splintered; and the rickety table and two chairs that comprised the principal furniture were made of unfinished deal, as if hastily put together by some drunken carpenter on the spur of the moment. If Mr. Cranks had any refreshment to offer his two guests, he did not make it known. Instead, he hurried to a trunk that lay in the corner of the room, and opened the lid, rummaging inside.

'Ah!' exclaimed Cranks, drolly pathetic, as he pulled out his care-worn costume of jersey and pantaloons. 'Here you have the tumbler's suit of armour, ma'am. All he has to defend his poor self from breaking his neck. And, here,' he continued, 'is proof all right . . . that's my name, ain't it? You tell me if it ain't!'

The proof was a sheef of bills from Astley's Amphitheatre and Vauxhall Gardens: *The Celebrated Cranks: Expert Posture-Master and Tumbler, pupil of Ducrow, he flies like a bird!* was commemorated in print on several occasions.

'Indeed, that is quite satisfactory,' said Mrs. Tanner, looking around the room with an appraising air. 'The Guild committee might well consider your case; I do not believe we have seen anyone more deserving as yet. Tell me, you said you have a family to support?'

'Well,' said Mr. Cranks, a little abashed. 'I don't think I said *that*, missus. My missus – she's dead and buried. My gal earns a few bob as a sick-nurse; the boy, he ain't got no regular occupation. I don't support them much; they keeps me – at least, Helen does. But she can't hardly afford to do it; I'm a sore trial to 'em. What would your committee say to that, do you reckon?'

'Why, I am sure it would count in your favour,' said Mrs. Tanner. 'You say your daughter is a sick-nurse? Is she in regular employment?'

'Aye, worse luck.'

'Worse luck?' said Mrs. Tanner, watching the acrobat closely. His face seemed to become suddenly darker; his expression swiftly clouded with anger.

'Aye, with a fellow what takes liberties; what pretends he's some kind of swell, when he ain't no more a gentleman than I am.'

'Indeed?' said Mrs. Tanner. 'And what sort of man is he, then?'

Bob Cranks picked up the sheath of theatre bills which Sarah Tanner had laid to one side.

'There!' he said.

She followed his pointing finger along the descriptions of Vauxhall Gardens' many delights.

'"The Hermit Seer"?'

'That was him, all right – telling fortunes in the Gardens; in an oyster grotto, with little prizes for the young'uns. Now he calls himself a bleedin' doctor – pardon my language, missus – and lords it all high and mighty over my gal! Still, I don't suppose your committee wants to hear about that, eh?'

Sarah Tanner looked at Arthur DeSalle.

'You'd be surprised, Mr. Cranks.'

'I knew it!' said Arthur DeSalle angrily, as they quit Windmill Court. 'The man is a complete impostor!'

'Does that truly surprise you?'

'My mother must be told; it cannot wait!'

'She must be told,' replied Sarah Tanner, 'but in a fashion so that she cannot help but believe it. Please, will you calm down? Wait – what's this?'

The interruption was, in fact, an elderly woman who stepped from a door near to the entrance to Windmill Court.

'Beg your pardon,' said the woman, 'but are you giving out tickets, ma'am?'

'No, not today.'

'Lord, that's a blessing,' said the old woman.

'A blessing?' said Mrs. Tanner, puzzled.

''Cos that party, who I saw you with, he don't deserve nothing.'

'Whyever not?'

'It's the drink, ma'am; makes him wild. Don't tell me you can't smell it on him? He drove his wife to an early grave; used to beat his daughter black and blue – worse than just a regular hiding – and the boy too, terrible afeard of his temper, until he got too big for him. He's an awful bully, ma'am. Now, if you do have tickets, and you want a temperance house, what keeps the Lord's day, you come and visit us . . .'

'Do you know where the boy lives? Or the daughter?' asked Mrs. Tanner. 'Their father seems to have no idea.'

'I couldn't say. And they won't tell him, ma'am – neither of 'em. Their own flesh and blood, and they won't tell him! Now, is that a man who deserves tickets?'

'Never mind your blasted tickets,' said Arthur DeSalle. 'Sarah – leave the wretched woman to her business.'

'Arthur, for pity's sake—'

'I tell you,' said DeSalle, 'I cannot stomach the foul stink of this place a moment longer. I wish to God you had not brought me here.'

Mrs. Tanner sighed and hurried after her companion. She caught up with him upon the corner of the New Cut, pacing back and forth, in search of a cab.

'The poor woman merely wanted something for her family.'

'And what about my family? My father – a peer of the realm . . . Damn me! what the devil are they plotting?'

'Arthur, I do not care one jot for your father or his

187

title. But I do know that if you want my help, you will go back and give that woman a couple of pennies for her trouble; she does not deserve your contempt.'

'For her trouble?'

'Yes. Arthur, you have always been generous to a fault; the man I know – the man I once admired – would not have treated a poor creature so badly.'

'That man did not fear for his family's future.'

'Arthur, will you go back?'

Arthur DeSalle took a deep breath.

'I suppose I must.'

CHAPTER TWENTY-FOUR

The cab deposited Sarah Tanner and Arthur DeSalle in a narrow lane off the Strand, not far from the Adelphi Arches, outside a small confectioner's, whose extravagant display of cakes and sweetmeats suggested a refined clientele. Mrs. Tanner did not, however, enter the shop but opened a side-door that adjoined the premises and hurried up a set of vertiginous steps. DeSalle followed close behind, bestowing a nervous backwards glance at the departing hackney. The staircase led to a locked door, which concealed a private apartment above the shop, let by the confectioner at sixpence an hour. The room itself was neatly kept, concealed from the street by Swiss lace curtains. Its furniture consisted of an iron-framed bed, a chaise-longue, twin marble wash-stands, and a painted wooden screen – over which was draped a moiré silk day-dress and petticoats, whilst, laid out on the bed, was a suit of smart black silk, a shirt, starched collar and cuffs.

Once inside, Mrs. Tanner locked the door behind her.

'Arthur, there is no-one following. You are quite safe – unless you consider me a danger?'

Arthur DeSalle sighed. 'Sarah, you never used to

make me the constant butt of your wit. Must I explain myself again? I cannot afford to be seen; not with you, and certainly not here.'

'I merely suggest that, in this room at least, you need not fear discovery by your wife,' she said, with rather deliberate emphasis on the last word, 'nothing more.'

'Sarah, please. If you intend to help me, I cannot see why I must endure these constant barbs about Arabella. Why do you try and rile me? You yourself said we were done. Would you prefer me to declare that I still love you?'

'Hardly. We are beyond that.'

'If that is the case, then why did you bring me here? There are a thousand such places.'

'Would you prefer to dress in the street? It's a respectable little house, as these things go. I am sure no questions will be asked.'

'That is not what I meant, and you know full well.'

'You remember it, then?' said Mrs. Tanner, whilst walking away from her interlocutor, and slipping behind the painted screen, reaching back to undo the buttons of her dress.

There was no reply, as DeSalle paced the room.

'Very well, I will say it out loud, if it pleases you,' he said, at last. 'Yes, I remember perfectly well. I remember the first night I spent with you, and the last; and I remember where we were upon each occasion. I can recall every moment and, God help me, the very thought of us together still fills me with a dreadful longing, though two years have passed. There, does that please you? Have I abased myself sufficiently? I swear, I did not realise that this slow torture would be the price for your help. I thought we put my marriage behind us at Vauxhall. I cannot believe you are so bitter.'

There was no reply. DeSalle tentatively stepped to the side of the wooden screen and peered behind. Sarah Tanner stood half dressed, in her cotton chemise, quite still, as if lost in thought, a frown etched upon her lips.

'You are right,' she said. 'I am sorry.'

'Truly?'

'I had thought I had sufficient self-possession; I will try harder.'

'Very well. Thank you.'

'But, still, if you don't mind, I would ask you not to stare.'

DeSalle smiled. Heedless of her admonition, he watched as she fastened a trio of embroidered petticoats about her waist.

'I think I cannot help it. If anything, I do believe you have grown more beautiful since I last saw you.'

'And I do not believe you,' she replied, 'not for an instant. You always had a silver tongue when it suited you. If you must stand there and ogle, will you pass me the gown?'

DeSalle obliged.

'Sarah – if you must know, I do still ache for you,' he said, as she pulled the fashionable dress down over her corseted waist.

'I am sorry to hear it,' she replied, flattening down her skirt with the palms of her hands.

'Are you sure that you will never consider—'

'No. Let us talk about your mother.'

❧

'I should simply tell her the truth,' said DeSalle, nervously pacing the room, as Sarah Tanner sat upon the edge of the bed. Twin glasses of champagne, bought for form's sake from the confectioner, stood untouched upon the mantel-piece.

'What? That the woman you introduced to her as your friend's cousin is in fact your former mistress? That she has found a drunkard in the New Cut who swears her doctor used to tell fortunes at Vauxhall? I should like to see her face.'

'She need not know how I came by the information.'

Sarah Tanner shook her head. 'She knows that you think very little of Stead; she wouldn't have kept the whole thing a secret, if you were in her confidence. And she did not believe you about Miss Smith's ramblings in the Haymarket; I am not sure she will believe this.'

'Then we need proof,' said DeSalle.

'Someone will know him at Vauxhall, but I cannot imagine your mother will visit the Gardens. I suppose we might find a more reliable witness to his former line of work, and drag them to Berkeley Square, but I wouldn't be too sure. At least we know that Miss Smith – Cranks – is his agent; he knows her background well enough, and she knows his.'

'I hardly think that is much comfort,' muttered DeSalle. 'Perhaps I should confront her – Miss Smith – tell her that I know her true colours.'

'Yes, but do you, though? We still don't know what is behind any of this – and if Stead has some peculiar hold upon your mother, then you'll only be alerting him to your suspicions.'

'Sarah, you seem to dismiss everything I suggest.'

'You forget, I know how these games are played. Her Majesty taught me a good deal.'

'Then where does that leave me?'

'I am one woman, Arthur,' said Mrs. Tanner, wearily. 'I cannot do everything. As things stand, if you want my advice, I would have a man watch Stead day and night; see where he goes, who his friends are. They say Inspector Field has opened a Private Inquiry Office – I expect he can be relied upon to find a good man, from what I know of him.'

'That is your best counsel? The police?'

'A former policeman. I suppose, in the meantime, we may still try and dent your mother's trust in Stead.'

'Ah! You have something in mind?' asked DeSalle.

'Perhaps if we were to surprise him. What if – for instance – a passing stranger, a respectable sort, were to recollect his face from Vauxhall?'

'You can engineer it?'

'I know a man who might oblige,' she replied, 'for a couple of bob. Still, we need the right circumstances. Somewhere in public; somewhere we can be sure of the outcome. Ah! I know just the place. Yes, I'm sure if I sing Dr. Stead's praises, your mother may deign to pay me a call at Mivart's; but perhaps you had better put in a good word for me, all the same.'

'Mivart's?'

She smiled. 'I think a little tea party is in order.'

———

The following afternoon, an exquisitely sprung landau, painted dark green, emblazoned with the DeSalle coat-of-arms, pulled to a halt outside Mivart's Hotel. The footman standing at the rear of the carriage, resplendent in plush and powder, jumped athletically down on to the pavement and opened the carriage door for his mistress. He accompanied Lady DeSalle into the foyer, and thence into the coffee-room, where Sarah Tanner sat waiting in a quiet corner. She hurriedly rose and curtseyed.

'Good afternoon, My Lady.'

'Mrs. Richmond. You are looking well.'

193

'Thank you, ma'am.'

Lady DeSalle dismissed her footman, whilst a hotel waiter materialised – with considerable haste – to offer her a seat.

'How are you finding Mivart's? I have not been here for some years. Yes, I do believe the Emperor of Russia took an entire floor and received guests, back in forty-seven or forty-eight; I remember my husband signing his visiting-book. The reception was a ridiculous affair, if I recall, but that is the Russian court for you.'

'A small suite of rooms is quite sufficient for my tastes, ma'am.'

'I expect it is,' said Lady DeSalle in a matter-of-fact tone, which rather implied that anything else would be utterly improper. 'I am glad to hear that is the case.'

Mrs. Tanner smiled politely.

'Will you take tea, ma'am?' said the waiter, who had hovered nearby, cautiously officious. Lady DeSalle, in turn, gave the slightest nod of her head, as if speaking would be utterly redundant. The waiter hurried away.

'I trust your time in London is proceeding in a satisfactory fashion, Mrs. Richmond?'

'You should know, ma'am,' said Mrs. Tanner, as the tea-service arrived, silver spoons surreptitiously replaced by gold-plated, in honour of the Viscountess, 'that I am brought to the capital by a legal matter, in connection with a relative's estate. It appears I am rather at the beck and call of the Court of Chancery.'

'You have my sympathy. I am thankful we have rarely had recourse to the law. And I suppose you have not had opportunity to see any more of the capital?'

'Very little, ma'am. I did, however, pay a call upon Dr. Stead, the man you recommended.'

'Ah, yes, you mentioned as much in your charming letter. How did you find him?'

Mrs. Tanner smiled and began to rhapsodise upon the skills and merits of the mesmeric physician, with the enthusiasm of an evangelical preacher. Lady DeSalle, in turn, nodded politely, as her companion described an astounding improvement in her physical well-being, attributable solely to the agency of Dr. Stead and his manipulations.

'He is a remarkable man,' agreed Lady DeSalle. 'There are so few medical men that may be relied upon.'

'You have used his services yourself, you said, ma'am?'

'In truth, Mrs. Richmond,' said Lady DeSalle, 'I am in quite good health. Dr. Stead has dedicated his powers to improving the condition of my husband. It is a delicate matter; but I have high hopes that much may be achieved, where others have failed. He assures me it is quite possible, if the magnetic influence is applied regularly under the correct conditions; and I have every reason to believe him.'

Sarah Tanner nodded sympathetically. Lady DeSalle, however, seemed to hesitate, as if fearing having said too much.

'And how do you find the London weather?' she said at last, changing the subject with consummate confidence. 'It is quite pleasant for the time of year; a little chill, perhaps.'

Before Mrs. Tanner could reply, however, the conversation was interrupted by the timid presence of the waiter, who bore a calling-card on a silver platter.

'Oh dear,' exclaimed Mrs. Tanner, picking up the

card and reading it. 'I fear Your Ladyship must forgive me. It is Dr. Stead. How ridiculous! I engaged him to call on me later this afternoon. There must be some confusion about the hour. I shall write him a brief note . . .'

'Such things happen, my dear,' said Lady DeSalle graciously. 'There is no need for that. Have the poor man come through.'

Mrs. Tanner nodded, and gave the requisite instruction to the waiter. It was not long before Stead strode purposefully through the coffee-room, ending with a low bow in front of his patroness.

'Your Ladyship,' said the doctor, 'I did not mean to intrude.'

'I expected you later in the afternoon, sir,' said Mrs. Tanner, with as much sincerity as she could muster. 'Did we not say four o'clock?'

'There must have been a misunderstanding, ma'am,' replied the doctor, plainly deeming it rather impolitic to disagree. 'My apologies.'

'Mrs. Richmond has just been singing your praises, sir,' added Lady DeSalle.

'You make me blush, ma'am,' said the doctor, with little sign of the affliction upon his cheeks.

'There is no need for protestation,' continued Lady DeSalle, imperiously. 'Mrs. Richmond is a woman of good sense. You will return later, I trust.'

'Why, of course, ma'am – anything for Mrs. Richmond.'

'And we shall see you tomorrow?'

'Of course, ma'am. All the arrangements are in place. I have the rooms prepared – decorated as per your instructions.'

Lady DeSalle nodded, with much the same air of dismissal as she had adopted with the waiter.

'I will not impose any further upon Your Ladyship,' said Dr. Stead, before turning to Mrs. Tanner, 'and a pleasure to see you again, ma'am. With your permission, I shall return at four o'clock?'

Sarah Tanner nodded. Stead made to bow once more, but as he rose, another man, seated in a lounge chair a few feet away, got to his feet. He was a portly, middle-aged individual whom residents of Holborn might have identified as one Charles Merryweather, Esq. Fortunately, no-one in Mivart's Hotel was likely to be in such a position; and so, dressed in a smart, if somewhat dandyish fashion, Charles Merryweather had merely passed as a gentleman, waiting on the company of a guest of the hotel.

'You, sir!' exclaimed Merryweather.

Dr. Stead turned, somewhat startled.

'Are you addressing me, sir?'

'Of course! I do believe I know you, sir!' continued Merryweather. 'Never forget a face! Will you shake my hand?'

Dr. Stead obliged, warily. 'I cannot recall—'

'I always said you were a fellow who'd prosper. My! Who's your tailor, eh?' said Merryweather, playfully, whilst reaching forward to rub the material of the doctor's jacket between thumb and forefinger. Stead brushed his hand away, astonished.

'Do you know this *gentleman*?' said Lady DeSalle, with icy emphasis.

'Know me, ma'am?' said Merryweather, before Stead could deny the connection. 'Well, perhaps he has forgotten. But I know him – why, he was the toast of Vauxhall Gardens; and Laurel House – my own residence, ma'am, a pleasant little villa in Kentish Town – not four summers ago.'

Sarah Tanner watched Stead carefully at the mention of Vauxhall. There was a glimmer of recognition – and fear – in his eyes, which he immediately subdued.

'I fear, sir, you mistake me for some other party.'

'Bertram H. Weatherspoon never forgets a face, sir,' proclaimed Merryweather, warming to his role. 'And my dear girl – Lizzie, ma'am, the finest daughter a man ever had – if she were here now, she would get down upon her knees, take your hand, and shower it with kisses!'

'There would be no call for any such unnatural proceeding,' protested Stead. 'I tell you—'

'You told her, my friend! You said "A dark man from over the seas will pledge his troth"! And didn't she attend to it! And didn't she meet the captain of a vessel at Greenwich Fair – an American, and none the worse for that! And did not they marry – they wed that very month! And don't they lived happy and content, with a babe-in-arms and a fine house down Deptford way – why, of course they do! You foretold it all, sir – and I thank you for it!'

'I fear, Your Ladyship,' said Dr. Stead, looking anxiously at his patroness, 'the man has quite taken leave of his senses. I am sorry that he should pester you – I will have him removed. Waiter!'

'Your Ladyship? Why! Begging your pardon, ma'am,' said Merryweather, with a bow. 'I hadn't realised how far my friend had risen. Well, I suppose we all want to know what the future holds, eh? I commend him to you, ma'am – take the word of Bertram H. Weatherspoon – you have the finest oracle as ever sat in Vauxhall's hermitage! Ask my Lizzie! We drink his praises every year, on her wedding day!'

As Charles Merryweather finished his soliloquy of

praise, he suddenly found himself surrounded by a trio of Mivart's staff, not least the doorman of the establishment, hastily summoned by the waiter.

'I say, sir! What do you mean by this?' protested Merryweather, ineffectually, as he found himself ushered from the room.

'My apologies, Your Ladyship,' said Stead, once Mr. Merryweather had been disposed off, 'that you should have to witness such a spectacle.'

'You have never met the man?' asked Lady DeSalle.

'Heavens, no! I fear, ma'am, there is a class of lunatic that are drawn to medical men. Perhaps he has attended a lecture and got to know my countenance; I cannot say. An unfortunate incident.'

'I suggest you write a strong letter to the management,' said Lady DeSalle. 'How they allow such individuals into a respectable establishment, I cannot imagine.'

'Nor I, ma'am,' agreed Dr. Stead. 'I will do so. Astonishing! Well, allow me to bid you good day once more; and you, Mrs. Richmond.'

Lady DeSalle nodded, as the doctor took his leave.

'Curious,' remarked Sarah Tanner.

'One cannot account for lunacy,' replied Lady DeSalle.

'You do not think the fellow was merely mistaken?'

'Mrs. Richmond, I hardly think that anyone of a sound mind could mistake a respectable medical gentleman for – what? – a fortune-teller.'

'No, ma'am, I suppose you are quite right,' replied Mrs. Tanner, a little despondent. For there was no mistaking the conviction with which Lady DeSalle defended the mesmerist.

'In fact,' continued Lady DeSalle, reflectively, 'I would say the doctor showed considerable self-restraint. A lesser man would have struck the fellow down. Next time we meet, I shall commend him for his self-possession.'

Mrs. Tanner nodded, recalling something that was said.

'You are seeing Dr. Stead tomorrow, ma'am?'

Lady DeSalle paused, if only for a second or two, as if deciding whether to say what was on her mind.

'Yes,' she said at last. 'I am going to inspect the doctor's new infirmary. I am hopeful that a few days spent there may improve my husband's condition. Berkeley Square is not entirely conducive to his recovery.'

'You put a good deal of faith in Dr. Stead, ma'am,' said Mrs. Tanner, taking care not to show her surprise at the news.

'Yes,' said Lady DeSalle. 'Still, I am sure you would concur that he has unique gifts, Mrs. Richmond?'

Sarah Tanner nodded.

'Indeed. In fact, I have a presentiment, Your Ladyship, that I may require further treatment.'

CHAPTER TWENTY-FIVE

Two days after the incident in Mivart's coffee-room, a highly respectable-looking couple walked arm in arm alongside the lake in St. James's Park.

'I am not sure I can allow you to do this,' said Arthur DeSalle, making sure that there was no-one in earshot. 'You may be putting your life at risk.'

'I think you should decide whether you want my help or not, Arthur,' said Sarah Tanner. 'I don't suppose you can pay for a suite at Mivart's indefinitely.'

'It is not a question of money; everything costs money. Perhaps we should wait. I will make arrangements to have Stead followed.'

Sarah Tanner shook her head. 'My plan is more likely to yield swift results.'

'It is not much of a plan – to put yourself at this fellow's mercy!'

'I can see no other method of working out what Stead is up to. I don't believe he is that dangerous.'

'But you believe the boy – the girl's brother – is a murderer!' protested Arthur DeSalle.

'I shouldn't think he will be part of the treatment. And there is no reason he should know anything about the matter; I have not seen him since that night on the Lane and he knows nothing of our connection. I am "Mrs. Richmond" now, if you recall.'

'They could murder you in your sleep.'

'It's rather unlikely that the man intends to do away with his clientele – what will *that* do for his business?'

DeSalle shook his head. 'All the same, I think my mother has lost her mind. To despatch my father to some retreat in Highgate – in the hands of that impostor!'

'No-one from the household will accompany him?'

'Servants? No – not even Winters. Apparently they might disturb the "magnetic conductivity of the Infirmary"! It will simply be Stead and Miss Smith – she will remain his nurse! – and whatever staff Stead keeps himself.'

'Who, of course, are all suitably "magnetic". And there are no other patients?'

'According to my mother, not at present. He has only just opened the place; my father will have a whole wing to himself.'

'It sounds contrived to isolate him entirely,' mused Mrs. Tanner.

'But to what end?'

'That is what I intend to find out,' she said, firmly. 'When I enrol myself as a patient.'

'Will he accept you?'

'I have dangled an inheritance in Chancery under his nose; he has all but suggested it himself.'

'The man is a villain!'

'And that is why, Arthur, I have no intention that he gets the better of you.'

'The better of me? Or is it that you won't allow any man to best you?'

Sarah Tanner smiled. 'A little of both. In any case, I am expected in Highgate this afternoon.'

—

Sarah Tanner's cab turned off Highgate Hill. She gazed out of the window, looking back towards the distant metropolis. The view from the hill was unobstructed, over the fields, across the terraces of new suburbs in Holloway and Islington, down as far as the valley of the Thames, with the dome of St. Paul's just visible amidst the lingering chimney smoke, and the Kent and Surrey hills looming obscurely in the distance. The main thoroughfare was lined with public-houses, seemingly every few hundred yards, a relic of when coaching provided the sole egress from the capital. But, as soon as the cab changed course, the inns disappeared, the smooth road gave way to a muddy lane, and the houses yielded to green fields, untouched by the speculative builder.

Her thoughts turned to Leather Lane. Nearly a week had passed since she last set foot in the New Dining and Coffee Rooms and a part of her wondered if she had grown too accustomed to the opulence of Mivart's, and the comforts that reminded her of her old life. Various recollections came unbidden to her mind – the night-houses on Regent Street; the rooms which DeSalle had taken for her, when she had been content to call herself his mistress – and it was only as the cab arrived at the ironwork gates of the Infirmary that she awoke from her reverie.

She had anticipated a newly constructed temple to Dr. Stead's prosperous practice; but the reality confounded her expectation. The house, which sat in several acres of garden, was an ancient one. The wall which marked the property's boundary was blanketed in a dense layer of ivy; the drive was at the mercy of weeds and over-grown shrubbery. The building itself, a red-brick mansion of two storeys, with a precipitous gabled roof and tall looming chimney-stacks, appeared weather-beaten and careworn. The only recent additions seemed to be a rather out-of-place Doric porch, and the tall sash windows upon the upper storey, which seemed either brand-new or newly painted. There was, arguably, a certain grandeur to the decrepit old house; but it struck her as a peculiarly shoddy place in which to accommodate a peer of the realm.

As the cab pulled to a halt, the front door opened, and an elderly man-servant, alerted by the racket of iron-shod wheels on gravel, stepped out to greet the driver. It was, Mrs. Tanner noted, as he opened the hackney's door, the self-same man whom she had seen in Upper Wimpole Street, the previous week.

'Good afternoon, ma'am,' said the old man. 'May I escort you inside?'

She accepted his hand as she descended from the carriage.

'I'm afraid Dr. Stead has been called away of a sudden, ma'am,' continued the old man, as he led her indoors.

'Oh dear, is that so?'

'He sends his apologies and has left you a brief note, ma'am – you'll find it on the mantel in your sitting-room. I'll have your luggage brought in, and Wright will show you up to the room.'

Wright proved to be a young girl in maid's uniform, who stood waiting in the hall. No more than sixteen or seventeen years old, she looked fidgety and nervous. The hall itself was rather gloomy and narrow. Its walls were painted a mustard yellow, that had long since faded; two panelled doors upon either side were of varnished oak; and the uncarpeted stairs were situated at the rear, with the banister of the same dark wood. There was no sign of dust or dirt; the drugget of warm crimson gave every impression of having being recently acquired; and yet the overall impression was rather lifeless and dull.

'If you'd care to follow me, ma'am?' said the girl.

She nodded and followed the maid upstairs. The age of the house was plain in the creaking floorboards and defects in the wainscotting, where sections of the carved wood seemed somehow to have shifted out of alignment with their immediate neighbours. If further proof of antiquity were needed, it became increasingly evident in the labyrinthine series of twists and turns – of abrupt corridors; of half-a-dozen steps up, then three down – that led from the principal stairs to Mrs. Tanner's accommodation.

'This is your rooms, ma'am,' said the maid.

It was a pair, similar in size to those at Mivart's. The sitting-room was furnished with a writing-desk, and twin armchairs arranged before the hearth; the bedroom with a substantial comfortable-looking bed supporting a tester draped in lace, a large wardrobe, a cheval glass and a marble wash-stand. There was nothing particularly lacking in the rooms – the bed-linen was plainly new; the hearths perfectly clean; the picture of a Scottish glen above the bedroom mantel perfectly charming – but there was nothing distinct or interesting in them, not unlike the hall downstairs. She idly wondered whether it simply suggested the lack of a feminine hand in the Infirmary's decoration or a particularly modest budget.

'Would you like a fire, ma'am?' asked the maid.

Mrs. Tanner smiled, turning from the bedroom

window, which had a view over the gardens of the house, some two or three acres of land.

'No, I am quite all right. Tell me, have you worked here long?'

'Just two weeks, ma'am,' said the girl.

'Two weeks? And were you in the doctor's employ before that?'

'No, ma'am,' said the girl, plainly a little puzzled by the interrogation.

'Forgive me – I soon require a new maid myself. Reliable girls are so difficult to find. Was it an agency?'

'Yes, ma'am. Mrs. Bolton's registry-office, Islington High Street.'

'Ah, well, I shall bear that in mind. Tell me, how do you find working here? Is it hard work?'

'Not too bad, ma'am, thank you.'

'Are there many other patients? I gather Lord DeSalle is here?'

'No, ma'am, no others yet, excepting you, ma'am, and His Lordship. Oh, begging your pardon, and another lady what's due tomorrow.'

'Another lady?'

'I don't know no more, ma'am. I don't like to pry.'

'Well, quite right,' said Mrs. Tanner, reaching inside her purse and retrieving a coin. 'There, that is for being such a good girl. Ah, now that sounds like my portmanteau on the stairs.'

'Should I help you with it, ma'am?' asked the girl.

'No, there is no need. I am quite content to unpack by myself. Do return to your work. But if you should hear any news of my fellow guests,' she continued, closing her purse rather ostentatiously, 'I should be most intrigued.'

The maid took the coin, curtseyed, rather clumsily, and retreated from the room. Mrs. Tanner, meanwhile, turned to the doctor's note, which lay in a white envelope on the mantel-piece.

My dear Mrs. Richmond,

My humblest apologies that I am not present to bid you welcome. In extenuation, I can only say that a medical matter *of the greatest urgency* demands my prompt attention *in propria persona*; I will say no more – I pray most sincerely that you can forgive me.

I trust your rooms are to your satisfaction; however, if there is any small item lacking for your comfort, rest assured, we shall acquire it. There is a morning-room with a modest library, at the end of the east wing; likewise, a music room and piano-forte. Small amusements of a domestic nature are, in my experience, conducive to a sound balance of magnetic fluid in the female constitution; should you wish to read or play, you will be doing yourself nothing but good.

It is customary that guests take their meals in their apartments. I hope to return early this evening; I trust I may present my apologies in person, therefore, after dinner.

Your humble servant,

J. Stead.

There was a knock on the door; the portmanteau appeared, dragged by the cabman, who looked distinctly weary.

'Where would you like your trunk, ma'am?'

⟶

Having unpacked her clothes, Mrs. Tanner returned to the portmanteau, and ran her hand over the base of the trunk until a click could be heard, revealing a small loose partition, which she removed. She did not take out the pistol that lay carefully secreted in the hidden compartment, but merely ran her hand over the barrel and examined the small pouch of powder that lay beside it, to reassure herself that it had remained sealed. Satisfied, she carefully slotted the wood back in place, then checked her appearance in the cheval glass that sat in the corner of the bedroom.

There was, she decided, little advantage in remaining in her room; she had, after all, been given leave to amuse herself and she determined to do so, if not precisely in the manner her absent host had intended. Consequently, she left her apartment, shutting the door quietly behind her, and began to explore the upper storey of the house. Although it was only four o'clock, the building already seemed dark and gloomy, sunlight having been banished by an occluded grey sky. Little thought seemed to have been given to illumination: for the house was too remote to benefit from a supply of gas; and she saw but one solitary oil-lamp, as yet unlit, resting upon a side-table by the upper landing. The over-riding impression, as she walked, was that of a house too long without inhabitants: there was nothing actually amiss – no wall that was damp or wood that was rotten – but every surface seem to bear the same dusty patina of age and genteel decay.

She spent half an hour or so familiarising herself with the maze of corridors and encountered neither the maid nor any other servant. Nonetheless, she was left feeling utterly thwarted: for every single door but her own had been left locked. She was about to continue downstairs, when she came to the sash window on the upper landing by the hall stairs. It looked out on to the gardens and there, along the

central path which lead to a circular pond and foun-
tain, surrounded by an unruly box-hedge, she saw
two figures: that of a woman in white-aproned
uniform, whom she immediately recognised as Helena
Smith – or perhaps the more mundane Helen Cranks
– and that of a man, seated in a wicker bath-chair,
pushed by the nurse.

Lord DeSalle.

She watched their progress for a minute or two: the
nurse drew to a halt by the pond, and sat down upon
a bench that faced the house.

Mrs. Tanner pulled back from the window and
hurried back to her room, to retrieve her shawl.

It was only as she walked briskly downstairs, a few
minutes later, that she realised she had no idea of how
to find a way into the garden. She pondered whether
to call the maid, but decided against it, fearing that
the outdoors might be prohibited as insufficiently
'magnetic' for her supposedly feeble constitution.
Instead, she tentatively made her way to the morning-
room, at the far end of the house, as described in the
doctor's note. She was gratified to find that the room
possessed twin doors in the French style, neither locked
nor bolted, which led out on to a paved terrace at
the rear of the house, and thence a flight of stone
steps down to the garden.

The garden itself showed few signs of care, much
like the property to which it was attached. There were
no blooms or bursts of colour; merely over-grown
gravel walks and hedging, once ornamental, that had
sprouted tall shoots in every direction and lost whatever form and shape man had once bestowed upon
it. The route to the pond, however, was clear enough,
and the bath-chair remained where Mrs. Tanner had
last seen it. As she drew nearer she could see that its

occupier was asleep, his head lolling slightly forward. She looked at the old man – for he certainly appeared old – for some family resemblance, some hint of Arthur DeSalle's noble features. But she could discern nothing in the thin, gaunt creature that dozed in the chair, nothing except a pitiful palsied twist to his mouth, from which a snail's trail of saliva ran down his chin. She realised that she had given little serious thought to the invalided man's condition. She suddenly felt a genuine sympathy for her erstwhile lover, picturing what it must have done to him, to see his father reduced to such a state.

A voice called to her.

'Good afternoon, ma'am,' said the nurse.

CHAPTER TWENTY-SIX

Mrs. Tanner nodded as the nurse addressed her. There was something rather forward in the woman's manner, not least in the fact that any decent servant would never have spoken first.

'Good afternoon,' she replied. 'I see His Lordship is sleeping? I trust I am not disturbing him.'

'His Lordship, ma'am?' said Miss Smith, as if temporarily forgetful of her charge's existence. 'Why, you'd as soon wake the dead from their grave. No, ma'am, when His Lordship sleeps, he sleeps.'

'I see,' continued Mrs. Tanner. 'Well, I am Mrs. Richmond. Perhaps Dr. Stead has mentioned my name? I thought I might take the air, whilst the rain holds off. You must be His Lordship's nurse. The doctor and Lady DeSalle both speak very highly of you.'

'That's very gratifying, ma'am,' said Miss Smith, although it was hard to be entirely certain of her sincerity.

'Tell me, can much be done for him, for His Lordship, along mesmeric lines?'

'I should hope so, ma'am. Otherwise, the doctor wouldn't try it, would he?'

'I expect not,' replied Mrs. Tanner, taking a seat upon a bench, on the opposite side of the little pond from the nurse. 'Poor man! And does the outside air do His Lordship good? The house is a little stuffy.'

'I give him a turn round the garden twice a day, ma'am; the doctor's instructions. I expect he feels the benefit.'

Sarah Tanner fell silent. In truth, having found her in the garden, she now had little certainty about what a conversation with the nurse might achieve. Undaunted, she tried another tack.

'In fact, Miss Smith, I believe I have seen you before. I attended one of the doctor's lectures in Marylebone not long ago. You were his mesmeric subject upon that occasion, were you not?'

'More than likely, ma'am,' said the nurse.

'It was a remarkable display. I was quite astonished.'

'Were you, ma'am?'

She looked at the nurse. She now understood Arthur DeSalle's instant dislike of the woman. There was a subtle measure of insolence, or at least a distinct lack of deference, in her voice. It was not in the words that she said, but the manner in which she spoke, and the clear, piercing gaze with which she turned her dark eyes on her interlocutor. Despite herself, she almost admired her for it.

'Of course. Why, I declare, you sound as if you doubt my word.'

The nurse did not so much deny the accusation, as ignore it.

'Only, the doctor says, ma'am, there can't be full sympathy if a party doesn't truly believe in the Science.'

'I am sure he's quite right.'

The nurse frowned, as if somehow discomfited by the reply.

'Begging your pardon, ma'am, but you're not sure,

are you? I don't mean to be contrary, but I have a gift, ma'am – you've seen it; and I can tell what you're thinking. I can tell, sitting here, you ain't sure, not at all.'

Mrs. Tanner shifted uneasily on the bench. She had the distinct feeling that the nurse had somehow turned the tables on her and found her out – even though she had said nothing remotely of significance.

'Of course,' she replied, 'one may have small doubts on certain matters.'

'Then it will be no use, ma'am,' said Miss Smith. 'If you have doubts, the cure's no good. You may as well go home, for all the good it'll do you.'

'Miss Smith, I am sure the doctor would not care for you to speak to me thus,' said Mrs. Tanner, trying to sound good-humoured.

The nurse merely turned her head away, and looked at her patient, who remained sound asleep. A rather frosty silence settled, until Miss Smith spoke out once more, as if struck by a sudden idea.

'I reckon I could cure them doubts, ma'am, if it's worth something to you, and if you weren't too particular,' she said, at last.

'Particular? Whatever do you mean?' said Mrs. Tanner, genuinely perplexed.

'If you'd like, ma'am, I could show you something that would make any female thank the Lord that they discovered the Science; and not doubt it for a second. But it'd have to be a secret, and kept dark, before and after; otherwise, well, I might lose my place.'

'Miss Smith, you talk in riddles. You quite unnerve me.'

The nurse smiled coyly, seeming to relish the idea. 'I can't tell you no more, ma'am, not unless you promise to keep it dark. Now I suppose I had better take him back inside. We don't want His Lordship catching his death, do we?'

Sarah Tanner hesitated as the nurse got up and took hold of the bath-chair. Finally, she spoke out.

'Very well – what is this secret of yours?'

The nurse looked round, a rather self-satisfied smile curling about her lips.

'Not now. I'll come to your room, ma'am. Tomorrow morning; I'll come.'

And, with those words, she pushed her patient back towards the house.

Mystified, Sarah Tanner watched her go.

⁓

'Mrs. Richmond – a thousand apologies, ma'am!'

Dr. Stead supplemented his plea with an extremely low bow. Mrs. Tanner, seated in an armchair in the doctor's study, situated upon the ground floor of the house, adjoining the morning-room, nodded in an aristocratic fashion, worthy of Lady DeSalle herself.

'You have every right to be displeased, ma'am,' professed the doctor. 'It does you great credit, if I may venture so bold, that you are not. Indeed, it shows an equanimity in spirits that will assist our endeavours. It was an urgent case, but I thank you, ma'am, and my patient thanks you for your consideration.'

Mrs. Tanner nodded obligingly once more, though privately wondering what manner of ailment might require urgent mesmeric aid.

'Now, pray, are you rooms to your liking?'

'More than adequate, sir.'

'Ma'am, you are generous. We are just beginning with the Infirmary, of course. A good deal of work needs to be done; I cannot deny it. But we have worthy patrons in Professor Felton and Lady DeSalle; I feel certain that the enterprise will flourish. Indeed, I expect another patient on the morrow.'

'Really, sir? Who?' said Mrs. Tanner, instantly regretting her question, which made her sound far too eager for the answer. Fortunately, the doctor seemed to ascribe her interest to mere feminine curiosity.

'You have every right to ask, Mrs. Richmond, but you must forgive me – I fear, in my exuberance, I spoke a little too freely. Suffice it to say, it is a lady of considerable distinction. She may wish to seclude herself from the society of others, but I will see if you can be introduced.'

'You are very kind, sir.'

'Now, as for your treatment, ma'am, I have personally magnetised a dozen bottles of mineral waters. Wright will leave them in your room. I urge you to consume two bottles a day; it will assist with our endeavours. I propose to apply the magnetic influence three times a day, at the hours of eight in the morning, two in the afternoon, and eight in the evening, commencing tomorrow. Does that suit, ma'am?'

'Eminently.'

'Then, ma'am, if you will forgive such a short interview, I fear I must bid you good night. I am rather weary in myself. I commend sleep, ma'am – nature's restorative!'

'Thank you, sir,' said Mrs. Tanner, getting up. 'Oh, I meant to ask – do you expect Lady DeSalle to visit at any time?'

'She will visit her husband daily, ma'am, I am quite sure of it.'

'You might mention that I would be happy to receive her, if you think it will not interfere with my treatment?'

215

'Interfere? Of course not, ma'am,' said Stead. 'I will be sure to let her know. Good night, then, ma'am.'

'Good night.'

Wright, seemingly the only maid-servant in the house, had stood patiently in the room throughout the conversation, a silent chaperon. At the doctor's signal, she opened the door to the hall and guided Mrs. Tanner outside, carrying a bronze oil-lamp in both hands to light the way. Mrs. Tanner followed her, in silence, back to her room. When they arrived, the girl halted on the threshold.

'I've laid the fire and lit your lamps, ma'am; there's water for the morning on the stand. Is there anything else?'

'No, I don't think so.'

'Thank you, ma'am,' said the maid, with another rather unprofessional curtsey.

'Tell me,' said Mrs. Tanner, 'have you ever been mesmerised, Wright?'

'Me, ma'am? I've seen people do it, ma'am; and it's a wonder, I'm sure.'

'But you've never experienced it?'

'Not me! I'd be afeared!'

'Of what?'

'That I shouldn't wake up!'

Mrs. Tanner smiled. 'That will be all.'

'Thank you, ma'am,' said Wright, retreating down the corridor. 'Good night, ma'am.'

Sarah Tanner stepped into the sitting-room and closed the door behind her. She walked over to the window, and drew back the damask, peering out into the gardens. But nothing was visible in the darkness, except the shadowy outline of a row of plane trees that, upon one side, seemed to serve as a natural boundary to the Infirmary grounds. She closed the

216

curtains, and walked through to the bedroom. Her thoughts had revolved principally around Helena Smith's curious promise for the morrow; but as she sat upon the bed, for the second time that day she recalled her own room in Leather Lane and wondered how the coffee-house fared in her absence.

―

In fact, the New Dining and Coffee Rooms had fared quite well, despite the loss of their guiding spirit. The horse-meat affair had long been forgotten and the little cash-box which sat under the counter was kept tolerably full by the determined efforts of Norah Smallwood and Ralph Grundy.

Norah, it must be admitted, found the shop particularly dull without her mistress for company, even allowing for being asked to play the role of lady's maid in Upper Wimpole Street; a performance which, to her slight annoyance, she had not been required to repeat. The old man, on the other hand, seemed to rather relish his authority over the waitress and took great pains to point out her failings in the cleaning of tables, and the stacking of plates, and general deportment. If Norah Smallwood did not down tools at once – or at least her dish-cloth – it was for one reason: that Ralph Grundy had also adopted an innovation for which she had long lobbied her employer. Under the old man's jurisdiction, the New Dining and Coffee Rooms had somehow begun to close at eleven thirty p.m., a full half-hour early. Norah, for her part, welcomed the opportunity to retire; in fact, a hot cup of gin at such an hour seemed to her an exquisite indulgence. Ralph, meanwhile, made a nightly point of gazing at his employer's mahogany clock, tutting quietly to himself, and 'popping out' to the Bottle of

Hay to 'check the time'. And if he indulged in a quick pint or two of porter, whilst referring to the landlord's most accurate time-piece, he concluded there was little harm in it.

Indeed, there was little harm in it. And yet, it might be argued that if he had not quit the shop and indulged his modest passion for liquor, he might have been a little more alert. He might, perhaps, on that first night that Mrs. Tanner spent under Dr. Stead's roof, have noticed the figure of a boy, lurking in the alley opposite the shop.

But, returning to the coffee-house in the company of Joe Drummond, who generously made a point of escorting the old man to the door, he did not see the boy. He merely bid his companion good night, unlocked the shop-door, went inside, and closed it behind him.

CHAPTER TWENTY-SEVEN

Sarah Tanner submitted to the mesmeric attentions of her host at eight o'clock precisely on the following morning. The treatment was performed in her own room and Wright, once again, was called upon to ensure there was no shadow cast over the morals of either doctor or patient. The maid, therefore, stood in a corner, watching the proceedings with a rather pained expression, perhaps fearful she herself might be called upon to participate or, worse, fall inadvertent victim to the mesmerist's powers.

The procedure differed not one iota from that performed the previous week, at Upper Wimpole Street. The same posture was adopted; the same outstretched hands to palm and forehead; the same intense expression of concentration. However, despite the unique magnetic properties of the Infirmary's mineral waters, Mrs. Tanner found herself no more overcome by the mesmerist's influence than upon the previous occasion. She obliged, after a judicious length of time had elapsed, with the correct responses; and she was quietly proud to elicit a similar gasp of awe from the maid-servant as she had from Norah Smallwood. Her only concern was the haste with which Dr. Stead conducted his magnetic passes: what had taken a half-hour in the previous instance seemed reduced to some twenty minutes. For the doctor seemed a little distracted. The reason, however, became evident as Mrs. Tanner found herself recalled from her feigned sleep to consciousness.

'There, ma'am,' said the doctor, with a degree of smug satisfaction, 'I am sure you feel the benefit already, do you not?'

'Indeed, just as I did in your office, sir.'

'It will take more, of course – much more. A constitutional weakness cannot be banished in an instant. You must trust me implicitly, ma'am. A greater sympathy must develop between us, if we are to succeed in this endeavour. Indeed, in mesmeric practice one should not think of "doctor" and "patient". You yourself, ma'am, are the necessary coadjutor to any success we may achieve; you must allow your will to be subject to mine. It is quite imperative.'

'Oh, I am sure, I shall do my best,' replied Mrs. Tanner, with the most charming smile that she could muster.

'Well, that is gratifying, ma'am. You must forgive me, however, if I do not remain. The new patient of whom I spoke yesterday is due within the hour; I have to make some essential preparations.'

'Of course, sir. Do not let me detain you.'

The mesmerist nodded and made his hurried departure from the room. Mrs. Tanner turned to the maid, who looked visibly relieved.

'What do you make of that?' asked Mrs. Tanner.

'Me, ma'am? I couldn't rightly say. Begging your pardon, but how does it feel, ma'am, when he does it to you?'

'I can honestly say, one does not feel a thing. You

would not like to try it? I am surprised the doctor has not tested whether you are sympathetic.'

'Not me, ma'am! Not for all the tea in China!'

Mrs. Tanner smiled, and dismissed the girl with a few words. But the maid hung back on the threshold of the room.

'Ma'am, I did hear something about the new patient.'

'Really?'

'I heard Delville – he's the footman, ma'am – say it's a lady – a proper lady, I mean – Lady Pennethorpe, I think he said.'

'I suppose you have been preparing rooms for her?'

'Yes, ma'am – on the ground floor, in the west wing.'

'Thank you, Wright,' said Mrs. Tanner. 'Thank you very much.'

Unsure precisely when she might expect Helena Smith, Mrs. Tanner spent the first hour of the morning simply observing the garden from her bedroom window, lost in her own thoughts, listening out for the nurse's footsteps in the hall. At length, she began to harbour doubts whether the nurse would appear at all, and whether the vague and mysterious promise was not some peculiar joke at her own expense. She concluded, therefore, that her only definite object for the morning was to observe the arrival of the new patient – the self-same woman whom Arthur DeSalle had told her had recommended the mesmerist to his mother. In truth, the impending appearance of Lady Pennethorpe rather undermined her conviction that Lord DeSalle had been removed from Berkeley Square solely to separate him from his family; it even suggested that the Infirmary was a genuine business venture.

She decided that to make an appearance downstairs at the moment of the Lady Pennethorpe's arrival might seem, at the very best, a patent and crass effort to make her acquaintance. But there was no window on the upstairs corridor, or the upper landing, that looked out upon the front of the house. After some deliberation, she quit her room and stood quietly outside the door, listening for any sound. There were no footsteps, nor any sign of Helena Smith, Wright or the other servants. Cautiously, she reached behind her back, undid the last but one button on her dress, and slipped her hand beneath the waistband of her petticoats, pulling two small items loose from a pouch concealed between the whalebone ribbing of her corset. One was a stiletto blade with an ivory handle; the other a narrow crooked finger of black metal, the length of a key. Pausing again to listen for the sound of creaking floorboards, and hearing nothing, she knelt down in the corridor, in front of the door opposite her own, and set to work on the lock.

A minute passed; a little more.

Then the lock yielded.

The room contained nothing but the skeletal iron frame of a bed and a wicker chair, missing half its weave. Heavy drapes blocked out all but a narrow shaft of light, which fell upon a bare floor encrusted with a thick layer of dust. The place had been undisturbed for months, if not years. She crept over to the windows, peering behind the curtains. There was an uninterrupted view of the drive, and of the house's front steps. She resolved to wait for whichever came first: the sound of footsteps upon the landing – on

222

hearing which she she would hurry back to her room – or the appearance of a carriage in the drive.

In the event, it was almost another hour, before Mrs. Tanner's plan came to fruition.

She heard the loud snort of a horse first, then the rattle of wheels. The carriage was a grand closed landau, painted a deep vermilion red, emblazoned with a gold-and-silver crest upon the door and pulled by two handsome bays. It came down the drive at a trot and swung round to the same spot where Mrs. Tanner herself had disembarked the previous day. The footman made haste to open the carriage door but the occupant seemed particularly slow to respond. At last, when Lady Pennethorpe – or, at least, a woman dressed in fine fashion – finally set foot on the step, her face was concealed by a heavy veil. But it seemed patent that she was ill – decidedly ill – since she climbed down with a hesitant, ungainly stumble, relying heavily on the footman's arm as she walked to the house, to be greeted by Dr. Stead.

Mrs. Tanner strained to listen; but the distance was too great to hear any of the brief conversation, as the new patient was ushered indoors. She was about to return to her room, when she was surprised to hear a second vehicle upon the drive. It was a smart black brougham, which pulled up immediately behind the landau. Without waiting for attendance, its occupant stepped out on to the drive, and hurried into the house. Mrs. Tanner saw him for only an instant; but it was long enough to recognise his face: the lecturer in mesmerism she had seen at the Marylebone Institute, Dr. Stead's patron, Professor Felton.

Then she heard the sound of footsteps upon the landing. She hurried back to her room; but it was merely Wright, come to inquire whether the fire might need lighting.

———

It was another hour before Helena Smith appeared at the door. She wore a sombre black outfit, and a grave expression to match.

'I've come, ma'am, like we agreed,' said the nurse.

'To speak the truth, Miss Smith, I am not quite sure what we agreed. Are you offering me some further "proof" of magnetism? I am sure I do not require it.'

'I think you do, ma'am,' said the nurse, flatly. 'I can see it plain. I think you want to know; otherwise you'd have dismissed it when we spoke. Besides, parties don't try the cure, not unless they're curious about the Science.'

'Is that so? You consider yourself a good judge of my character?'

'I told you, ma'am, I have a gift.'

'Then tell me why should I pry into Dr. Stead's affairs? I am sure he will reveal whatever is appropriate in the course of my treatment.'

'Not this, ma'am. You won't have seen the like of it.'

'Well, whatever is it?'

'There's terms first, ma'am, by your leave.'

'You require money?'

'A guinea,' said the nurse.

'A guinea? I do not have that much to hand.'

'I'll take your word, ma'am. I expect you can send to your bank.'

'I expect I can.'

'And you'd keep it dark – you swear?'

'I still have not said I am interested in this intrigue of yours, Miss Smith.'

224

The nurse shook her head. 'I can see it in your eyes, ma'am. You're bold enough. Now, do you swear or don't you? It's worth knowing.'

Mrs. Tanner hesitated. In part, she had decided not to be too eager with the nurse.

'Very well,' she said at last.

'There! That's a bargain,' said the nurse, with a look of sly triumph. 'Only you'd best follow me, ma'am, because there ain't much time.'

Mrs. Tanner followed her, as the nurse turned and left the room.

'You must tell me what we are about,' she demanded, as Miss Smith walked briskly down the corridor.

'There ain't the time,' persisted the nurse, clearly enjoying her advantage, as they came to the main stairs. 'They'll be starting any minute. Only tell me first, ma'am – you have a strong stomach, don't you? I reckon you do.'

'Strong enough, I suppose,' said Mrs. Tanner, a little taken aback.

'I thought so,' replied the nurse. 'Now, if anyone asks, I'm showing you the morning-room.'

Mrs. Tanner nodded. Miss Smith, meanwhile, led the way downstairs to the end of the east wing, and the room in question. One corner served as a small library, with two substantial bookcases, containing various sets of leather-bound volumes, which looked never to have been opened. The nurse, however, sidestepped the bookcase that lay against the wall, and pushed against the oak wainscotting with both hands. At first, Mrs. Tanner could not fathom her purpose; but then a section of a wall seemed to come loose – a door, covered in the same oak panelling and trellised wallpaper as the bricks and mortar on either side. It swung open on its concealed hinges, revealing a narrow passage.

'The doctor didn't build it, ma'am, if that's what you're wondering,' said the nurse, observing Mrs. Tanner's surprise with some amusement. 'I reckon it's always been there. Only you must promise now – you'll keep absolutely quiet? On your honour?'

Mrs. Tanner nodded. The nurse, satisfied, beckoned for her to follow, as she slipped into the darkened passage.

The corridor, in fact, was barely wide enough for two persons, certainly not two women in petticoats, and so she was obliged to follow in the nurse's wake. Sarah Tanner wondered idly whether it was some ancient priest's hole; but discounted the idea, as the floor was level and boarded, the walls papered. More likely it was the addition of a previous owner, with time and money to spend; an amusing novelty. In fact, it did not extend more than a few feet before they encountered a steep set of stairs. The nurse gestured for silence and led the way to the top. There the corridor widened. It was only as her eyes became accustomed to the darkness that Mrs. Tanner realised they stood behind a door. The nurse spoke, whispering quietly in her ear.

'Behind the door is the gallery to the old library. Hold the door an inch ajar – no more, or you will be seen.'

'And what shall I see?' said Mrs. Tanner.

'Just look down, ma'am. It will become clear. But you must swear – do not make a sound.'

'You have my word.'

The nurse nodded, and stepped back from the door, allowing her companion to slide past her. Mrs. Tanner, for her part, took a deep breath and opened the door.

The room was a library at one time, that much was instantly clear. The walls of the iron-railed gallery were lined with shelves, though all were quite empty, distinguished only by the occasional cobweb. Below lay a great marble fire-place where the comfortable chairs of a country gentleman had once been placed before the hearth. But the room had been cleared of all furniture; there was no rug or drugget, and the bare boards had been polished to a shine. There were only two exceptions: a screen placed before the tall sash windows, which served to conceal the interior from anyone who might pass by the front of the house, but still allowed some light to enter; and a long wooden table, which had been covered in a white linen cloth.

Mrs. Tanner could make little sense of the arrangements; she was about to turn back to the nurse, when the library door opened and three figures entered the room: Dr. Stead, the Professor and Lady Pennethorpe. There was nothing remarkable about the two men. Lady Pennethorpe, on the other hand, seemed quite out of place: for she was dressed in a loose silk gown, more suited to the boudoir; and she walked in a stiff, automaton-like fashion, holding the Professor's arm. She was, most likely, a similar age to her acquaintance, Lady DeSalle; her features, moreover, bore the same aristocratic imprint. But her face looked gaunt, weary and distinctly vacant.

'Everything has been done, as I instructed, Stead?' asked Felton.

'The maid assures me, sir. It is quite in order; washed twice over.'

'Then we had best begin. Are you sure you are happy to assist?'

'I hope to learn something, sir.'

'I hope you shall. Very well,' continued the Professor,

227

turning to the woman who still clutched his arm. 'Your Ladyship will please sit upon the table; allow me to assist you.'

Lady Pennethorpe obliged, quite mechanically, and sat upon the linen, without any remark, as if it were the most natural thing in the world. Her eyes, in particular, remained fixed ahead of her, as if oblivious to what they saw.

The inference was obvious: that the woman was mesmerised.

Was it possible? To what end?

As Mrs. Tanner pondered the question, she was distracted by the Professor removing something from his pocket and laying it on the mantel. It appeared like a roll of cloth; but she could not make it out, as he turned his back. Dr. Stead, meanwhile, simply stood awkwardly to one side, appearing distinctly nervous, clasping and unclasping his hands with alarming frequency.

The Professor turned back to face his subject.

'Please drop your gown, ma'am,' said Felton.

Lady Pennethorpe did as instructed; the silk fell from her shoulders and, to Mrs. Tanner's astonishment, there was neither shift nor corset beneath, merely bare flesh. Stead could not suppress a crimson rush of blood to his cheeks. The Professor, on the other hand, seemed quite unmoved. Then, as Felton moved, she could make out what he had laid out upon the mantel-piece.

A gleaming row of sharp steel knives.

CHAPTER TWENTY-EIGHT

'Your Ladyship will forgive me,' said Felton, as he leant forward and touched her breast. Lady Pennethorpe, for her part, seemed to feel nothing; her face remained resolutely unflinching and expressionless as the Professor touched her.

'Well,' continued Felton, turning his head to address Dr. Stead, 'there can be little room for debate. The skin is taut and cannot be folded; the veins are dilated; you can see the purple-red mass? There! I can feel it, I am sure. A hardened scirrhus; I should say about the size of half an orange.'

'It might not merely be a cyst?'

'You asked for my opinion, Stead. I am happy to assist your practice here, upon occasion, but you must take my advice.'

'And you will operate?'

'Immediately; it cannot be left to flourish unchecked. It is Her Ladyship's wish, is it not?'

'Indeed.'

'Of course,' added Felton, 'if I had but seen her a little earlier . . .'

The Professor's tone was gently remonstrative. Dr. Stead blushed for a second time.

'Her Ladyship did not confide in me until recently,

sir,' said Stead. 'Another physician had prescribed compression; she had trusted his advice.'

'Compression indeed!' said the Professor, with a snort of disgust.

'I do not believe she has even told her husband of her condition. And she rather feared going under the knife.'

'Well, you have removed that obstacle, at least,' said Felton, approvingly.

'Another triumph for the New Science, sir.'

Professor Felton nodded, and returned to the mantel-piece, where he retrieved one of the knives that lay ready, then turned back to his patient.

'Very well. If Your Ladyship will turn and lie back upon the table?'

Lady Pennethorpe wordlessly obliged.

'And place your right arm over the side, ma'am. Yes, quite – now let it drop . . . good . . . and keep it fixed and straight.'

Mrs. Tanner looked on; the woman's arm lay over the side of the table, taut and straight, as rigid as if tied to the floor by an invisible skein of rope. Felton, meanwhile, placed the knife on the table, took off his jacket, removed his cuffs, and rolled up his shirt-sleeves.

'You have the dressings ready?' asked Felton, picking up the knife once more. 'I shall need you to compress the subclavian artery.'

Stead nodded. There was a distinct bead of sweat forming on his brow.

'Come on then, sir – step forward,' said Felton, impatiently, as Stead approached the table. 'Good Lord! The artery is there – place your fingers there! On my oath, Stead, you do not have the makings of a surgeon.'

'Mine is a humbler calling,' said Stead, rather queasily. 'You must forgive me.'

The Professor smiled, a faintly indulgent look upon his face. 'Well, you have done your part; our patient will feel no pain. That itself might have been considered miraculous not many years ago. The rest is the surgeon's domain; there are some limits to mesmeric practice. It is those who claim otherwise who have damaged its reputation. Now, watch closely – if it is to be done, it must be done swiftly.'

Felton raised the knife, and cut deep into the breast. Mrs. Tanner gazed at the scene played out before her: the blade was plainly real, as were its effects, but the woman upon the table did not even blink. There was something horribly unnerving about it: both the ease with which the steel sliced into the patient's pale skin; and her dispassionate, unfocused gaze.

'An oblique, elliptical incision, Stead, above and below the nipple. Then a strong deep movement as far as the pectoral muscle.'

'There is much blood,' murmured Stead, his face quite contorted with disgust.

'A mere trickle. It is simply a matter of ligating the bleeding vessels, once I have removed the tissue,' said Felton, quite calm. 'Thankfully I can see no induration in the axilla . . . it is a straightforward matter of excising the tissue of the breast . . . Not long now! . . . Ah! There – it is free.'

Felton worked with professional rapidity and, finishing, his voice had a hint of triumph. Sarah Tanner, however, had no wish to dwell upon his success; she could not help but look away. For the sight of the sloughing, ulcerating mass of red and yellow matter, which the Professor deposited into an unseen container beneath the table, made her stomach turn. By the time

231

she brought herself to look again, Felton had a needle and thread, and had already begun to close the wound.

'I would make a fine seamstress, would I not, Stead?'

'Quite so, sir,' muttered the mesmerist, swallowing hard. 'Is Her Ladyship . . .'

'Ask her yourself, sir.'

'Does Your Ladyship feel any pain?' said Stead, timidly.

'No,' replied the patient, in a still, quiet voice, seemingly quite unmoved.

'She has done well. And with your assistance, I trust she will recover.'

Sarah Tanner felt a tug at her sleeve.

'We must go now,' said the nurse, in an urgent whisper. 'I will be missed.'

❧

'You look a little pale, ma'am,' said the nurse, as she closed the door in the morning-room. She said the words quite plainly, but there was a distinctly mischievous look to her face, which left Mrs. Tanner convinced that she took some pleasure in her unease.

'You misled me, Miss Smith. Whatever I anticipated, whatever I thought you had planned, I did not expect to see a surgeon's butchery at first hand.'

'Butchery? If you like. They were removing a cancer of the breast. She took that blade peaceful as anything, didn't she? You can't deny it.'

'You are telling me that she was mesmerised?'

'I saw it done, ma'am,' said the nurse proudly. 'I helped the Professor prepare her.'

'I expect aether or chloroform might accomplish the same result.'

'I suppose they might, ma'am, if you trusted to 'em and knew the dose – but I don't expect you'd find a party as could sit bolt upright having taken 'em, and talk and all.'

Sarah Tanner said nothing.

'There's no point denying the Science, ma'am,' said the nurse, with some satisfaction. 'I can see it in your eyes; there ain't any room for doubt, is there? That's worth a guinea of anyone's money! Anyhow, I'd best go; they'll need me. We can talk about it again, I expect.'

And with those words, and the hint of a smile, the nurse hurried off down the corridor, leaving her interlocutor somewhat lost for words. Sarah Tanner's immediate thoughts on the events in the library – and Helena Smith's part in it – were, however, put to one side, when she noticed the nurse's progress interrupted by the appearance of Wright, walking in the opposite direction from the hall. The maid immediately stood to one side as Helena Smith bustled past, but it struck Mrs. Tanner – watching them both – that there was a distinct look of anxiety upon the girl's face, as the nurse caught her eye.

'Oh, I'm sorry, ma'am,' said the maid, who came armed with a duster and damp cloth, 'I didn't know you were here; I'll come back later.'

'There is no need. I was just returning to my room. Please, carry on.'

The maid nodded and began, rather self-consciously, to apply her duster to the furniture.

'Tell me,' asked Mrs. Tanner, on the threshold of the room, 'I am curious – what do you make of Miss Smith?'

'Make of her?' said the maid. 'Why, nothing, ma'am. It ain't my place.'

'I confess, I myself find her a rather odd creature. What do the servants think of her?'

233

'Well, we do find her a bit queer, ma'am. But we don't have much to do with her; she keeps her own company. Now, Cook reckons . . .'

'Cook reckons what?'

'No, I suppose I shouldn't say, ma'am. I shouldn't repeat gossip.'

'You may be frank with me, you have my word,' said Mrs. Tanner. 'I have good reasons for asking.'

'Well, Cook says she's got gipsy blood in her. Offered to tell her future!'

'Is that so?' said Mrs. Tanner. 'I shouldn't be at all surprised.'

—

Mrs. Tanner took a plain lunch of bread and cheese in her sitting-room, and received her mesmeric treatment at the appointed hour. The doctor seemed more relaxed and in good spirits but said nothing of his new patient, whilst Mrs. Tanner, for her part, had resolved to maintain a discreet silence upon the subject. Once the mesmerist had left, she spent the afternoon secluded in idleness, pondering the events of the morning. Her reverie was only interrupted by the appearance of Wright and the announcement that a visitor awaited her in the morning-room. She took the card which Wright bore in her hand and appeared surprised to discover it contained the name of Arthur DeSalle. It would have been a suspicious mind that wondered if the impromptu visit of the young nobleman had been pre-arranged. Certainly, the young maid suspected nothing of the sort, but merely reported back to the morning-room that 'Mrs. Richmond will be down shortly'.

Some five minutes later, having exchanged suitable pleasantries, Mrs. Tanner, in company with the gentleman in question, began a tour of the Infirmary's gardens.

'You do not believe we can talk safely in the house?' said DeSalle, as they ambled down the over-grown path.

'It might be unwise, to say the least. And the maid is watching us from the kitchen. Can't you see her? Perhaps she thinks we are sweethearts.'

'She may think what she likes. You think she is spying on us?'

'No, I don't believe she is in Stead's confidence. Most likely she is just curious. So, have you seen your father? I assume you gave that as the purpose of your visit.'

DeSalle scowled. 'I have. He is neither better nor worse; it is a kind of dreadful limbo. I swear, Sarah, I would rather he were dead.'

'You might be careful what you wish for,' she said, quietly.

'You think his life is threatened?'

'It might be in danger; at least, if Stead plans some form of mesmeric surgery.'

'Surgery? What the devil do you mean?'

Mrs. Tanner recounted the events she had witnessed in the library. DeSalle listened in astonishment.

'Good Lord!' he exclaimed. 'I have read an account of something similar in Paris, a year or two ago – an amputation; I rather disbelieved it.'

'Apparently it can be done. Her Ladyship barely blinked.'

'Then Stead actually possesses some peculiar power he can bring to bear? I cannot believe it! I am not sure if it makes matters better or worse!'

'Arthur, if your mother has seen something similar, that might explain her faith in him. She has not been ill herself?'

'No, no – I do not think so. Do you suppose he intends to operate on my father?'

235

She shrugged. 'He is no surgeon himself; he positively blanched at the sight of blood. Whether Felton might consider it, I cannot say. From what I saw, at least the Professor is not a quack.'

'I am not sure that is a comfort. What about Stead?'

'I can only repeat what I saw; that the woman did not flinch or complain, though he cut away at her like a joint of meat. If Stead can do that much, can snatch away her senses to such a degree, then he may not be the utter fraud I first thought him. And your mother may not be such a dupe after all.'

'Unfortunately, Sarah, I still have every reason to question his motives.'

'Of course. I do not think for a minute—'

'No, wait,' continued DeSalle. 'You have not heard me out. I have some news of my own. You suggested I have Stead followed—'

'You hired a man?' interjected Mrs. Tanner.

'I followed him myself.'

'Arthur!'

'I am not a fool; I do not believe he saw me. I hired a cab and followed him all day yesterday; you are not the only one who can play detective, when the need arises.'

She sighed. 'He was here in the evening; I can tell you that much. And he had a patient to visit in the afternoon.'

DeSalle shook his head. 'No, I don't think so. I was outside his house in Wimpole Street. He was about to leave, most likely to come here and receive you – it was a little after one o'clock – and then a cab drew up. I knew the passenger immediately.'

'Who?'

'Wilmot. I could tell Stead was surprised to see him. They went inside together, then Wilmot came out, a

236

half-hour later. He looks ghastly at the best of times, but yesterday he looked like he was ready for the grave. I have never seen a man turn so pale. Stead came out again a short while later. I had thought he would go directly to Highgate, but he took a cab and went through Mayfair, towards the Thames. He crossed it at Vauxhall and went down to Lambeth.'

'Lambeth? And what then?'

DeSalle blushed. 'I'm afraid the cab-driver lost him.'

'Ah. No wonder Stead did not see you.'

'Sarah! Don't give me that look. Do you not see? Stead – Wilmot – Miss Smith and your Lambeth roughs . . . you were right from the start – they are all connected. There is some dreadful web being woven about my father.'

'Well, I am not sure I have done much to penetrate it.'

'You may yet have a chance,' he insisted. 'Am I right in thinking that my mother has not yet paid him a visit?'

'Not to my knowledge.'

'You are probably right. I received a note from Winters this morning. My mother has made arrangements with her coachman to travel to Highgate this evening, at nine.'

'Nine o'clock? A rather late hour to call on an invalid. Whatever for?'

'I have no idea,' he replied. 'But I suspect that whatever Dr. Stead has planned – whatever purpose he hopes to accomplish by bringing my father here – I fear it happens tonight.'

CHAPTER TWENTY-NINE

———

After Arthur DeSalle's departure, Mrs. Tanner spent the remainder of the afternoon deep in thought. She had fancied, before arriving at the Infirmary, that she might have an opportunity to investigate Dr. Stead's affairs; but his continued presence in the building, the careful locking of every door, and even the situation of her own room, all conspired against the possibility. There was, she concluded, little chance that she might discover anything further about the arrival of Lady DeSalle, not without an ally. And there seemed only one likely candidate.

Wright arrived with the evening meal at seven o'clock. It was a beef stew, with an appetising aroma that would have tempted any palate. Mrs. Tanner, however, put the dish to one side and turned to the maid. She had thought of several stories which might serve her purpose; all of them more unlikely than the next. In the end, however, she had determined on the last resort open to her, a rather desperate gamble. She had resolved – in broad terms, at least – to tell the truth.

'Are you not hungry, ma'am?' said the maid.

'I am very uneasy.'

'Ma'am?'

'Can you answer me something, and be quite frank?'

The maid looked distinctly uneasy herself, but nodded.

'Do you think your master is an honest man?' continued Mrs. Tanner.

'Dr. Stead, ma'am? Well, I'm sure he's a gentleman.'

'I wish it were so. Unfortunately, that is not the case.'

'Ain't it, though, ma'am?'

'No, it is not. You may ask what possible cause I might have to say such things. Perhaps I had best explain myself. I expect you saw me talking this afternoon with Lord DeSalle's son, the future Viscount.'

'I weren't prying, ma'am!' protested Wright. 'I was just in the kitchen and—'

Mrs. Tanner waved her hand dismissively. 'I did not think that you were. But I must make a confession to you, Wright, and I must do it in the hope that you will keep my confidence.'

'I'm sure I will, ma'am.'

'Very well. In recent weeks, Mr. DeSalle has come to suspect that his father and mother are the victims of a dreadful imposture, perpetrated by your master. I cannot vouchsafe a full explanation – suffice it to say that both the doctor and Miss Smith are not who they seem; and that Mr. DeSalle is certain that their practice of mesmerism, perhaps even the very creation of this Infirmary, is a cloak for plans of the most heinous and immoral nature.'

'No!' exclaimed the maid, in open-mouthed astonishment.

'Unfortunately, it is quite true. The matter is a delicate one, which cannot yet be brought before the police; the family's honour and reputation is at stake.

239

But Mr. DeSalle has entrusted me as his agent, and had me come here to gather evidence that may allow him to settle the matter in a discreet fashion.'

'Like a detective?'

'Well, let us say, I am an intimate acquaintance of several inspectors of the detective police, and I have been known to assist in their investigations; that is why Mr. DeSalle employed me.'

'Then you ain't ill?'

'Not in the slightest. Indeed, I have been obliged to feign the mesmeric state, to gain the doctor's confidence.'

'My head's swimming, ma'am!'

'You said yourself you had doubts about the character of Miss Smith; I can assure you that her employer is no better. Indeed, if the matter goes to the police, you may yet see him in Newgate as a convicted fraud.'

'Don't say that, ma'am!' protested the maid, increasingly agitated, as the prospects of her own future employment began to weigh heavy on her mind.

'I am afraid it is true. I am telling you this, my dear, for your own welfare. You are an honest girl, and I should hate to see you embroiled in a police matter. I said as much to Mr. DeSalle and he agrees; indeed, he was generous enough to say that, if my estimation of your character was correct, he would ensure that you were found a place, and should not suffer because of the doctor's infamy.'

'Oh, I am honest, ma'am!' exclaimed the maid. 'I don't know nothing about none of this! What can I do?'

'Mr. DeSalle informed me that his mother was arriving at a late hour this evening,' continued Mrs. Tanner. 'Tell me – have there been any preparations made?'

'Preparations?'

'In the old library, for instance? Miss Smith confided in me that Professor Felton carried out surgery there this morning. I expect the room must be cleaned.'

'Oh, I've cleaned it, ma'am. But I don't reckon the doctor's making use of it tonight; he hasn't told me nothing and we ain't expecting the Professor again – leastways, not as I know about it.'

'And there has been nothing out of the ordinary this evening? Nothing I should report back to Mr. DeSalle?'

The maid shook her head, then hesitated before speaking out. 'Only, it's a silly thing, ma'am . . .'

'What?'

'The doctor – he made a point this afternoon of saying I needn't clean in Lord DeSalle's study this evening. Not that it matters, of course. The poor old soul can't do nothing for himself, anyhow – begging your pardon, ma'am.'

'Tell me, is there a room adjoining the study where one might overhear a conversation within it?'

'I won't eavesdrop, ma'am!'

'I wouldn't ask you to do it, my dear,' said Mrs. Tanner, calmly. 'But for the honour of one of the foremost families in the land, I may have to sacrifice my morals. Will you help me?'

'The young Viscount – he said he might find me a place?'

'I would make it my personal mission to ensure that he did. And I am sure a small gratuity, a token of his thanks, might be arranged. But you must say nothing to the other servants – I cannot be sure who is to be trusted.'

The maid thought for the moment; there was a gleam

in her eye that suggested a degree of excitement at being co-opted into the unexpected intrigue.

'I'll do what I can, ma'am. For the family's honour, like you say.'

'Of course.'

~

Mrs. Tanner's evening mesmeric treatment occurred at eight p.m., as arranged. Her own anxiety, if truth be told, was that Wright might give her away. For, having conceded that her trance was a deception, she felt sure that the maid watched the process with a peculiar intensity, like a small child trying to fathom the secrets of a magic show. Dr. Stead, however, seemed quite oblivious to the maid's mood, and possessed of the similar nervous urgency which had gripped him at the start of the day. There was, Mrs. Tanner concluded, another mesmeric experiment which weighed heavily upon his mind.

Once the performance was over, Wright left the room with her master, carrying a lamp to light his way. She returned some ten minutes later, knocking on the door so quietly that Mrs. Tanner barely heard her. After a brief interrogation, the maid led the way along the dark corridor, past the upper landing, to the opposite wing of the house. There, she pulled out a bundle of keys, and hesitantly unlocked the door to one of the rooms. Again, the interior was barren and covered in a layer of dust that had settled like fine sand, which rose in clouds as the maid's skirts brushed the floor.

'There is nowhere better?' said Mrs. Tanner.

'It's right above the study, ma'am,' replied Wright. 'I reckon you'll hear anything through the chimney, if you leans into it.'

'Unless they start a fire,' said Mrs. Tanner.

'The master ain't asked for coals, ma'am.'

'Very well, it will have to do. You had better leave. Take the light and close the door behind you. If anyone asks why you were here—'

'I'll say I thought I heard a bird trapped in the chimney,' said the maid.

Sarah Tanner smiled. 'Yes, I suppose that will do.'

The maid nodded, visibly enjoying the air of conspiracy; silently, she crept from the room, closing the door slowly behind her, leaving the room in darkness. Mrs. Tanner leant into the chimney breast, her shoulder brushing against the brick, but there was no sound from below. Treading softly, she crouched down on the hearth-stone by the fenderless grate and waited.

Her patience was rewarded some fifteen or twenty minutes later, as distinct sounds began to be heard. A rumble; then scraping of wood upon bare boards, as if furniture were being moved. Then, a few minutes later, voices. She recognised them immediately: the first was Stead; the second the nurse.

'You are sure he will not wake?'

'An ox would not wake; another drop will kill him. Will you leave me in peace? I've learnt the lines. You're like an old woman!'

'It must be done well, if it is to be done at all. Are the lamps ready? It must be at the right time.'

'Be calm! There – that is her carriage. Give the bitch a brandy first, if you think it helps.'

'I have no wish to steady her nerves,' said the mesmerist, sarcastically.

'Go, then, for pity's sake.'

The sound of footsteps. Mrs. Tanner could hear the carriage herself; it drew to a halt outside. Then, a minute or two later, the distant booming sound of Stead's voice in the hall, effusive with welcome. Then the nurse spoke in the room below.

'We'll put on a good show, eh, Billy boy?'

Helena Smith was not alone: Lord DeSalle was in the study.

You are sure he will not wake?

Had the old man been given something to keep him down?

The sound of footsteps again; the mellifluous tones of the mesmerist.

'Everything is in readiness, ma'am. You are quite right; there is nothing achieved by delay. Will you take a seat?'

Lady DeSalle, her flawless accent unmistakeable, accepted.

'Every magnetic property is in alignment, ma'am. There could not be a better location; nor a better hour. From my research, I can assure you that this room is at the centre of a veritable whirlpool of magnetic forces. Can you not feel something in the air?'

'I am sure of it.'

'Now, I have already placed your husband in sympathy; the state resembles the deepest sleep, as you will see.'

'He looks quite at peace,' said Lady DeSalle.

'He is, ma'am. You may be sure of it. It is a serene state of equanimity which will allow the disjunction between mind and body to which I have so often animadverted.'

'And you are willing, Miss Smith, to put yourself through this trial?' said Lady DeSalle.

'I am, ma'am. I consider it my duty as a Christian.'

'Excellent,' said Stead. 'Then, with your permission,

Your Ladyship, I shall begin to place Miss Smith under my influence.'

The room fell silent or, at least, whatever might have been Lady DeSalle's response, it did not carry. Mystified, Sarah Tanner listened intently. The mesmerist's manipulations were, however, carried out without a sound. It was only some ten or fifteen minutes later that Dr. Stead spoke out.

'There, we have our subject, ma'am. Are you sure you wish to continue the experiment? It may cause you distress.'

'No, I wish to go on. It has been too long.'

'Very well. I shall place Miss Smith's hand in the water; it is already magnetised and will establish a conduit for the fluid. There. Now, Miss Smith, can you hear me?'

'Oh, yes, sir.'

'Good. Now, you know your task. Where is Lord DeSalle?'

'Lord DeSalle? I cannot see him. There is a mist,' said the nurse.

'Where is Lord DeSalle?'

'I tell you, there is a fog, silly!'

'Miss Smith, you must bend to my will. Where is Lord DeSalle?'

'There is a . . . no, wait, I see a man, coming through the mist. A handsome man.'

'Is it him? Is it His Lordship? Draw closer.'

'He is walking so slowly.'

'William?'

It was the voice of Lady DeSalle, trembling with emotion.

'Yes, I see him now,' continued the nurse, unprompted. 'His true form; a manly handsome youth. He says he would talk.'

'William, is it you?'

A pause. A choking sound.

'Yes,' said the nurse, an alteration, a slight timbre to her voice. 'Yes, I am here, my love.'

CHAPTER THIRTY

'William, is it you?'

'Yes. I have been wandering for so long, my dear. I am so glad to find you again.'

'Can you see me?'

'No, I can only hear your voice. There is a fog – it will not clear. The wretched mist; I cannot seem to escape it.'

'You must, my dear, for my sake,' said Lady DeSalle, earnestly. 'We want you back. The doctor can bring you back.'

'Can he? Blessed man! Caroline, I . . .'

A choking sound again.

'Do not fear, ma'am,' said the doctor. 'Miss Smith is up to the task.'

'Caroline?'

It was Miss Smith's voice again, the same harsh tone.

'William?' said Lady DeSalle, eagerly.

'I remember . . . do you recall that night at Almack's? I had known you but a month. The night we danced?'

Lady DeSalle's voice almost seemed to give way. 'I do.'

'You wore that beautiful dress. The red silk. Wear it again. It suited you so well.'

'That was many years ago, my dear,' she replied. 'I do not think it would fit.'

'Would it not? Forgive me, my love, I have forgotten. Ask the doctor . . . make sure that the doctor . . .'

Again, the same choking sound.

'I fear the strain is becoming too much, ma'am,' said Stead. 'I must bring Miss Smith back.'

'No! One more minute, I beg you!' exclaimed Lady DeSalle.

'My love . . .'

'No, ma'am. It is dangerous territory upon which we encroach; you must permit me – I cannot endanger Miss Smith's constitution. There! You see how the light flickers – the connection must be broken!'

'Very well,' said Lady DeSalle, her voice muted.

Silence.

A minute passed; then two.

'Miss Smith?' It was the doctor's voice.

'Sir?'

'Are you with us? Are you well?'

'I feel a little tired, sir.'

'I am not surprised. You cannot find fault with the girl, Your Ladyship. She reached the very limits of her powers; she has surpassed herself.'

'No, you are quite right.'

'Perhaps you might like to be alone with His Lordship, ma'am?'

'Yes, I should like that very much.'

Sarah Tanner tiptoed from the room, lest her footfalls reveal her presence. The bizarre secret of Lady DeSalle's confidence in the mesmerist suddenly seemed patent: the conduct of a living séance, with Helena Smith as medium, that allowed her a form of communion with her husband which would otherwise be denied her. It was plain from the conversation between the nurse and her employer that it was a fraud. Indeed, even without such proof, Mrs. Tanner would not have doubted it, whatever she had witnessed that morning. But it was not until she quit the room that she realised what lay at the root of the mesmerist's power, and enabled him to snare the grief-stricken woman so completely, the explanation that connected the horse-meat riot of Leather Lane and the ruthless exploitation of a loving wife's desperation.

The question remained: what was to be done?

At first, she contemplated going directly downstairs; but she concluded any attempt to explain herself – or how she had come by the information – might resemble the actions of a lunatic. A letter might serve her purpose better, but was there time? She thought the matter over. It could be left to the next day; it could easily be put aside. And yet the prospect of delay – the prospect of leaving the old man in Dr. Stead's power for any longer than necessary – seemed abhorrent.

She would make the attempt. She hurried to her room, sat down at the writing-desk, and began to write, as swiftly as was possible. The note was finished within a matter of minutes, the paper blotted, and placed within an envelope which she hastily addressed and sealed. She rang the servant's bell and, without waiting, walked briskly back to the gloomy landing and the heart of the house. As she came down to the ground floor, at the back of the main hall, she encountered the maid, ascending from the kitchen to answer her summons.

'Ma'am!' said the girl in a whisper. 'What happened? Did you hear anything?'

'Never mind for now. Is she still here, Her Ladyship?'

'She just rang the bell for her servants. She'll be on her way.'

'Servants? How many of them are there?'

'A coachman, and two footmen.'

'The servants – did you speak to them? Did you catch their names? Was one named Winters?'

'He was, ma'am, I heard the coachman call his name. Do you know him?'

'Wright, would you do something for me – something important? Mr. DeSalle will reward you for it, you have my word.'

'What is it, ma'am?' said the maid, peering nervously down the hall.

Mrs. Tanner pressed the letter into the young girl's hands. 'Take this and give it to the man, Winters. Tell him it is a private communication from me to his mistress, concerning His Lordship.'

'There ain't time for that, ma'am – I can't go through the front, and if I go back through the kitchens they'll be gone before I'm half-way there. That's them now!'

The sound of footsteps could be heard approaching the hall.

'Just go, and I will make sure there is time . . . I will not blame you if you are too late, but go now!'

Wright yielded and hurried back down the stairs, just as a door opened and Dr. Stead, accompanied by his elderly footman, ushered Lady DeSalle into the hall.

'Why, Mrs. Richmond,' exclaimed the mesmerist, briefly at a loss, before swiftly regaining his composure. 'I trust there is nothing amiss?'

'Mrs. Richmond,' said Lady DeSalle, with a polite nod.

'No, sir – ma'am – you must forgive me,' said Mrs.

250

Tanner, hurriedly. 'I did not mean to disturb you. I was merely going to see if I might borrow a book, to read in my room.'

'A book? But you do not have a lamp, ma'am,' said the doctor.

'A lamp! No, I am so foolish. How ridiculous! I followed the maid downstairs, and then she was wanted in the kitchen. I forgot I should need my own light.'

'I fear it is you who must forgive me, ma'am,' said the doctor. 'My servants have grown used to making trivial economies, since we had no other patients until your arrival. We need not stint on illumination, I am sure. Nor should the girl have abandoned you in such a fashion. I will speak to her.'

Mrs. Tanner nodded, and addressed Lady DeSalle. 'Ma'am, I am sorry to intrude; I hope His Lordship's health is improving.'

'As well as can be hoped,' she replied tersely. 'The hour is late. I will bid you good night, Mrs. Richmond.'

'And you, ma'am.'

The footman opened the front door. Mrs. Tanner glanced outside but saw no sign of Wright. The doctor, meanwhile, led Lady DeSalle to the waiting carriage and watched his patroness depart. Once the carriage had vanished from view, he returned to the hall.

'Now, let me ring the bell – wherever can that girl have got to, eh? I cannot imagine what she was thinking, ma'am! Not waiting to light your way! The very idea!'

Mrs. Tanner smiled affably. But, for a moment, she had the idea that the doctor looked at her with a peculiarly quizzical expression. He said nothing more, however, and a few seconds later, Wright appeared in the hall once more, looking distinctly breathless.

251

'Ah! There she is!'

'Sir?' said the maid.

'You left Mrs. Richmond standing here without a light! What were you thinking, girl?'

'Sir?' said the maid.

'It is not the girl's fault she was required in the kitchen, sir,' interjected Mrs. Tanner. 'I'm sure she will not make the same error again.'

'I should hope not. Show Mrs. Richmond to the morning-room, will you – she requires some reading matter. Ma'am, my apologies. It has been a long day and I will bid you good night, if I may. We shall meet again in the morning.'

'Of course, sir,' replied Mrs. Tanner.

Dr. Stead gave a low bow, as was his custom, and left the hall. The maid, in turn, waited until her master had left, and motioned for Mrs. Tanner to follow her.

'I did it, ma'am!' she said in a conspiratorial whisper. 'I gave him the note!'

⁓

For a second night, Mrs. Tanner retired to her bedroom. She had almost resolved to quit the Infirmary on the spot; there seemed little else she could accomplish. A further conversation with Wright had revealed that Lady Pennethorpe had already been taken home; and Lord DeSalle was unlikely to provide her with any information. She even had a nagging fear that Dr. Stead now entertained some suspicion of her. Moreover, if her letter to Lady DeSalle – and the accusations it contained – was not proof in itself of Stead's deception, she felt sure there was enough for any woman with an ounce of sense to uncover the truth. And yet to leave on foot, under cover of darkness, was dangerous; to persuade her host to provide some form of transport at such an hour was unthinkable. In consequence, she resolved to leave in the morning, under pretext of a walk to Highgate village; her trunk, she decided, could easily be abandoned.

As she went to close the curtains, she looked out into the wild expanse of the house's gardens. The darkness was almost complete, except for the faint light of a crescent moon. Yet, in the periphery of her vision, she had a vague impression of a man, standing by one of the plane trees on the garden's boundary. When she looked closely, however, there was no-one to be seen.

She recalled Jem Cranks, whom she had last seen lurking on Leather Lane.

Was it the boy? She could not be sure.

She drew the curtains and walked back into the sitting-room. After more thought, she laid hold of one of the armchairs that sat by the hearth, and dragged it slowly into the bedroom, then shut the door and wedged it against the door-handle. Satisfied that it would hold, she opened the trunk and reached down into the compartment that contained the pistol. Having loaded it with a bullet and powder, she placed it on the bed, with a small tin of percussion caps laid carefully beside.

Then, with the lamp still burning, she lay down to rest her head.

It was half-past twelve that night, when the Bottle of Hay public-house finally closed it doors. Midnight was the appointed hour, but the landlord, despite possessing a famously accurate clock, was willing to stretch the point, if sufficient good-will pervaded the bar, and sufficient customers looked likely to run to another round of drinks. Amongst those finally evicted on to the street was Ralph Grundy, accompanied by Joe Drummond. As was his custom, he turned his steps – albeit in somewhat meandering fashion – towards the New Dining and Coffee Rooms.

He did not dream that he was being watched by a dozen eyes.

As he approached the door, he tripped on the cobbles and the coster caught his arm.

'There, old chap, watch your step!'

'Don't "old chap" me, Joe Drummond,' murmured the old man. 'I know I've old bones; I don't need you reminding of it.'

The coster merely smiled. If truth be told, a pleasant pint or two of intoxicating liquor warmed his belly, and made the old man's customary belligerence bearable, even amusing.

'Well, good night, Joe Drummond, and you watch your step and all,' muttered Ralph Grundy, as he let himself inside the shop.

'Aye, old chap, I will,' said the coster, with a wink, and turned about.

It was but a minute or so later, as he walked down the narrowest part of Back Hill, a steep little road that dropped away from the market, that Joe Drummond heard footsteps behind him.

'Halloa! Who's there?'

'Don't you know me?' said the boy, stepping from the shadows. 'I'm ready to make a match of it now, if you like.'

The coster spun round, fumbling for his pocket-knife.

'What's the matter, old man, lost your chiv?' said Jem Cranks, grinning. 'Maybe one of my pals can help you out, eh?'

Joe Drummond peered into the darkness, suddenly sober. There were two boys behind Cranks.

Another noise; more footsteps. He turned his head and saw three more youths behind him.

'Not so big now, are you, old man?'

The coster made to speak but something held him back; a realisation, as the gang of boys moved towards him in concert.

It was not just Cranks.

All of them had knives.

CHAPTER THIRTY-ONE

Sarah Tanner woke, though it was still perfectly dark. The bed was a comfortable one, and it took a few seconds to remember where she was and then identify the sound. It was a knock at the bedroom door; and then the murmur of a woman's voice.

'Ma'am? Are you there?'

It was the maid-servant.

Another knock.

'What hour is it?' she asked.

'Just gone five, ma'am,' said Wright. 'May I speak with you?'

'Will it not wait 'til daylight?'

A pause.

'It's important, ma'am. About what you told me about the master.'

Mrs. Tanner rose from the bed. The lamp had burnt out and so she fumbled for a match to light a candle, which she placed upon the mantel-piece. She had not removed her dress from the previous night and, upon looking in the mirror, she frowned at her dishevelled appearance. Nonetheless, she walked over to the door and removed the armchair that had spent the night tilted against the handle. Upon opening it, she found the lamp in the sitting-room already lit, and the maid standing before her, her hands clasped nervously together.

'What is it?'asked Mrs. Tanner.

'Won't you come through and sit down, ma'am?' said the maid.

Sarah Tanner hesitated. There was something peculiarly forced in the maid's tone that made her wary. Instinctively, she began to step back, reaching to grip the door, ready to close it.

But it was too late.

Hands reached out from either side of the doorway, grabbing hold of her, pulling her sharply into the room, then pinning her arms behind her back. One man she recognised instantly as the mesmerist's elderly footman, whose grip was firmer than she could have imagined; the other, wearing a brown fustian suit, seemed strangely familiar, even though she did not catch a glimpse of his face in the dim light.

'What is the meaning of this?' she exclaimed, struggling vainly against the men's hold.

'It is for your own good, ma'am.'

It was the voice of Dr. Stead, who stepped into the room from the hall.

'Is this the woman, Mr. Smith?' continued the mesmerist, his voice directed to one of the men who restrained her.

'Oh, it's her all right, sir.'

Mrs. Tanner twisted her head, but she knew the voice well enough: Jem Cranks. Her heart sank.

'Wright,' she said, her eyes pleading with the maid, 'I do not know what they have told you—'

'Please!' interjected the mesmerist. 'Mrs. Richmond, calm yourself. We mean you no harm. Young Mr. Smith here has come to take you home. I have done my best with the treatment, but I must admit defeat. We cannot allow these perverse freaks of your imagination to take hold once again.'

'Wright – listen to me . . . his name is not Smith, it is Cranks—'

'There, my dear,' continued Stead, stepping forward, 'there is no need to indulge in these wild fancies. You must forgive me, ma'am; you need to calm yourself.'

And before Mrs. Tanner could say another word, Stead covered her mouth with a cambric handkerchief.

She thought, at first, he intended to gag her.

At least, until the stinging, sickly sweet scent overwhelmed her senses and a suffocating, oppressive stillness smothered her thoughts.

———

Where was she?

Naked, she lay upon the table in the old library.

If I could only sit up, she thought to herself. If only I could sit up; I could stop him.

Helena Smith stood on one side; Arthur DeSalle on the other. The nurse looked at her with the same self-satisfied, knowing gaze; DeSalle turned his head.

'It is a triumph for the New Science, sir,' said the nurse. 'She does not feel a thing.'

'There is so much blood.'

'That does not matter. It grows bigger by the day; it must be removed. Cut deeper.'

'I cannot do it. I have not the skill.'

'Come, sir. You almost have it.'

'She will die!'

'What the devil does that matter? There! You have it!'

258

She leant her head forward. Her belly was red with blood; the knife lay beside her upon the table.

The child lay dead in his hands.

———

Sarah Tanner awoke slowly, half-remembered dreams ebbing away, to leave a terrible headache that made her temples throb with pain.

Where was she?

She was in the corner of a room, her back against the wall. The room itself was black as pitch; the wall felt like rough exposed brickwork; the air dank and heavy. It was a cellar, she was quite certain of it.

She suddenly realised that she could barely move her limbs: her legs had been tied with rope; her arms were constrained by a garment wrapped tight around her upper body, pinned to her sides by tight straps.

She thought of Jem Cranks's appearance at the Infirmary and wondered why she was not dead.

She tried to move her body, shifting her weight. The floor, however, was hard and uneven. As she tried to move forward, she lost her balance and toppled over, barely managing to twist so that she did not fall face first on to the stones.

No, not stones – odd pieces of coal. For her fall generated a great flurry of sulphurous dust that left her choking for breath.

As she lay coughing on the ground, she heard the sound of footsteps above; then the creaking of wood. A light shone into the room, revealing its dimensions. It was a coal-cellar; no more than five and a half feet from floor to ceiling and ten wide. She found herself being dragged roughly back into the corner.

'Watch yourself, missus! You might do yourself an injury, eh?'

It was the boy. With a grin, he returned to the narrow set of wooden steps from which he had descended. At first, she thought he intended to take away the lamp he had left at the top and shut the trap-door behind him. Instead, Jem Cranks was replaced upon the steps by the figure of Dr. Stead.

'Well, my dear,' he said, 'I see you are awake. Excellent! I am not overly familiar with the properties of chloroform. I rather feared I had lost you for good. I must offer my apologies.'

'You'll forgive me if I don't accept them.'

'My dear Mrs. Richmond – or should I say Mrs. Tanner? – there is no need for such ill-feeling. I merely had to remove you from my affairs as swiftly as possible; there is no need to make matters more awkward than necessary.'

'How did you find me out? Was the boy at the house? Did he see me?'

'Young Jem? Ah, yes, you are well acquainted, are you not? No, it was not the boy; not quite. You see, when I met you in the hall last night, I noticed there was a mark – a scrape of soot or ash – upon the shoulder of your dress; that seemed rather peculiar, as did your rather hasty explanation of your presence. I started to wonder how a lady might come by such a mark. And the girl was so flustered when I spoke to her; well, let us say I have a suspicious mind.'

'It was Wright, then?'

'I questioned her later in the evening; she confessed the ridiculous story you had told her and what you had been up to – I do believe she thought I would murder her, poor girl! A lady detective, though! What a credulous little creature she is!'

'You have not killed her, then?'

'My dear woman! You must take me for a monster!'

Mrs. Tanner held her tongue.

'As it happened,' he continued, 'it was my good fortune to receive a nocturnal visit from our mutual friend, young Cranks, and he told me that a certain Mrs. Tanner had been absent from Leather Lane for a week or so. I began to think matters over; and, of course, then I recalled that peculiar incident at Mivart's – I assume that was your doing?'

'I thought it might shame you.'

'What, out of paying court to Lady DeSalle? Why, my dear, it would take a good deal more than that. I have spent several months establishing myself in the good graces of the finest families in London; I don't intend to be done down by a petty adventuress, even one of your calibre.'

'Adventuress?'

'My dear, please, we are fellow-travellers along the same highway. Your motives are quite transparent, even if you are a marvellous actress. You need not maintain the flimsy pretence you constructed for the benefit of Miss Wright.'

Sarah Tanner paused, her thoughts racing. 'I do not believe I am so transparent as all that.'

'Come,' said Stead, jovially, 'it is quite obvious. You are a woman of unique talents – my young friend has told me as much – and, as luck would have it, you have acquired certain incriminating documents which are rightfully mine. You obviously possess some experience in these matters. You thought you could make something of it. Perhaps sell them back to the family, once I was out of the way? It was bold, ma'am. I give you full credit. And, I freely admit, I have no idea how you inveigled yourself so swiftly in their lives. I suppose you have the advantage of youth and beauty, which I cannot lay claim to, eh? But I have invested too much in Lady DeSalle, my dear, to let you ruin it.'

'Ruin what?' said Mrs. Tanner. 'Stealing love letters from a man who's half-way to the grave?'

The mesmerist smiled. 'I don't know what you mean, my dear. Miss Smith is an expert medium.'

'I know what I heard,' muttered Mrs. Tanner. 'I suppose at some point, some years ago, Lord DeSalle entrusted his private correspondence to his lawyer for safe-keeping – including letters from his wife. I do not suppose he expected Wilmot would sell it on to the likes of you; doubtless he was a more sober individual in those days. Miss Smith makes it all sound fresh, I'll grant you, but there is nothing mystical about it.'

'The likes of me! Why, you sound positively outraged!' exclaimed the mesmerist, visibly amused. 'I think you should consider the proverbial pot and kettle, my dear. If it is any comfort, poor Mr. Wilmot has never been a willing confederate of mine. He merely has an unfortunate weakness which places him in my power.'

Mrs. Tanner blinked, as pieces of a jigsaw clicked into place.

'A fondness for liquor, or a fondness for boys?' she said.

Stead raised his eye-brows in surprise. The voice of Jem Cranks, out of sight in the room above, could be plainly heard.

'There! Didn't I tell you?'

The mesmerist, however, recovered his composure.

'My young friend thinks you are "a mighty fine piece of work", my dear. I am beginning to agree with him. He thinks we should do away with you.'

'Then why haven't you?'

'Good Lord! Nothing unnerves the woman!'

exclaimed the mesmerist. 'My dear, I must profess my sincere admiration!'

'Then release me from this strait-waistcoat of yours.'

'Ah, do you like it? A nice touch, I thought. Miss Wright believed implicitly that you had been transported to an asylum.'

'What did you do with her?'

'I told you, I am no monster. I gave her six months' wages, a mediocre character, and told her to take her leave. She was quite grateful for such largesse.'

Mrs. Tanner fell silent.

'Let me be blunt,' continued Stead. 'You have certain letters which poor Grubb sold to the butcher; your interference in this business brooks no other explanation. I should still like to acquire them. I am willing to pay a decent premium – namely, your freedom.'

'And if I refuse your offer? What will happen then?'

'Nothing,' said the mesmerist.

'Nothing?'

'Nothing at all. I shall simply leave you here to . . . well, to reconsider.'

'Or to rot,' said the gloating voice of Jem Cranks.

'If I tell you where they are, your boy will kill me.'

'You have my word he will not,' replied Stead.

'Is that what you told Charlie Grubb, when you thought he might give away your little scheme?'

Stead shook his head. 'I am sorry you cannot be more co-operative, my dear. Perhaps you need a few days' solitude to think upon it. Because I do not think you will get a better offer.'

And, with that, Stead blew out the lamp, and closed the trap-door.

CHAPTER THIRTY-TWO

A‌s her eyes adjusted to the darkness, Sarah Tanner considered her situation. She tried to focus her thoughts solely on her escape, on the chances of obtaining her freedom. Nonetheless, her spirits sank. She was certain that Wright had been dealt with by the mesmerist, and prayed that the girl had come to no harm. She could not rely upon her for rescue, that seemed quite clear.

Arthur DeSalle, on the other hand, would immediately suspect any fabrication concerning her disappearance from the Infirmary. And yet, with the maid already despatched, who would testify to the manner of her departure? She had already done what he asked: her letter to Lady DeSalle was, she assumed, sufficient to derail Stead's plans. How long would Arthur search for her? She had vanished from his life once; perhaps he might eventually conclude she had vanished again, of her own free will.

And what of Dr. Stead? She cursed her own impatience in writing to the Viscountess with such haste. If Lady DeSalle withdrew her husband from the mesmerist's care, would he still want the missing letters? What if she told him the truth – about her connection to Arthur DeSalle; that she had never seen the letters in the first place; that every motive they had ascribed to her actions was wrong?

Would he still place any value on her life?

She might call out, of course, but she doubted if she could be heard. Her imprisonment was planned; they would have gagged her if they thought she might draw attention to herself.

She took a deep breath then tried to move again, more carefully than before. She still wore her clothes from the Infirmary; she still possessed the slim stiletto, artfully concealed behind her back, in a pouch between the whalebones of her corset. If she could simply move her hands . . .

No. It was quite impossible. The strait-waistcoat was swathed in leather straps that bound her upper arms firmly to her sides. However much she attempted to twist and turn, however much she strained the tendons of her wrists, she could not reach the handle of the blade, which lay a couple of inches beyond her grasp.

Frustrated, she gritted her teeth and tried to wriggle backwards against the brickwork, hoping that she might rub the leather against some jagged surface. But the walls, though rough and unplastered, seemed to afford no opportunity.

It was, she concluded, foolish to ignore the obvious.

'Help!'

'Murder!'

She called out loudly a dozen times, her voice echoing around the low chamber. At last, she heard the pad of footsteps for a second time and the trap-door opened, illuminating the cellar with a shaft of light. To her disappointment, if not surprise, it was Jem Cranks who appeared at the opening. Without waiting for him to speak, she cried out louder still, reasoning that, with the trap lying open, her voice might carry further.

The boy shook his head, amused, waiting until she stopped for breath.

'That caterwaulin' won't get you far, missus. There ain't no-one to hear you.'

'You cannot keep me here for ever. Someone in the house will suspect.'

'"Someone in the house"?' mimicked the boy. 'Where do you think you are, anyhow?'

'Some cellar in your master's blessed Infirmary, I imagine.'

The boy shook his head.

'First off, he ain't my "master" – me and old Johnnie-boy is partners, see? Second, we ain't so green as to keep you in that house, with respectable parties coming and going. No, we brought you here, missus – where there ain't a soul to hear you; not if you shouts or screams, not on any account.'

As the boy spoke, he raised his hand. It contained a small pistol, which he pointed at his captive.

'Bang!' he said, playfully. 'See? I learnt my lesson, dealing with you, missus. You won't catch me out again. Except Johnnie says leave you be: starve it out of you. But I reckon I could make a party talk all right, if I had a mind, and spare us the waiting.'

She stared at the boy. He spoke in a detached, matter-of-fact fashion that, in any other youth, she might have taken for a mere show of bravado. Yet she was sure that he was in earnest. His eyes possessed the same grim malevolence which she had seen at their first encounter, and the only hint of emotion was a certain self-satisfaction in his voice. She tried desperately to focus her thoughts, despite her aching head.

266

A mere boy must have a weakness. What was it?

'Perhaps we could make a bargain, you and I,' she said.

'Not likely. You ain't got nothing I want.'

'If you let me out of this place, now, I will take you to the letters. And I have some money put by . . . it's yours. Stead need not know about that . . . it is a tidy sum.'

The boy walked down the wooden stairs, and shuffled forward, crouching before her. He put the gun to her chest, prodding her with it.

'You must think I'm a proper Sam, missus.'

'No, I don't,' she replied, hesitantly, the nerves in her voice quite unfeigned. 'I'm telling you the truth.'

The boy shook his head and raised the gun to within an inch of her face.

'See this? This says you better tell us about that money now, before you goes anywhere. Then I'll think on it.'

Mrs. Tanner kept her eyes fixed on the weapon.

'Stead told you to leave me alone.'

'And I told you,' he said, running the barrel down her cheek, scraping her skin, 'he ain't my guv'nor. And if my hand slips on this 'ere trigger, well, I don't reckon he's that particular. You know, come to think of it, I ain't never seen anyone get shot. I bet there's a bloody awful mess, eh?'

She froze. The boy's hand did not look steady; it was a thought she found hard to put from her mind.

'Cat got your tongue, eh?' said Cranks, grinning, touching the scratch on her cheek with his free hand.

The boy seemed enthused by his power over her. She could sense what was coming next; she had seen it before in others; it was written in his face, an awful admixture of childish excitement and malice.

He leant closer and, pushing the barrel roughly into her neck, forced his lips upon hers.

Instinctively she flinched, tried to twist her head away, which only seemed to delight the boy all the more, as he pushed his lubricious mouth insistently upon her own. His free hand, meanwhile, clumsily groped at her legs, making her thankful for the tightly drawn bonds that suddenly seemed her only protection.

A mere boy!

She willed herself to submerge the sickly feeling of disgust in the pit of her stomach; to ignore the gun. She knew it was her opportunity; and it required all her self-possession.

She kissed him back.

It was not delicate; it was not passionate. But it was a kiss, all the same, and, astonishingly, as she responded, the boy started in surprise, scrabbling back in the coal, seemingly shocked at the outcome. It was not quite the result she had anticipated; she wondered if he'd ever even kissed a woman before.

'Are you quite sure I've nothing you want?' she said.

'What's your game?'

'I'll take you to the letters and the money, if you just untie me and let me out of this wretched hole. And then I'll do more besides, if that's what you fancy; I reckon that is what you fancy, ain't it? I can tell. What's that worth to you?'

'Fancy? From where I'm sitting, missus, I can do what I damned well like, can't I just!'

'I suppose you can,' she said quietly. 'But have you ever had a woman? One who was willing.'

'Course I 'ave,' replied the boy, before adding hastily, 'twice.'

'You liar! I'll bet you've never even seen a pair of bubs. Why, you're blushing right now.'

'I ain't. An' I've seen lots of girls.'

'Well, girls, perhaps,' she replied dismissively, trying to goad him. 'Shame I'm all trussed up, ain't it? We could make a nice little arrangement, just you and me. Your pal wouldn't have to know about it, neither.'

The boy seemed to hold back, then scrambled forward, thrusting the barrel of the gun against her lips.

'Shut up,' said Cranks.

But, instead of forcing himself on her again, he ran his hand down to the trio of leather straps that bound her arms, pulling at the buckles. Once they were free, he stepped cautiously backwards, holding the pistol outstretched, until he could seat himself half-way up the wooden steps that led to the trap-door.

'Go on then, missus,' he said with a broad grin, as if struck by his own ingenuity. 'If you're so game, you make us blush, eh? Let's see what a fellow's missing – show us, eh?'

'What? Take off my clothes? In this place?'

'All of them. Cast your skin and let's have a look,' said the boy, with relish. 'Then I'll think about it, if I like the goods.'

'What if I don't?'

'Then I reckon I'll try my aim,' said the boy, waving the pistol.

With a show of reluctance, she wriggled free of the loosened waistcoat. She leant forward, crouching over the rope tied around her legs, pulling at the knots.

'What you doing?' said the boy.

'The dress is all of a piece; I can't get it off if it's tied to my legs, can I?'

The boy thought the matter through, weighing the problem in his mind.

'Keep it slow,' he said at last. 'I want to see your hands.'

She nodded, and worked at the rope. She wondered if the knots were the mesmerist's work, since they were not done particularly tight; she somehow imagined the boy would be more skilful. At last, she was free.

'I'll have to undo the buttons at the back, though,' she said.

The boy beamed at the prospect. 'Go on then, missus. I don't mind.'

She nodded, and reached both hands behind her back, opening a button of the dress, reaching between her stays. In a second she had the ivory handle of the stiletto in her hand, concealing the blade beneath her cuff.

'One's stuck, you'll have to do it for me.'

'Turn about, then,' said the boy, getting off the steps. 'Slow.'

She did not wait for him to reach her. As he moved, finding his footing on the coal-strewn floor, she lunged at Cranks with the knife, leaping forward to catch him off guard, slashing at the arm holding the gun, then back into his body. Her first strike made contact; there was a fine spray of blood from the boy's hand as he squealed in pain. He dropped the weapon, which clattered noisily to the ground, discharging its shot harmlessly into the cellar wall with a puff of foul-smelling smoke.

But the boy, agile as ever, somehow managed to roll to one side, avoiding her second thrust. As he turned, leaning back on the steps, he kicked out wildly with his foot, catching her square in the belly, sending her flying backwards.

The shock of the blow was such that, as she fell back, the knife tumbled from her hand. She watched with dismay as it fell at Jem Cranks's feet.

The boy picked it up in an instant.

CHAPTER THIRTY-THREE

'You're a proper sneak, missus!' said Cranks, taking the knife. 'But I'm wide awake to your tricks, ain't I just!'

'You're wounded,' said Mrs. Tanner, looking at the boy's right hand, clumsily tucked under his left arm to stem the bleeding.

'What?' said the boy. 'You going to kiss it better, then, missus? It's just a nick, anyhow. I've 'ad worse.'

'I'll make it worse if you come any closer.'

Cranks shook his head. 'You're a viper, you are! And I won't get bit twice, not likely!'

The boy began to edge backwards up the steps, keeping a wary eye on his erstwhile captive, the knife held out like a talisman. Sarah Tanner, in turn, tried to scramble to her feet. But the pieces of coal that littered the floor caused her to stumble. She hurriedly picked one up and flung it at the boy's head.

Cranks dodged it with ease.

'Johnnie was right,' said the boy, now perched on the top of the steps, one hand on the trap-door. 'I reckon we'll give you a day or two solitary, like in the jug. Then you'll be on your hands and knees a-beggin' us to let you out, eh? No-one crosses Jem Cranks – not you, nor no-one.'

272

Mrs. Tanner's tongue faltered; she could see no hope of escape – her best chance ruined. It was just as the boy heaved at the trap, however, that her spirits rose: for there was the sound of a heavy knocking, somewhere above; the sound of a man's voice.

'Police! In the name of Her Majesty, open up!'

The trap-door closed; there was the sound of rapid steps. Then the muffled report of another gun being fired.

A few seconds passed; then the creaking hinges of the trap stirred into life, and the door was pulled open once more, albeit slowly. She grabbed two more lumps of coal, ready to hurl them with all her might.

A man stood at the top of the steps, dressed in a woollen overcoat, a scarf pulled around his face.

'Sarah!' exclaimed Arthur DeSalle.

～

The cellar, it seemed, belonged to the kitchen of a small cottage that squatted by the edge of a hedge-lined dirt road, with the rear of the building backing on to open fields. Sarah Tanner peered outside into the daylight. Grateful to be free of the foetid air of the basement, she took a deep breath. A minute or so passed, until Arthur DeSalle returned indoors, coming back from the lane outside.

'Damn the boy!' exclaimed DeSalle, red-faced with anger.

'He stole the horse?'

'My best mare! Worth fifty guineas!'

Mrs. Tanner could not help a wry smile at Arthur DeSalle's indignation.

'You can't trust anybody, can you?'

'Well, never mind that,' replied DeSalle, tetchily. 'What the devil happened at the Infirmary?'

Mrs. Tanner sighed. 'Stead grew suspicious; it was my own fault – I shouldn't have trusted in the maid. She told him I was spying on him; I just hope he hasn't killed her for her trouble.'

'You think he might have?'

'I doubt he has the stomach for it,' she said. 'His young friend does, though; mark my words. But the question is how on earth did you find me?'

'I was watching the house—'

'You!' interjected Mrs. Tanner. 'Of course! I saw you in the garden. I thought it was Cranks! Except, I suppose he should have managed to go unnoticed.'

'In point of fact, Sarah, I do not believe I was seen; at least, not by anyone else,' said DeSalle. 'You had best be grateful I was there. I had not intended to linger all night, but I could see the lamp still burnt in that wretched man's study, so I kept watch. I had a feeling something was up. Then I saw them removing a trunk from the house; just before dawn.'

'A trunk?' said Mrs. Tanner ruefully. 'Charming. Stead gave me a dose of chloroform.'

'I had no idea you might be the contents! But they seemed in such a hurry that I followed the carriage.'

'And where are we?'

'I don't know the name; somewhere in the country, a couple of miles west of Hampstead. There is a small village not half a mile back. I managed to follow them at a distance whilst they kept to the main road; but then they disappeared from sight. I would have been here sooner but I have spent the last two hours searching every wretched lane and by-way in the district. It was only by sheer good fortune that I saw Stead's carriage coming back out of this very road. I thought I would come down and investigate the house. Then I heard a gunshot as I came up.'

274

'And so you decided to impersonate a police officer?'

'I thought it might provide an excuse to enter the place.'

Mrs. Tanner smiled. 'Arthur, more than likely you saved my life. But I heard a shot . . .'

'I had my pistol,' replied DeSalle. 'The boy was too quick; he bolted as soon as I came in. It was as much to scare the devil off, as anything; I don't think I even scratched him. I don't have your aim.'

'More's the pity. Well, let us have a quick look around the house, although it appears quite empty at first glance. Then we had best be off; Cranks will be too quick on that nag of yours – I have no wish to see him again, if it can be avoided. It looks like we can cut through the fields to the village.'

'Sarah,' said DeSalle, putting an arm on her sleeve, 'are you quite all right? They did not harm you?'

'No, they did not,' she replied briskly, glancing at her hands, examining the layer of coal dust that coated them. 'Though I suppose I look like a chimney sweep.'

'A little.'

'I don't suppose there is a pump in the yard?' she said.

'I don't think so. I saw a trough outside . . .'

'Then that will have to do. And when I'm done, I can tell you a good deal about Dr. Stead.'

The land behind the cottage began as rough scrub, but then yielded to a cornfield, its boundaries delineated by a hedgerow, that seemed to mark a gently undulating path down to the nearby village. As they walked Sarah Tanner outlined her experiences at the Infirmary, and, at length, her conversation with Stead.

'So he has obtained these letters, between my mother and father?' asked DeSalle.

'Private correspondence your father had entrusted to Wilmot's care. Perhaps Grubb merely copied them, I don't know. But then the boy lost some in his enthusiasm for making a few pence by selling old paper. And that is how the business on Leather Lane began. I suspect Wilmot had no inkling what Grubb was doing until his death. In any case, it allows Miss Smith to maintain an authentic performance; your wretched mother believes she is in touch with your father's spirit. It gives her hope he may be revived. False hope, I fear. I expect she is contributing a good deal to the man's finances. Does she have money to draw upon?'

'My father's money, most likely, in some form or another. But your letter that the girl passed to Winters—'

'Assuming that she told me the truth,' interrupted Mrs. Tanner.

'Granted. But if we assume that, and my mother reads it, then your letter exposes Stead?'

'I elaborated a little on the pure facts. But I told her I had overheard Miss Smith and Stead plotting the deception; and how it was carried out.'

'You did not mention me?'

'Why, of course. "Dear Lady DeSalle, as your son's former whore, I beg to inform you that I have been masquerading as a respectable woman in a good cause . . ."'

'Sarah,' protested DeSalle, 'don't be so coarse. It's not worthy of you.'

'I said nothing. I said I was leaving Stead's care, as I feared for my own safety – not far wrong, as it proved – and that I enjoined her to consider her own

276

well-being and reputation; to consider the possibility she was in the hands of villains of the blackest dye.'

'That must suffice – she cannot be so blind to the truth. But I must speak to her; Wilmot must be obliged to confess . . .'

DeSalle halted, pausing besides the hedgerow. She examined his expression.

'You're thinking about the consequences, aren't you?' she said. 'The police.'

DeSalle nodded. 'The whole sordid affair will have to go through the courts; the family will become a laughing-stock. I am not sure I can countenance it.'

'You needn't go so far. Once your father is removed from Stead's power, isn't that enough? That's what you wanted, after all.'

'And leave the man free, to prey upon others?' asked DeSalle. 'To blackmail and bribe? To kill, when it suits him?'

'Does that make much difference to you?'

DeSalle waved his hand dismissively.

'No, it will be the police. There is nothing else for it.'

'Why are you suddenly so certain?'

'It doesn't matter.'

'No,' she persisted, 'tell me. I am curious.'

'Very well,' said DeSalle, 'if you insist on it. They know who you are, Sarah; they know where you live. From everything you tell me, the boy, at least, will not baulk at persecuting you for the defeats you've inflicted on him. Stead may feel much the same, not least since he has no idea of my involvement.'

'You do not think Cranks saw you at the cottage?'

'I took care that he did not; I had the scarf wrapped about my face. Besides, he turned and ran the instant I forced the door. No, they will blame you for everything. If I do nothing, then I will have profited at your expense and made some of the worst villains in London your sworn enemies.'

'They'll be in good company.'

'No, Sarah,' continued DeSalle, shaking his head, 'you cannot make light of it. You would not have gone so far, if it was not for me; you would not have placed yourself in mortal danger. My family will have to bear the consequences of my mother's credulity; and if she will not bring the matter to the police, then I shall do it myself.'

'You'd do that for my sake? You swear?'

'I think it must be done. We could concoct a story about your part in it . . . I don't know . . . say that you were an actress whom I hired as my agent! It need not be too far from the truth.'

Mrs. Tanner smiled and gazed up at him.

'What?' said DeSalle. 'What are you looking at?'

'A man I once admired.'

And with that, she drew close to him, and kissed Arthur DeSalle lightly upon the lips.

———

It was two hours later that Sarah Tanner got down from a hired carriage – paid for by Arthur DeSalle – and set foot upon Gray's Inn Lane, for the first time in over a week.

If truth be told, she felt quite buoyant; and if she could not immediately explain the sensation to herself, there was a part of her that knew the answer: *she had kissed him*. The memory of it played at the edge of her consciousness; distracted her from the world about her, as she cut through the alleys. At length, she chastised herself for such girlish excitement; a mere kiss, after all, from a man with whom she had shared every intimacy. And yet it thrilled her all the same, pushing aside thoughts of the New Dining and Coffee Rooms; even of the threat posed by Cranks and Stead.

But there was something amiss, almost imperceptible at first, that roused her from her reverie. Strange looks from some of the costers; whispered conversations as she passed by.

Was it her clothes?

No. Whilst the soiled condition of her dress and the coal-dust in her hair militated against re-admission to Mivart's Hotel, once wrapped in a cheap shawl, they were perfectly suited for Leather Lane.

A woman spat nearby.

Did she spit *at* her? It made no sense.

At last, unnerved, she reached the New Dining and Coffee Rooms to find them shuttered, even though it was barely four in the afternoon. Hurriedly, she opened the door and went inside. She found Ralph Grundy seated behind the counter, a bottle of brandy, half empty, beside him; Norah Smallwood, meanwhile, sat at a table, rubbing her eyes, her cheeks red with tears.

'Missus!' exclaimed the old man.

'What's going on?' she asked. 'What in heaven's name is going on?'

'I thought it best to shutter the shop, missus,' said Grundy, drunkenly apologetic. 'Folk ain't happy; and I thought it'd be a mark of respect.'

'What do you mean?'

'You ain't heard then?' said the old man.

'Ralph, just tell me what's going on.'

'I'll tell it plain, missus. Joe Drummond died this morning. They thought he might pull through, being such a big man and all, but he didn't.'

'Joe's dead? How?'

'Stabbed. Cut up bad.'

279

Mrs. Tanner blanched.

'Who did it?'

The old man hesitated. 'I ain't told no-one, missus. There's some on the market who'd have your guts, if they knew for certain; a few as think you're mixed up in it, anyhow. The Peelers have been sniffing round the Lane all day. I suppose they can't know nothing. But I was the one that found him, see?'

'What haven't you told anyone?'

'It was the last words he ever spoke, I reckon.'

Sarah Tanner steadied herself against the counter.

No-one crosses Jem Cranks.

'It was the boy, wasn't it?' she said, at last.

'Aye, it was,' said the old man, grimly, taking another swig of brandy.

CHAPTER THIRTY-FOUR

The reason given for the complete closure of the New Dining and Coffee Rooms that very evening was the death of Sarah Tanner's mysterious relative, which, Ralph Grundy let it be known, was unexpected, as the party in question had been thought to be recovering. There was, it must be said, a degree of skepticism amongst the market-folk; and it was not diminished when Ralph Grundy quit his usual lodgings that same night. But no-one could quite say what link, if any, there was between the closure of Mrs. Tanner's premises, the movements of her employees, and the dreadful murder of Joe Drummond. For the coster had been a quiet, unassuming individual, who had not said a word concerning his first encounter with Jem Cranks, not even to his closest friends, perhaps thinking it beneath his dignity to boast of besting a mere boy. The closure of Mrs. Tanner's shop, therefore, merely served to heighten the impression that *there was something queer about that woman*, which was already the prevailing impression amongst many of the inhabitants of the district.

Ralph Grundy was, of course, obliged to attend the coroner's inquest the following day. He gave the briefest of evidence and, right or wrong, said nothing of the few words which the coster had spoken to him, as he struggled for breath on Back Hill. He was not interrogated for very long and, as the verdict of 'unlawful murder by person or persons unknown' was delivered by the jury, he slipped quietly from the Wesleyan Chapel where the coroner had established his dominion, and walked in the direction of Holborn. There, he went over to a carriage parked upon the road-side of the busy thoroughfare, exchanged a few words with those inside, and went on his way.

'You could have gone yourself,' said Arthur DeSalle, as the vehicle pulled out into the noon-day traffic.

'I only wanted the verdict,' said Sarah Tanner, peering out of the window as Ralph Grundy's figure disappeared into the market crowd. 'And to know Ralph and Norah are safe. It was good of you to pay for their accommodation.'

'It is nothing.'

'It will be the funeral tomorrow, but I don't expect I would be that welcome.'

'You'll keep the shop shut?'

'Until this whole thing is over. I will not have them . . . I will not take that risk. Especially not Norah – not again.'

'You don't think we should go to the police?'

'About poor Joe? What proof do we have?'

'Let the police find their proof. *You* were drugged and abducted! It is not just my word . . . the maid, Wright, she can testify to it.'

'If she can be found. Besides, it is too late for all that. If we went to the police, it would all come out, Arthur. You spoke some fine words the other day, and I am sure you meant them, but I don't want to appear in the *Police News* any more than you, even if our reasons differ.'

'Then you would have a murderer go unpunished?'

'No.'

'Then what?'

'That is my affair. Come, tell me again, about your mother.'

'Why?' said DeSalle, as the carriage rolled onwards. 'What good will it do?'

'I am not quite sure I believe it,' she replied. 'There is something we are missing.'

'It gets no better with repetition.'

'Nevertheless.'

'Very well,' said DeSalle with a sigh. 'When we parted yesterday, I went directly to Berkeley Square. I spoke to Winters and he swore that he had delivered the note the night before, just as you had intended, as the girl had instructed him.'

'So your mother had the night to think the matter over?'

'Quite. And, in the morning, she went to Wilmot's office – he heard that from the coachman.'

'Was she there long?'

'No, a few minutes, from what I could gather. I rather assumed Wilmot had confessed his guilt; or, at least, admitted how Stead had made use of him.'

'And then you attempted to see her?'

'She would not admit me!' exclaimed DeSalle. 'My own mother!'

'Perhaps she was ashamed of herself. But, still, she had your father returned to Berkeley Square, later in the afternoon?'

'You make him sound like a parcel.'

'I meant no offence. But in Stead's hands, he is merely a commodity to be exploited. So you left your mother a note?'

'I said precisely what we agreed – nothing of your

283

true background. I wrote that you had expressed your concerns to me before you left the Infirmary; that I knew about that note, that I trusted your word, that I had my own concerns as to Stead's probity, *et cetera*. I gave her every opportunity to—'

'What? Fall upon her hands and knees and crave your forgiveness for her sins? Not everyone is so keen to admit their faults, Arthur.'

'It is not simply a matter of pride!' exclaimed DeSalle. 'Somehow they have contrived to convince her—'

'Calm yourself. It does no good.' Mrs. Tanner sighed. 'Show me the note again.'

Arthur DeSalle wearily shook his head, and reached inside his jacket pocket, to recover a letter in his mother's hand, which he passed to his companion.

Berkeley Square
23rd May

My dearest Arthur,

You must forgive your poor mother for not receiving you earlier today. I had a severe head and had been much tried by the events of the day, and by the unfortunate atmosphere of suspicion that seems to have suddenly permeated our relations.

Whence does this poisonous cloud arise? Let me say first that I do not blame Mrs. Richmond. Dr. Stead informs me that, in more volatile females, the mesmeric state may act upon the nerves so as to produce fantastical delusions. Her letter to me this morning can only be an instance of such self-deception; she has convinced herself that this plot she describes *must* be true; therefore it *is* true. I am quite sure that she has since had cause to reflect upon her letter, and regret it.

Nor, Arthur, are you greatly at fault, though I was surprised to receive your note. If I lay any blame at your feet, it is only that it must be *your* suspicions and fancies that have been nurtured in the impressionable mind of a susceptible young woman.

No, the fault is mine. I have kept my dealings with Dr. Stead a secret; I have feared the disapproval and vilification of those who deride mesmerism, but know nothing of its practitioners or its powers. I have been fearful of what my own son might think of me; and it is surely for this reason that you feel constrained to address me in such heated terms.

What is to be done? It seems to me that it is my duty as a mother to allay your fears, however groundless, and to put things right. I have therefore taken two steps, of which I am sure you will approve.

In the first instance, I have brought your father back to Berkeley Square. You do not imagine, I trust, that he can come to any harm whilst under my roof?

Second, I have invited Dr. Stead to visit us tomorrow night and, in conjunction with Miss Smith, perform the small miracle which he has worked upon several previous occasions. I should like you to attend at eight o'clock. For I am quite certain that the evidence of your own eyes will erase any doubts you may harbour. Will you do this for your mother's sake?

If so, with your permission, I shall also write

a suitable letter to Mrs. Richmond, extending my forgiveness and understanding – for I believe she is deserving of it – and inviting her to the same demonstration. I can see no better way in which this awful misunderstanding can be laid to rest.

Believe me always,

Your loving mother

'She is quite the devotee of mesmerism,' said Mrs. Tanner, 'if she considers me a lunatic and will welcome me into her home to prove a point.'

'You think Stead has said nothing of your true identity?'

'If he acknowledges who I am, he risks the exposure of everything that happened on Leather Lane. Better to paint me as a harmless lunatic; that way, there will be no questions, and everything I have said can be ridiculed. But there is something wrong in your mother's note, I'm sure of it.'

'Sarah, I swear,' said DeSalle, 'the fellow has mesmerised her! You said he has some powers . . .'

'I cannot explain what I saw with Lady Pennethorpe, that much is certain. I suppose if your mother has seen a similar procedure, that may have confirmed her faith in the man.'

'It is more like he has bent her to his will; no-one can gainsay him!'

She shook her head.

'I do not believe that. Your mother has twice the backbone of that wretched man.'

'What then?'

'I told you, we are missing something – some crucial fact. I just cannot imagine what it might be. You should go and see Wilmot.'

'His clerk – if he can be trusted – claims nothing

has been heard of him since my mother called upon him yesterday morning,' said DeSalle. 'Apparently, he left the office quite abruptly, not long after she spoke to him. I will try again, but I don't hold out much hope.'

'He may be the one man who can help us. It's odd that your mother doesn't mention him in her letter.'

'Presumably because he denied everything!'

Mrs. Tanner shrugged, as the carriage rattled to a halt. 'Ah, here we are.'

DeSalle gestured towards the dingy street outside. 'I would happily have settled you back at Mivart's.'

'No, I don't want Stead or his young friend to find me. Calthorpe Street will do; I was quite comfortable here those few weeks last year.'

DeSalle nodded, but said nothing.

'You'll have your man call for me at half-past seven?' she said, gathering her skirts up, ready to go.

'Wait a moment. The man will open the door. Sarah – are you sure that you can stomach this wretched charade tonight? I am not sure that I can bear it.'

'Stead won't be expecting me. I may have escaped his trap, but I am sure he believes that he has seen me off. It will put him off his guard. Let him play out his party piece with your poor father, if that is what has been arranged, and then confront him with everything you know – about Miss Smith, about Wilmot, about Cranks – and tell him you'd rather bring in the police than see your mother so despicably imposed upon. He will crumble, I am sure of it.'

'Very well, I will attempt it. But do not blame me if I strike the fellow down.'

She smiled and put her hand gently upon his arm.

'One way or another, we shall put an end to it tonight.'

DeSalle nodded once more, seemingly reassured. Instinctively, he clasped her hand with his own. A peculiar hesitancy seemed to overwhelm them both. Neither moved until the driver appeared at the side of the carriage, and reached to open the door.

Mrs. Tanner pulled her hand away, and stepped down on to the pavement.

'Tonight, then,' she said.

'Indeed,' said DeSalle. He watched her ascend the steps to the lodging-house; and even when the door closed behind her, he gave no order to the coachman, keeping him waiting, quite lost in his own thoughts.

CHAPTER THIRTY-FIVE

Sarah Tanner stepped beneath the pendulous gas-light, supported by the ironwork arch that graced the front steps of Lord DeSalle's town-house. She was dressed after the latest fashion, in a barège evening gown which Arthur DeSalle had included in her Mivart's wardrobe. In other circumstances she might have relished the opportunity to wear such an exquisite outfit. Instead, as she was ushered into the hall, and permitted the Balmoral cloak that hung about her bare shoulders to be removed, she suddenly felt strangely vulnerable.

'Lady DeSalle is expecting you in the morning-room, ma'am,' said the maid, the cloak having been despatched to some discreet hiding-place. 'If you'd care to come with me?'

She followed the girl to a small room at the rear of the house. The maid announced her and returned to her duties, leaving her in the company of Lady DeSalle, who sat by the fireside. The fire was unlit, the room illuminated by twin gas-lamps that projected from opposing walls. She tried to fathom the Viscountess's features for some indication of her mood but was met by the same refined *froideur* which she had seen on each occasion they had met.

'Mrs. Richmond, please take a seat.'

'Thank you, Your Ladyship.'

'Do you admire gas-light?' said the Viscountess, not expecting any reply. 'I consider it rather unflattering myself; but my husband insisted we take it. I trust you had a pleasant journey? I gather you are no longer staying at Mivart's?'

'No, ma'am. The hotel is forwarding my post. My affairs in London are almost resolved, and an old friend, with whom I had not corresponded for many years, has been generous enough to accommodate me. In short, I'm afraid I only received your letter this very afternoon.'

'I see,' replied Lady DeSalle. 'Well, I am glad you did. I trust you do not object that I have taken this opportunity for us to speak *tête-à-tête*?'

'Not at all, ma'am.'

'Good. For, truly, Mrs. Richmond, your note at the Infirmary caused me a great deal of consternation and has put me to a good deal of trouble.'

'I am sorry to hear that, ma'am.'

'It placed grave imputations upon the character and actions of a man in whom I have placed implicit trust.'

'I should have spoken to you in person, ma'am, but—'

'Wait,' interjected Lady DeSalle, 'I have not finished. In other circumstances, I would warrant that such rash and groundless accusations might lead to court; they might well be considered a gross libel. Dr. Stead, however, assures me that your letter and its more fantastical elements were, in all likelihood, the product of an agitated nervous system, one that will have since settled back into its natural equilibrium. Another man might have considered a prosecution. He suggested that we let the matter rest. Now, that is a man of generous spirit, surely?'

'Indeed, one might suppose so.'

'I, however, would prefer to set matters to rights. I cannot abide inaction. Now, it seems likely to me that you have had time and opportunity to contemplate the patent absurdity of the claims you made in that unfortunate missive. Indeed, it seems quite clear to me that they were the aberrant product of disordered nerves. Am I correct in my assumption? You appear in possession of yourself at present, at least.'

'It is difficult to pass judgment on one's own state of mind, ma'am,' said Mrs. Tanner, cautiously. 'But if you are quite certain that there is no truth in what I wrote, then I can see no other satisfactory explanation.'

'Quite,' said Lady DeSalle, seemingly taking the remark as a tribute to her own character and perspicacity.

Sarah Tanner said nothing. It was, she suspected, another of those instances when the Viscountess expected no interruption.

'I must admit, my dear, I do not hold you entirely at fault,' said Lady DeSalle, her tone softening a little. 'You may be quite frank with me, Mrs. Richmond – has my son spoken to you about Dr. Stead? I do not say he is at the root of this mischief but I believe he harbours grave doubts regarding the adherents of mesmerism.'

'I would not care to betray his confidence, ma'am.'

Lady DeSalle smiled. 'You need say no more. Very well, let us call this interview at an end and put any misconceptions or ill-feeling behind us. I think we shall go up to the drawing-room: Dr. Stead is waiting for us there. There need be no great awkwardness

291

between you, I am sure. And then, my dear, I shall keep to what I wrote in my letter: you shall have every proof of the man's true character.'

Mrs. Tanner indicated her agreement and followed the Viscountess as she led the way back into the hall, and then upstairs to the drawing-room where she had been received on their first meeting in the house. Dr. Stead stood waiting, removing his hands from his waistcoat pockets and effecting a small bow.

'Your Ladyship. Mrs. Richmond, how charming to see you again.'

'Are the arrangements in order?' said Lady DeSalle, imperiously.

'Miss Smith is putting everything in place in the library, ma'am, rest assured,' said Stead, though his gaze wandered to examine Sarah Tanner's countenance.

'Nonetheless,' replied the Viscountess, 'there are a couple of small matters I should like to superintend in person, before my son arrives. Mrs. Richmond, you will forgive me? I shall not be long.'

'Of course.'

And with that, Lady DeSalle left the room, closing the door behind her.

'I do believe,' said Stead, with a rather sickly smirk, 'that Her Ladyship has delicately given us this time to remove certain misunderstandings that may have arisen between us.'

'I think I understand you well enough.'

'Is that so?' said Stead, lowering his voice. 'I cannot believe it, my dear Mrs. Richmond – shall we call you that? – or you would not have dared come here tonight.'

'Whyever not? Or is your boy lurking in the chimney?'

'Ah, yes, young Cranks. You gave him quite a scratch, you know. He did not take it kindly. He describes you as a veritable she-devil. Tell me, my dear, who was your friend with the pistol – not the police, at any rate, eh? They do not travel on such fine pieces of horse-flesh.'

'Only if you tell me the purpose of this charade.'

'Why, to persuade dear young Mr. DeSalle of the virtues of mesmeric treatment, of course! I gather he is somewhat skeptical. I believe Her Ladyship is quite eager to have her son bear witness to my genius; and it would be to my advantage if the young man thought his mother were spending her money wisely. I admit, when she told me of the idea – and that I might convert *you* at the same time – I did not imagine that he would accept the invitation.'

The mesmerist paused, listening for any sound of movement upon the landing outside.

'Listen,' he continued, urgently, 'there is little time. There is no need for us to be at loggerheads, no need at all. An orchard may contain rich pickings for all, if you catch my meaning. Surely we may come to an amicable arrangement?'

'An arrangement? One that does not involve me being "left to rot"?'

'An idle threat, my dear,' said Stead, dismissively. 'Come, you and I are cut from the same cloth; we both wish to make the best of things. Fate has given you the possession of certain items, containing certain information, which might be considered rather valuable. I, on the other hand, am best situated to exploit said information to a pecuniary advantage.'

'Is that so?'

'Let us strike a bargain, Mrs. Richmond. A fixed sum, for you to relinquish your property and not to hinder me in word or deed. A hundred guineas – what do you say? Hurry, there is the bell! That will be Mr. DeSalle!'

'I will think on it,' said Mrs. Tanner.

'Excellent!' said the mesmerist. 'I am glad to hear it. You are no fool, ma'am. I know that full well.'

———

The library – once a modest retreat for the master of the house, not more than fifteen or sixteen square feet – was lit by two wall-mounted lamps, similar to those in the morning-room downstairs, except that the gas was turned down to the lowest possible degree, leaving much of the room in shadow. Lord DeSalle himself, the same inanimate creature Mrs. Tanner had seen at the Infirmary, was carefully positioned in an armchair by the hearth, his eyes closed, his head tilted a little to one side. Beside him, on a plain mahogany dining-chair, sat Helena Smith, her eyes demurely lowered; and, between them, a corner table upon which rested a cut-glass bowl, three-quarters filled with water. Dr. Stead led the party into the room, his patroness at his side, followed by Mrs. Tanner and Arthur DeSalle.

'I do not think I can bear it,' said DeSalle in a whisper.

'Hush. Let it play out. Wait until I speak.'

Three chairs were arranged in a semi-circle. Stead took his place in front of them, with the same bravura air of control and self-importance he had manifested at the Marylebone Institute. Mrs. Tanner rather marvelled at his belief in his own abilities.

'Please, if you would care to take your seats. Lord DeSalle – you must forgive me – I have aligned them along magnetic principles; I would be grateful if you do not move your chair from the appointed spot.'

Arthur DeSalle returned the mesmerist's words with a rather contemptuous glance.

'I will do as you ask, sir, for my mother's sake; but that title belongs solely to my father at present. Please do not be so free with it.'

'Forgive me, sir,' said Stead. 'I meant no offence.'

'There is none taken.'

Mrs. Tanner cast an admonitory glance at Arthur DeSalle; his eyes, however, remained fixed on the mesmerist.

'Very well. Let me explain the procedure. First, sir, I must place Miss Smith in sympathy. That will take some minutes; but it will produce the necessary spiritual dislocation which allows her to act as a conduit between this earthly plane and a higher realm; which enables the communion that Her Ladyship desires. The magnetised water provides a medium for the magnetic fluid, allowing the current of communication to flow, if you will, like the wire of the electric telegraph, upon which our words travel so freely.'

'My mother has explained your peculiar theology,' said DeSalle, with unmistakeable sarcastic emphasis. 'I remain to be convinced.'

'Then I had best begin,' said Stead, with a glance at Miss Smith, his confidence seemingly undaunted. 'If I may, ma'am?'

Lady DeSalle gracefully gave her permission. Stead, in turn, adopted the same posture which he had adopted at Marylebone, kneeling unmoving before his subject, one hand upon her temple. Seconds passed into minutes. Mrs. Tanner felt the unease of Arthur DeSalle beside her, his posture as tense and static as that of the mesmerist, albeit for different reasons. At last, just as she was certain that DeSalle could take no more, the same effect was produced: Helena Smith's countenance was distorted by spasms, her eyes shut, her head fell to one side. Stead, satisfied by the spectacle, raised her head upright.

'There!' he exclaimed. 'Miss Smith is in sympathy, sir. Her spirit may travel where it will; but it is my influence that will guide her. We shall create a channel. It will seem strange at first, but I beg your indulgence.'

As he spoke, the mesmerist placed his subject's hand in the bowl with reverential care.

'If I may, Your Ladyship?'

'Of course.'

With the same theatrical care, Stead placed Lord DeSalle's hand in the same container.

'Now, Miss Smith, will you speak?'

'Readily, sir.'

'Do you see Lord DeSalle?'

'No. It is the fog, sir. Always there is a fog.'

'This is commonplace, sir, do not concern yourself,' said Stead, as an aside to Arthur DeSalle, before turning back to his subject. 'Where is His Lordship? Where is Lord DeSalle?'

'There is something . . . out of reach . . . a man or woman . . .'

As Helena Smith spoke, Lord DeSalle's breathing – no louder than a whisper when they had entered the room – seemed to take a different turn, a throaty rasp emanating from his lips.

'He knows you are near, my dear,' said Stead, with a would-be conspiratorial glance at his audience. 'Can you see him? Look closely now.'

'It is a man, I am sure of that much . . .'

The old man's breath became more guttural. Then, to the mesmerist's patent relief – for it clearly ruined the rhythm of his exhortations to his subject – the sound seemed to diminish and vanish altogether.

'Come, Miss Smith, draw closer,' exclaimed Stead.

Helena Smith, however, scowled. A spasm seemed to distort her face; a look of shock and disgust.

'No!' she exclaimed, her eyes still shut.

'Miss Smith! I command you—'

Sarah Tanner knew instinctively that this was not part of Dr. Stead's plan: the mesmerist's face was a picture of anxiety. Helena Smith, meanwhile, opened her eyes wide, sharply pulling her hand from the water, as if bitten by a venomous snake. Her head turned towards the recumbent body of Lord DeSalle.

'Lord,' she whispered.

'What the devil do you mean by this display?' said Arthur DeSalle, unable to contain himself any longer. 'If you truly believe that—'

But a small voice interrupted him.

'It was not my doing,' Helena Smith said, shaking her head.

'Now the girl is babbling nonsense!' exclaimed DeSalle. 'Really, Mother – this is the man in whom you place so much confidence! This is the man—'

Sarah Tanner, however, ignored Arthur DeSalle's rant; it was not the reasoned interjection they had planned. She had been watching Helena Smith's face; she had formed an idea as to what the mesmerist's subject might mean. Impulsively, she leant forward, taking Lord DeSalle's hand, grabbing tight hold of his wrist.

'It was not my doing,' repeated Helena Smith.

'I think that will be a matter for others to decide,' said Mrs. Tanner, quietly.

'Sarah?' said DeSalle.

'Unless I am very much mistaken,' she said, releasing her grip, 'I am afraid His Lordship is dead.'

CHAPTER THIRTY-SIX

Arthur DeSalle leapt from his chair, clasping his father's hand, inclining his head to the old man's lips. But there was nothing: no breath, no sound. He did not notice that the old man's skin was already cold and peculiarly moist to the touch. He merely knew that whatever spark of life had remained in his father's ruined frame had been utterly extinguished.

'Murderer!' cried out DeSalle, turning to face the mesmerist, who, for the first time, seemed at a loss for words. 'This charade of yours – this heathen mumbo-jumbo – has cost a man his life!'

'Sir!' retorted Stead, finally recovering himself a little. 'I hardly think that you can blame myself or Miss Smith. I commiserate with your tragic loss, of course. You have my deepest sympathy—'

'To the Devil with your sympathy!' exclaimed DeSalle. 'I shall see the pair of you hanged!'

Stead blustered in reply; Helena Smith remained quite silent. But the mesmerist's words were interrupted by a softer voice.

'He is dead, then?'

Lady DeSalle spoke in a flat monotone; even her husband's death did not seem to penetrate the cool façade she presented to the world.

'Mother – I am sorry . . .' said DeSalle.

'Your Ladyship,' interjected Stead, 'I fear your son is so stricken by grief, he believes me somehow culpable in this tragedy. You have my word, if His Lordship has paid the debt of nature, it cannot be laid at the door of his doctor!'

'I do not know what to think, sir,' said Lady DeSalle. 'I fear this experiment has gone dreadfully awry.'

Sarah Tanner glanced at her erstwhile lover, then back to his mother. She had held her tongue; but she decided it was time to speak.

'It was the laudanum,' she said.

DeSalle turned his head. 'What do you mean?'

'The doctor has been administering laudanum in addition to his mineral waters; that is his method of putting your father in "sympathy". He must have given him too much for his constitution.'

'The same fantastical notions all over again, ma'am!' protested Stead.

'I've seen it before. His skin is already cold, clammy; and there is a slight blue tinge to it – you can see it, even in this light, if you look closely. You must have given him too large a dose, sir.'

'Are you a doctor, now, ma'am?' asked Stead.

'Mother,' exclaimed DeSalle, 'can you not see? Surely it is plain to you now – this man is the vilest of impostors!'

Lady DeSalle clasped her hand to her forehead, closing her eyes, as if trying to blot out the world about her.

'Very well,' she said, her voice faltering a little. 'Arthur, you may call the police. Do whatever you think best.'

'No!' exclaimed Stead. 'Your Ladyship, I beg you, if only I might speak to you in private?'

'No, no more talk, sir. It is over. I wish to be alone with my husband; I should be grateful if you would oblige me. Arthur, the rest I leave in your hands.'

Arthur DeSalle said nothing in reply. For, even in the dim gas-light, he could see a solitary tear fall down his mother's cheek, and then another, until she hid her face in her hands.

<hr />

It was little more than an hour after Lord DeSalle's death when the door-bell rang. The detective inspector was a man of average height, with a tweed suit and well-cared-for whiskers, accompanied by two constables whom, for want of anything better to do in the first instance, he stationed at the door. He surveyed the well-appointed hall with an appraising look, then allowed himself to be led into the adjoining dining-room, to be greeted by Arthur DeSalle. The conversation that followed took some ten or fifteen minutes. It led, in turn, to a steady progress through the house, which began with an examination of the deceased, followed by a kindly but protracted interview with the deceased's wife – who had retired to her room – and an interrogation of Dr. John Stead and his female companion, who had both been sequestered in the drawing-room and watched by two servants, upon Arthur DeSalle's most particular instructions.

It was during the latter discussion that DeSalle slipped downstairs, and quietly entered the morning-room where Sarah Tanner sat by the fire, in the same spot Lady DeSalle had sat upon her own arrival in the house.

'It is the police, I suppose?' she said. 'I presume they wish to speak to me.'

'I am sorry, Sarah. What else could I do? Perhaps you should have left.'

'And how would you explain that, on top of everything else? Do not worry, you are not to blame for it. What have you told them?'

'They know nothing of Sarah Tanner; only Mrs. Richmond. I have told them about what you heard at the Infirmary, the note you wrote to my mother. I mentioned Stead's connection with Wilmot; said I had discovered it for myself – which is practically true. I am sure they can find out Stead's background for themselves; it should not take much doing. I have given them every hint.'

'Arthur, that will not do. You're upset; you're not thinking things through. There is little point trying to protect me. Stead knows who I am, even if he does not know of our connection. It will all have to come out, there is no way round it.'

'Sarah, please, I did my best. Will you . . .'

'What?' she said.

'Will you just let me hold you?'

She silently rose to her feet. The sight of her erstwhile lover's eyes, red with tears, stung her deeply. She beckoned him forward. He came close, hugging her body as if he might fall, his head resting upon her shoulder.

She had no idea how long she held him. At last, the embrace was interrupted by a knock at the door. Immediately, DeSalle pulled back, straightening his jacket, quickly wiping his eyes with his cuff. Mrs. Tanner was instantly reminded how peculiarly boyish his features were; she fought an urge to hold his arm, to comfort him.

'That will be the inspector.'

'Then you had best tell him to come in.'

The door opened. The detective inspector came directly into the room but drew up short, as he caught sight of Sarah Tanner, a look of recognition passing between them.

'My, my!' he exclaimed. 'I did not expect to see you again, my dear. I can see this is going to be a long night's work.'

'Inspector Murdoch,' said Mrs. Tanner, drily.

———

'You see, sir,' said the inspector, having taken a stroll around the room and sat down, albeit without being asked, 'Dr. Stead tells a very interesting story. He claims that he has always administered small amounts of opiate to his patient, for medicinal purposes.'

'And my mother knew of this?'

'Well, she denies it; that is true. Now, the good doctor also dropped many heavy hints, shocking heavy they were, that I might do well to investigate the background of another of your guests – one Mrs. Richmond. Almost went so far as to lay the business at her door, so to speak. You can imagine my surprise, therefore, when I discover that myself and the lady in question are already acquainted.'

'I am sure you are mistaken, sir,' said DeSalle. 'Mrs. Richmond is a relative of a friend of mine.'

'Richmond, sir,' said the inspector, 'or Richards? It was Richards, ma'am, was it not, when we last met. Why, it must be a year ago. But I never forget a face.'

Sarah Tanner shrugged.

'A peculiar thing that,' continued the policeman. 'Mr. Ferntower – you recall the gentleman, ma'am? – made a point of contacting me the week after our little encounter, to say he did not want to bring any charge. Curious.'

'Then I have nothing to answer for,' said Mrs. Tanner. 'And my name is my own affair.'

'Nothing, ma'am? Why, forgive me, but on the occasion of our parting, I believe you struck a police officer in the course of his duty – this police officer, to be precise. I walked with a limp for a week.'

'My foot slipped.'

Inspector Murdoch, despite himself, smiled, dispelling the rather dour impression given by his severe whiskers; it was a smile that broadened, until he burst into a laugh.

'Good Lord! I should like to bring you before a judge, just to hear you tell the story. "My foot slipped." Priceless! Now, come, my dear, less of your chaff; don't forget I have seen your moves, as they say. You are no more a relative of this respectable member of the aristocracy than I'm Prince Albert, God bless him. Now first of all, does this young man know that for himself, or is he more of a gull than I take him for?'

'Inspector!' protested DeSalle. 'You forget yourself.'

'Oh, begging your pardon, sir, I speak in my professional capacity; please don't take offence. Now, will you tell me the truth? Or must we all visit the Yard?'

'Sarah, you are not obliged to say anything,' said DeSalle.

'Oh, "Sarah" is it?' said Murdoch, suggestively.

Mrs. Tanner sighed. 'Very well, Inspector, I will tell you the full story.'

'That's fine, my dear. I like a good story,' said the inspector, gesturing to the seat opposite. 'Take your time, we have all night.'

Mrs. Tanner looked briefly at DeSalle then sat down. Gathering her thoughts, she gave her account, commencing with the horse-meat riot in Leather Lane and finishing with the living séance that resulted in Lord DeSalle's death. The only thing she omitted was the death of Joe Drummond; and if Arthur DeSalle noticed the omission, he kept silent. Inspector Murdoch, for his part, listened attentively to the tale, only interrupting to question a couple of points. When she was done, he leant forward in a thoughtful fashion, and spoke as if still evaluating the facts.

'So you'd have me believe that you and this young gentleman are "old acquaintances"?'

'If you must know, Inspector,' said DeSalle, tetchily, stung by the policeman's words, 'we were lovers.'

Mrs. Tanner smiled to herself; it was an admission she had never thought she would hear from Arthur DeSalle's lips. Even under the circumstances, she somehow took a certain pride in hearing him say it.

'Really?' said the inspector. 'And you, my dear, following this queer set of events on Leather Lane, took it upon yourself to play detective, and act on your former "acquaintance's" behalf.'

'Is that a crime?'

'That depends,' said the policeman, 'but I should certainly consider it a grave error of judgment. Still, what's done is done, I suppose. I suggest you leave such work to the Detective Branch in future.'

'The question is, Inspector,' demanded DeSalle, 'what will you do now?'

'It's an odd tale, sir. I cannot take your word for it – everything must be checked. I suppose the crux of it is your Mr. Wilmot – if he will confess to this fraud with your father's correspondence, that might be something. You claim the Grubb boy was murdered – well, that is an inquiry in itself. I suppose we had better find this boy Cranks. And as for His Lordship, first things first, a doctor must see the body.'

'But do you think he was poisoned?' persisted DeSalle.

'By laudanum? Likely as not; your "acquaintance" here was right about the signs – and I won't inquire how she knows of them. Still, if it was, then likely it was a mistake upon Stead's part, or that girl of his. Murder? I'm not so sure, sir, even if the fellow is the fraud you say he is. What's his motive? Who'd kill a man in front of half-a-dozen witnesses, after all, eh? We'll have them spend the night at the Yard, don't you fret. In the meantime, I will need to talk to all the servants. Lord! I said it'd be a long night, didn't I? I don't suppose, sir, you have any brandy? Fortifies the nerves.'

'What about me?' said Mrs. Tanner.

'You, ma'am? Why, you didn't do for His Lordship – begging your pardon, sir – did you now? Stands to reason. We'll talk again tomorrow, by-and-by, I should think, assuming this address of yours ain't a piece of nonsense.'

'I am staying at Calthorpe Street, you have my word.'

'And mine,' added DeSalle.

'The word of a peer of the realm, eh? Well, I suppose that will have to do. We'll need you at the inquest, of course. The coroner will be most particular. Now, did you say you had a brandy, sir? Helps me think.'

———

The morning after Lord DeSalle's death, a hansom pulled to a halt on Calthorpe Street, just as dawn was breaking. Arthur DeSalle jumped down from the carriage on to the pavement and paid the driver. He rang the second of three bells, and, not waiting for a reply, opened the front door and hurried inside and up the stairs. Sarah Tanner met him on the first-floor landing, still in her barège dress of the previous night. Without a word, she ushered him into her rooms.

'The inquest will be tomorrow,' said DeSalle.

'Murdoch has finished at Berkeley Square, then?' she said.

'For now. When I left, they had come to remove . . .'

Arthur DeSalle's mouth dried up.

'They must examine him, Arthur. It will settle the matter.'

'I could not stand to watch them take him away, like a piece of meat. And my mother cannot be consoled; there are no words. She blames herself, I can tell. God forgive me, for I know she loved him, I blame her myself. If she had not invited that creature – that worm – into her home!'

He spoke quickly, as if he could not control his thoughts.

'Hush,' said Mrs. Tanner, taking his hand.

'I came here – I wondered – I could not think of where else to go . . .'

She put her hands gently to his face, pulling him towards her.

'Hush,' she said, kissing him lightly on the lips, just as she had done in the field.

Was it an impulse or what she had intended all along? She was not certain herself.

'Sarah, I cannot bear this. You are the only one I could come to, and yet . . .'

'Hush,' she said again, kissing him a second time. 'You are here now. Come to bed.'

CHAPTER THIRTY-SEVEN

They lay naked upon the bed, side by side, covered only by a coarse sheet of creased linen. They had made love; she could not quite believe it herself. She had sworn that she would not let it happen; she had broken every silent promise she had made to herself. She knew now that those oaths had been ridiculous, a poor means of concealing her true sentiments. They had made love and a part of her told her that she had been utterly foolish. But any regret, any confusion, was smothered, extinguished by the warmth that still suffused her limbs; and the thousand passionate, fond memories rekindled by Arthur DeSalle's touch.

She had little sense of time passing. At last, she propped her head with her arm, and with her right hand, idly traced the contours of his body beneath the rough material. DeSalle turned to face her, his face quite earnest.

'You've been thinking,' she said.

'A good deal.'

'About what?'

'You are still in love with me, Sarah,' he said. 'You cannot deny it.'

'You always were a conceited creature,' she said.

'Please, do not make a joke of it.'

'Very well, perhaps I am.'

'I need you, Sarah. Without you, my life is a sham, worthless. You are the only happiness I have known. Why must we be parted?'

'Must we talk of this now?'

'Listen to me,' said DeSalle insistently. 'Forget the wretched coffee-house; that is no life for a woman like you. You could have satin sheets instead of cheap cloth; the latest fashions; you could keep rooms in any part of London you chose—'

'I know what money can buy, Arthur. That is not the difficulty. You know it.'

'What, then?' said DeSalle, sitting up.

'Countless things. For a start, the small matter of an inquest – a trial! Do you imagine that my name can be kept secret; that our connexion will not be made known to the world?'

DeSalle frowned. 'I talked to Murdoch after you left; I may be able to procure his discretion. He may even be persuaded to say that he recommended you as my agent.'

'You mean you intend to bribe him? To paint me as your spy, some adjunct of Scotland Yard?'

'Is that so unreasonable? I did not think you would be so scrupulous. There will be a scandal; I know that well enough. I am resigned to that; my mother's actions have all but guaranteed it. I just do not wish to make it worse. And all this will pass. It need not contaminate our chance of happiness.'

She did not reply but merely rose and picked up her chemise from the drugget beside the bed.

'I had best get dressed. I cannot say what hour Murdoch intends to call upon me. It might be better if you were not here, don't you think? And you might consider shaving.'

DeSalle, unconsciously, put his hand to his chin. He followed her example, beginning to collect his clothes that lay scattered upon the floor, dressing as he talked.

'I know why you have grown cold,' he said at last. 'You are thinking of Arabella.'

She sighed. 'I suppose your wife is no obstacle either?'

'Not to my affection – my love – for you.'

She frowned. 'What if I told you I want to keep the coffee-house; to stay in Leather Lane?'

'Then I would visit you there, whenever I could, dressed in rags. I'd learn coster slang and carry a bag of weights, and a sack of potatoes! Upon my honour, I would do anything to keep you.'

'And your wife? What would she say?'

'Please! How often must I say it – there is nothing between us. It is a marriage of convenience, nothing more; a link forged between two families. You know how such things are arranged. Why, for pity's sake, she has spent the last three weeks in the company of her mother!'

She looked away. Part of her rebelled at the thought; another part wanted to run to him.

'Give me time to think.'

'I see. Well, you are right, I suppose: I had better go. Lord! I am not sure I can face my mother.'

'I think you should talk to her.'

'Doubtless you are right about that, too. Sarah . . .'

'What?'

'Thank you. If you had not been here, I do not know what I should have done.'

She smiled.

'Come back tonight, we can talk then.'

The door-bell rang as the afternoon turned into evening, a little short of six o'clock. Sarah Tanner had remained at Calthorpe Street all day and was glad that Inspector Murdoch had finally deigned to make his appearance. She descended the stairs and opened the door. There was, however, only a youthful liveried messenger, bearing a note in a fine hand, that looked familiar.

'Mrs. Richmond?'

'Yes?'

'Telegram from Lady DeSalle,' said the messenger. 'Mivart's sent me here.'

'I see. Does it want a reply?'

'I'm told it does, ma'am.'

'Let me read it.'

She took the envelope and opened the contents.

Mrs. Richmond,

Will you call upon me this evening? Eight would be a suitable hour.

Yours, Viscountess DeSalle.

'You may tell her "yes",' said Mrs. Tanner, perplexed.

'Thank you, ma'am.'

She folded the telegram and returned indoors, unable to fathom the Viscountess's motive. She was far too curious to ignore the invitation, and yet the note had left her with a peculiar irrational sense of foreboding.

She tried to think of other things, but it was two hours before she needed to quit Calthorpe Street and they passed terribly slowly. In particular, whenever she heard footsteps upon the pavement below, she half expected the bell to ring, whether for Inspector Murdoch or, as the day grew longer, Arthur DeSalle.

But neither man appeared and she was left back with her own thoughts.

For a long time, she pondered Arthur DeSalle's words that morning. Even if he was quite sincere in his love for her, she felt far from certain that she could allow herself to become his mistress for a second time, no matter what the terms. For he had a wife; that much had changed, whatever his protests. She might have a prior claim upon his affections but she could make no demands upon his time; none, at least, that could not be overturned in an instant, upon the whim of a woman she instinctively despised.

But she loved him. She could deny it no longer.

Was that enough?

It seemed an impossible puzzle; there was no answer, no right or wrong conclusion, that relieved her of a nagging anxiety that she would suffer for it, whatever her decision.

She consciously tried to put the question to one side and turned her thoughts to the events of the previous night. For there was something there that troubled her. Inspector Murdoch had said it could not be murder.

Who'd kill a man in front of half-a-dozen witnesses?

An answer had occurred to her; not one that she much liked.

—

'Mrs. Richmond, ma'am.'

The maid announced Sarah Tanner's presence with the same diction and gravity as if she were the master of ceremonies, calling out arrivals in a grand ballroom. But the only person present was Lady DeSalle herself, dressed in deepest mourning, her face pale and drawn, in stark ghostly contrast to the rich black silk

311

of her gown. She dismissed the maid with the slightest wave of her hand.

'I will not ask you to sit down,' said Lady DeSalle, without any preliminary social nicety, 'as I do not believe this will be a pleasant interview.'

'Indeed?' said Mrs. Tanner.

'I expect you are curious as to why I should have asked you here, to a house in mourning.'

'In all honesty, I have no idea, ma'am.'

'No, I expect not. Do you know, this very morning I endured the sight of my husband's body being removed by two porters, to be anatomised by some butcher, "to establish the cause of death"?'

Her voice was calm, focused, albeit bitter. Mrs. Tanner said nothing.

'You warned me, of course; that hastily scribbled letter. Not that I wish to address you on that subject.'

'Then why am I here, Your Ladyship?'

'I have called you here, "Mrs. Richmond", to demand the truth.'

'The truth?'

'Are you a parrot, ma'am, that you must repeat what I say? I demand to know what you are to my son.'

'Your son?' she said, surprised. 'I am sure I am nothing to him.'

'You are a liar, ma'am. I saw him look at you last night; I saw the looks you gave him back. I heard him call you "Sarah"! I know my son, Mrs. Richmond, even if you think me a fool.'

'I have never thought that,' said Mrs. Tanner, warily.

'Will you answer my question?'

'I have no answer.'

'That is not good enough,' said the Viscountess, firmly. 'I have brought disgrace upon this house; I have let sentiment blind me to the actions of a gross impostor. I see that now. But I am free from Dr. Stead's mesmeric spell and I will not be trifled with – not if my son's future is at stake.'

'What would you have me tell you?'

'You might tell me your name and why my son felt obliged to bring you into this house.'

'My name?'

'I spoke today to the Countess Stanhope, the Earl's grandmother. She is elderly; given to forgetfulness. But she knows her family well enough; you are no more the Earl's cousin than I. Why did my son set in motion such an imposture; or does he truly believe you are Stanhope's cousin?'

'I am sorry to have deceived you, if that is any comfort.'

'Are you his mistress?' demanded the Viscountess.

'No, not that.'

'I do not believe you.'

'I shall be frank, if you like. He thought I might persuade you to abandon your devotion to mesmerism; that I could unmask Stead as a fraud. He has always doubted the man, you must know that. I did my best to help him, as a friend.'

'A friend? What sort of friendship can a peer of the realm claim with what . . . an actress? a whore? What does it say of a man that he should bring such a woman into this house?'

'A whore? Is that what you think of me, ma'am?'

'What else am I to think?' said the Viscountess, icily.

'And what would Arthur say if he knew you killed his father; could he understand that?'

Lady DeSalle gasped.

'Do not worry, ma'am,' continued Mrs. Tanner. 'I

313

do not think that Murdoch has thought of it, not yet, at least.

'No, you are talking nonsense—'

'Your face says otherwise, Your Ladyship. I wondered what perverse hold Stead must have over you, so that you discounted everything I wrote down at the Infirmary so readily. I even wondered if I had been wrong, if he actually wielded some mesmeric influence that kept you in his power. But it was quite the opposite, wasn't it? You went to Wilmot and he confessed; he admitted his connection to the man; he admitted his clerk had been rifling through every piece of precious correspondence entrusted to him, passing the choicest information to his true master. You are an intelligent woman; you saw how he had played upon your emotions, the memory of the man you loved. I expect you wanted revenge. I know I should.'

Lady DeSalle fell silent, but when she spoke, her tone had changed.

'I am beginning to see, Mrs. Richmond, why my son has come to rely upon you.'

'You gave your husband the laudanum, after Miss Smith had administered the usual dose. You saw how easy it would be to place the blame on their shoulders.'

Lady DeSalle shook her head. 'My husband had suffered enough. It was for his sake, as much as anything.'

'Except you thought you might see Stead hanged in the process; or, at the least, a good many years in gaol.'

'Will you tell the police?'

'No.'

'Why not?'

'In the first place,' said Mrs. Tanner, 'the man has done things, has set events in motion, which merit the

314

worst punishment. Second, I would not wish to see your son hurt any more than he has been already.'

'You give me your word?' said Lady DeSalle.

'Yes, if you can trust it.'

The Viscountess looked visibly relieved. Indeed, for the first time in Sarah Tanner's memory, her upright posture seemed to slump a little, and a brief smile played about her lips.

'I think I may have misjudged you.'

'I should like to think so.'

'Do you love him?' said the Viscountess.

'Does it matter?'

'Perhaps you do not understand me. He is now Viscount DeSalle. He has inherited land; a title; a proud history. This catastrophe – there is no other word – will tarnish all that, but it cannot be allowed to destroy it. *His* reputation, at least, must remain intact. It is not so terrible, after all, to be the son of a witless old woman, misled by a charlatan; Society will forgive such things, in time. But there cannot be another scandal; it would ruin the family; it would ruin him. If you love him, you will do nothing to damage him. You will let him be.'

'I can only promise that I will never, knowingly, do him harm.'

The Viscountess sighed in frustration.

'That is not enough.'

'It will have to do,' said Mrs. Tanner, somewhat curtly.

'I see I can say nothing more to prevail upon you. So be it. May I ask one favour?'

'If I can grant it, I will.'

'If you ever speak to him of this, tell him that I have always done what I have thought best for the family; tell him that I am sorry.'

'You may tell him that yourself.'

'No,' she said, ringing the bell for the maid, 'I think not. Now I am suddenly rather tired; I think you had better go.'

———

As Sarah Tanner quit the house, and walked beneath the gas-light that hung above the steps, dimmed to a mere glimmer as a token of mourning, she saw a figure emerge from the opposite side of the road, hurrying forth to intercept her before she got into the cab that sat waiting. She recognised it as that of Inspector Murdoch, who greeted her with a rather curious expression upon his face.

'I am surprised to see you here, ma'am,' said the inspector.

'I was equally surprised to be invited.'

'I don't suppose you'd care to tell me what you might have been discussing with Widow DeSalle?'

'A private matter.'

'Is that so?' said Murdoch. 'Curious hour for social calls. You know, Mrs. Tanner – may I call you that? – I'm beginning to wonder about this affair.'

'In what way?'

'Well, let's just say that your gentleman friend told a good tale last night; and you matched it word for word. To tell the truth, I shouldn't be half surprised if your pal Stead is exactly what you say he is. In fact, I've spent much of the day finding that out. He's not on the square, as they say, that much is plain to me. But there's a few things that don't add up. And, well, you know the police, ma'am, we like our arithmetic done proper.'

'But you speak in riddles.'

Murdoch smiled. 'Well, for instance, we carried out

the post-mortem examination this morning. Her Ladyship insisted she come to the Yard to hear the result. She's a tough old bird; not many would do that, eh?'

'No, I suppose not.'

'I told her it was the laudanum; spared her the worst. She took it well enough. Said she wanted to see Stead face to face, before we packed him off to Newgate; to ask him before God why he had deceived her. Now, I wouldn't stand for it; but it turns out that a viscountess trumps a detective inspector down at the Yard – at least with my chief.'

'I'm sorry to hear it.'

'Not as sorry as I was when I found out she got the constable to put him in cuffs and leave them alone. She has that way about her, eh? Whatever she says, goes. That got me thinking – what did she have to say to him, that couldn't be heard by no-one else?'

'It's a mystery to me.'

'And do you know what she did, as soon as she got back?'

'I have no idea.'

'I think she sent for you, ma'am. Now, why is that?'

Sarah Tanner tried to form an answer. And, in that very moment, a loud percussive crack echoed through the night air.

It came from inside the house.

The crack of a pistol.

CHAPTER THIRTY-EIGHT

Murdoch dashed up the steps to the front door and pulled the bell repeatedly. Even though the door was made of solid oak, chaotic sounds could be heard from within, not least a woman's piercing scream. Mrs. Tanner stood behind him, helplessly, peering at the upper floors of the house.

'Police!' shouted Murdoch. 'Damn you, open this door!'

At last the door was opened, by the same maid who had ushered Sarah Tanner inside. Her face was streaked with tears, her manner frantic.

'What the devil has happened?' exclaimed the detective.

The girl struggled to speak through her tears, gesturing upstairs. 'It's Her Ladyship . . . I can't . . .'

Her voice faltered, but Murdoch did not linger in the hall, hurrying up the stairs to the first floor. Halfway, he turned back to address his involuntary companion.

'You'd best stay there.'

'Of course, Inspector,' replied Mrs. Tanner.

She followed him as soon as his back was turned.

The drawing-room was much as she had left it. One of the family's man-servants stood upon the threshold,

318

speechless, his face white with shock. The inspector brushed past the man and entered the room. The once imperious figure of Lady DeSalle was seated, slumped awkwardly in a high-backed armchair, in a loose posture that she could never have willingly adopted in life. The cause of death was plain enough. Her dress was burnt where the bullet had pierced her breast; the black silk suddenly tarry and viscous, heavy with clotting blood. The pistol lay upon the floor, the smell of smoke still hanging in the air.

Murdoch leant across to close the Viscountess's sightless eyes, then bent down to examine the gun. As he did so, Mrs. Tanner noticed a single sheet of paper that lay folded upon the nearby mantel. She stepped forward, attracting the detective's attention.

'Now, you leave that be!' exclaimed the inspector.

'Damned if I will,' she replied, hurriedly snatching the paper from its resting place, glancing at the name written on the exterior, then reading the contents. She was surprised to find it addressed to the very man who hurried to snatch it from her fingers.

Dear Inspector Murdoch,

It was I who killed my poor husband. I could not bear to see him suffer any longer. I administered the laudanum to DeSalle in secret, without assistance. You will find, if you wish to inquire, that I had procured it from Partridge, the druggist in South Molton Street, on the pretence of wanting something to help me sleep. Dr. Stead and Miss Smith are, therefore, innocent of any crime. You must forgive me for misleading you, just as I must ask forgiveness of the Almighty.

Viscountess DeSalle

Murdoch grabbed the note and read it through himself.

'Blow me,' he said. 'Well, I never! Now, ma'am, perhaps you'd care to tell me what this poor woman had to say to you. Because, from where I'm standing, assuming this *is* her hand, this whole case has just been turned on its head.'

'If you must know,' said Mrs. Tanner, her mind racing, 'she warned me off her son.'

'Humph!' exclaimed the inspector, gesturing with the letter in his hand. 'That's all well and good, but what about this? Did she say anything? The truth now!'

'She confessed it to me, not fifteen minutes ago. I put it to her that she killed her husband and she admitted it.'

'You put it to her?' said Murdoch, incredulously.

'Surely it had occurred to you, Inspector?' said Mrs. Tanner, rather relishing the detective's surprise. 'Stead had been giving Lord DeSalle laudanum for weeks; he would not mistake the dose. And why should he kill him? His Lordship was the golden goose. The Viscountess was paying his bills; funding his schemes. The only persons who might want Lord DeSalle dead were his wife, to put him out of his misery, or . . .'

'Or your young man,' said Murdoch.

'She admitted it,' replied Mrs. Tanner emphatically. 'It was not Arthur. But I don't understand the note; it makes no sense.'

'In what way?' said Murdoch, skeptically.

'She had talked to Wilmot, you see; she saw him yesterday and he confessed to everything. She told me as much: she knew how Stead had been imposing upon her. So she killed Lord DeSalle; but she planned

320

for the blame to fall on Stead's head. That was why she did it at the séance; she wanted witnesses.'

'I think you're wrong, my dear,' said Murdoch. 'Because this little note here says the fellow's innocent.'

'Not true – he may not have killed the old man, but he's not innocent, not by a long chalk. I've told you what he's done—'

'You've told me a good many things. But why should I take your word about Dr. Stead, when this poor woman – the very creature whom you say he's been defrauding – declares him a saint, eh?'

'Even the dead can tell lies.'

'Now why should she do a thing like that?'

Mrs. Tanner looked at the detective, as if weighing her words carefully.

'I'll answer you, if you'll answer me. What do you make of Stead? What have you learnt about him? Be honest with me; it may be worth your while.'

The detective sighed, but nonetheless responded. 'From what I can make out, he hadn't been heard of in London until twelvemonth ago. The fellow rents rooms in Wimpole Street and an old house in Highgate; doesn't pay his bills too promptly but that's no great crime. If he's a doctor of anything in particular, I can't find a medical man to answer for it; mind you, that's not to say he ain't. Nailed his colours to a surgeon by the name of Felton – I haven't had a chance to talk to that gentleman as yet – but I gather he's quite respectable, if a little eccentric. Great believer in the mesmerics. Lectured on it for years. Even claims to have amputated a fellow's leg under it.'

'I told you as much,' said Mrs. Tanner, thinking back to the old library at the Infirmary.

'Well, that's as maybe. He seems to have made Stead

his apprentice in the mesmerics and Miss Smith his exhibition-piece.'

'You mean Miss Cranks.'

'I only have your word on that, at present, my dear. The name Cranks doesn't put a smile on the face of the Lambeth constabulary, that's true enough. But we ain't found this boy of yours. Listen, that's all by-the-by: if you want to hear what's in my gut – well, I expect the fellow's a fraud, like every other quack in Mayfair. But it's plain he didn't kill His Lordship; and I've only your word on his having done much of anything else. Now, you tell me, why should I believe you?'

'Because you asked me before why Her Ladyship might have wanted a private word with Stead. Well, Inspector, I believe I have a shrewd idea.'

'Go on then,' said the inspector.

'I'd like to speak to Arthur first.'

'His Lordship?' said Murdoch, pointedly. 'I don't think you'll get the chance.'

'Why, do you intend to arrest me?'

'I could find a reason, I'll warrant. But what I meant was, I think the new Viscount might not have much time for you at present. Last thing I heard, he was meeting a certain party off the South Western Railway.'

'Who?'

'His wife, up for the funeral. Well, they can make it a double now, eh? I suppose I had better speak to him smartish, mind you. Now, why don't you tell me this "shrewd idea" of yours. I'm all ears.'

———

It was an hour later that Sarah Tanner left Berkeley Square and returned to Calthorpe Street. She stayed in her rooms and waited in vain for Arthur DeSalle to appear, as he had promised. In all honesty, she did not truly expect him. Indeed, Inspector Murdoch's revelation, and the tragic events in Berkeley Square, had put paid to her hopes. She could hardly imagine the turmoil that the news of his mother's death would create in his mind. Yet she still felt stung by his absence, however justified it might be, and she spent the remainder of the night in a fitful sleep, perpetually hearing footsteps by the door.

Nonetheless, the following morning, she rose early and quit her rooms not long after dawn broke. If anyone had observed her fretting the previous night, they would have noted a change in her manner, as she walked with great determination in the direction of Leather Lane.

Her appearance in the market was noted by certain females who made it their business to remark upon the doings of *that woman*, and they were surprised to note that her destination was not the New Dining and Coffee Rooms, but rather the premises of Geo. Sanders, Pork Butcher. It was noted, too, that she entered into a private conference with Mr. Sanders for some quarter of an hour. Indeed, there was, amongst the coster-women, a degree of speculation as to what such intimate colloquy might signify. Some ventured the nonsensical slander that *there was something in that horse-meat after all*; others that *Sanders' missus ought to keep an eye on him*, with the inference that, otherwise, the portly butcher might all too easily succumb to the coffee-house keeper's siren charms.

If Mrs. Tanner had any intimation of the romantic interpretation attached to her meeting with George Sanders, however, she gave no sign of it. Instead, she next turned her steps eastwards, down Holborn Hill, crossing the old Fleet valley and up the curve of Snow Hill to St. Sepulchre's Church, facing the monolithic walls of Newgate gaol. The sky above was a miserable one, clouded and black, pregnant with rain and soot. She recalled it had been much the same on the single occasion she had stood upon the same spot to watch a Newgate hanging, although then the crossroads had been packed with serried ranks of curious humanity. She shuddered slightly at the memory.

She turned her attention to the great iron-studded door that marked the prison lodge.

It was still an hour until nine o'clock, but she did not wish to miss her chance.

She decided to wait.

<hr>

John Stead appeared at the prison gate precisely as the chimes of St. Sepulchre's began to toll. He seemed to bid his gaoler a cheerful farewell, and strode on to the pavement of the Old Bailey with the confident air of a gentleman exiting his club in Pall Mall. It was only as he saw Sarah Tanner approaching that his countenance darkened a little, before resuming his normal facetious good humour.

'Why, dear Mrs. Richmond – you have come to wish me well, I expect!' said the mesmerist, with a bow.

'After a fashion. You must count yourself lucky.'

'The Viscountess confessed to her little misdemeanour; I suppose I might consider that to be a spot of good fortune for Miss Smith and myself. I certainly bear no ill-will, though I would not recommend Newgate to anyone seeking comfortable accommodation in the capital. Now, my dear, why are you here? Forgive me – I must be blunt – we did not part on the best of terms. Indeed, one might animadvert to the fact that you were rather keen to brand me a poisoner.'

'As you were to shift the blame for His Lordship's death to me.'

'Ha! I merely made certain suggestions to that fellow Murdoch. He cannot have acted upon them, or you would not stand here today. Still, I did not think him particularly sharp. Well, here's to British justice, my dear – a fine institution! Now, I say again, do tell me, what do you want of me?'

Mrs. Tanner timed her reply carefully.

'I still have the letters,' she said, at last, 'or, at least, I know where to obtain them. Are they still worth your one hundred guineas?'

It was Stead's turn to fall silent, as if deliberating the offer.

'If anything, my dear, they may have increased in value.'

'Then one hundred and fifty,' said Mrs. Tanner, swiftly.

'You are quick as a trap, ma'am!' said Stead, amused. 'But the risk has increased proportionately. One hundred, I can offer no more.'

She let him wait. She could see the greedy glint in his eye; the prospect of future wealth.

'Well,' she said, 'I suppose the deal was already struck. You have me. Meet me by Sanders' shop, in the alley, at midnight tonight. The place will be empty; I hear he has arranged a holiday for the sake of his wife's health.'

'Wait! The butcher's? Never! I do not believe it.'

'The letters are there, you have my word. Your boy is not so clever as he imagines; they are in the place where I concealed them. He could ransack the shop a dozen times and not find them.'

'My! Young Cranks will be very disheartened to hear it.'

'I don't care to hear about his moods. And I warn you – come alone. I have no wish to make his acquaintance again.'

The mesmerist hesitated.

'Can I trust you, Mrs. Tanner?'

'Can you not read my thoughts?'

'There has never been true sympathy between us, my dear. You know that.'

'A hundred guineas would buy my sympathy,' she said, flatly. 'How do I know you have the money?'

'Please. Lady DeSalle was a very worthy patron.'

'Midnight, then?'

Stead nodded.

'A bargain! You are a fine piece of work, ma'am. Young Cranks was right! Midnight it is!'

Chapter Thirty-Nine

That very night, Sarah Tanner returned to the New Dining and Coffee Rooms. At a little before midnight, she slipped out of the front door and walked down Leather Lane. The market stalls had already been abandoned but for a solitary individual, his barrow loaded with fried slices of plaice and pots of whelks. She did not recognise the man, but he seemed determined to garner nocturnal customers, perhaps thinking of those who would shortly wend their way home from the Bottle of Hay.

'Plaice dabs? Two for a penny?' said the street-seller, ever optimistic. She shook her head and carried on.

She came at last to the butcher's shop, just as distant bells began to toll the hour. At first she could not tell if the mesmerist had kept his appointment. But there was someone loitering by the solitary gas-light on the corner of Dorrington Street, although he stayed firmly in the shadows. It was only when she drew close that she discerned the features of the mesmerist, partially concealed by the collar of a shabby fustian overcoat.

'Good evening, ma'am,' said Stead. 'I risk a good deal coming here. I hope you will not disappoint me.'

'Not if you have the money.'

'Of course. On receipt.'

She walked quietly past him and beckoned him further along the alley, to the wooden gate that opened on to the butcher's back yard.

'It is locked,' said Stead.

'You tried it?'

'I thought it would do no harm,' said Stead.

'No matter,' said Mrs. Tanner, 'it's merely a latch, a poor one at that.'

Glancing left and right along the alley, she dug the toe of her boot under the bottom of the gate, pushing it up on its hinges. At the same time, she took a slender, crooked piece of metal from her pocket, and wedged it between the gate and its wooden jamb. There was a rattle as the latch sprung free of its fastening.

'Well,' she said, in an urgent whisper, 'are you with me? Or do you think it best to stand about in the street?'

Nervously, Stead followed her through the gate. 'You must forgive me, my dear, I have little experience in such matters.'

'Is that so?'

'Quite. I see, once again, that my young friend Cranks did not under-estimate your abilities.'

'I'm flattered,' she replied, closing the gate behind them, looking around, then walking briskly to the ramp that led to the butcher's basement. 'The letters are in the cellar, but he keeps the place padlocked. It will take me a minute or two to spring it; you must tell me if you hear any sign of danger.'

The mesmerist nodded, peering after her as she descended the ramp and set to work on the lock.

'You do not need a light?' he whispered.

'It would only give us away. He keeps a lamp inside in addition to the gas; that will suffice, once I am in.'

'I must say, I am surprised, my dear, to find a woman of your talents in such humble surroundings. They could be put to much better use.'

'I enjoy the retired life.'

Stead chortled to himself. 'I doubt that very much.'

'There! Now, wait for me.'

She removed the padlock and slipped inside, leaving the mesmerist crouched anxiously in the yard above. She returned a few seconds later, the dimmest hint of lamp-light visible through the gap between the doors.

'I shall need your help.'

'I am no burglar, ma'am. Nor do I intend to learn the trade.'

'The letters are secreted under a stone flag, part of the floor,' she said in an urgent whisper. 'Sanders has placed his mincing machine on top of it. I cannot do it by myself. It needs the strength of two to move it.'

'How did they come there in the first place?'

'I told the butcher to put them there for safe-keeping. He showed them to me. After your boy began turning his house upside down, he had some idea they might be of value. Listen! I have no time for this. We may call it quits if you prefer. I cannot stand here all night.'

The prospect of a lost opportunity seemed to spur the mesmerist into action. Gingerly, he began to descend the ramp.

'If I break my neck, my dear, you shall answer for it.'

'I am sure,' said Mrs. Tanner.

The cellar was much the same as on the night of the horse-meat riot. The cast-iron, crank-driven grinder dominated the centre of the room; on the right was a doorway, with steps leading upward to the shop and rooms above; on the left were half-a-dozen sides of beef, strung up on great hooks. A single lamp hung from the ceiling, its light turned low.

'I can barely see a thing,' complained Stead.

'Look,' said Mrs. Tanner, pointing to the small window, high up on the farthest wall, designed to allow a narrow shaft of daylight from Leather Lane into the basement room. 'Any more and we will be seen.'

'Where is this hiding-place, then? I hardly think we can shift that contraption!'

'It is merely the foot of it; the stone you see there. If we both push . . .'

Stead shook his head, but still followed Mrs. Tanner's lead, leaning his weight against the mincing machine. It shifted a fraction.

'One more push,' she urged.

Stead obliged. The machine shifted a little more.

'Not quite,' she said, urging him to push again. 'Tell me, I suppose you have heard what became of the Viscountess. I expect you are sorry to have lost your patroness.'

'Sorry? We had a pleasant arrangement, my dear. I told her what she wished to hear; she gave me money. I suppose I am sorry. It could have lasted a good deal longer, if her son could have been persuaded.'

'But she found you out, didn't she? She found out how that boy of Wilmot's passed you all those useful pieces of paper.'

'My dear, Mr. Wilmot enjoyed the company of boys, as I believe you somehow discovered. He was quite happy to employ them, in various capacities. A certain youth merely went on to supply me with some trivial details concerning certain individuals. There – are we done?'

'A little more – I cannot free the slab, not yet. Tell

me, I am curious, what did you say to the Viscountess? What persuaded her to confess, and obliged her to take her own life?'

'Perhaps I mesmerised her. Now, surely that is enough?'

'Not quite. It is heavier than I thought. It was Grubb who ruined it for you, I suppose. Old Wilmot was too drunk to see what was going on, wasn't he? Then I stuck my nose in, and Grubb got agitated.'

'Poor boy. You quite frightened him, my dear. He was going to confess to his master.'

'And he might have given it all away; not just the waste paper, but everything he'd done for you. All those letters he'd copied! So you did for him.'

'Humph,' said Stead, straining, 'that was not my doing.'

'Cranks, then.'

'Perhaps.'

'Wilmot found out after the boy died, though, didn't he? Then he came to you. But you knew enough about – well, let's say his habits – to keep him quiet.'

'Are we done?'

'And Wright – the maid. Was that Cranks's work?'

'I told you, my dear, I merely gave her notice.'

'I went to her employment office,' said Mrs. Tanner. 'They have not heard of her since that night.'

'My!' exclaimed Stead, exasperated. 'Of what consequence might the girl be to you?'

'I like to know who I am dealing with, sir. Besides, we are partners now, are we not? You need not be so coy.'

'If you must know, I left her to the boy. What he did to silence her, I cannot say.'

'Do you intend to do the same with me?'

'Not if you deliver upon your promise. There – we

have shifted it a good two feet. And I am rather tired of your questions. I am not here for your amusement or edification, ma'am, rest assured. That will suffice, I trust?'

'I think it might.'

She crouched down in the semi-darkness, feeling around the stone slabs on the floor with her hands. At length, she took the same piece of metal she had used on the gate and prised one of the slabs a little loose.

'Do you have them?'

'Here,' said Mrs. Tanner, holding up a bundle of careworn papers.

Stead grabbed them from her hand. He unfolded the first sheet and held it up to the lamp-light. He picked a second sheet, and repeated the process. A look of incomprehension, then anger, grew upon his face.

'These are not the letters,' he said.

'I know,' she replied calmly. 'Looking at it, I should say it is Wilmot's account with his tailor. Another of his employer's scraps that poor Charlie disposed of. I got them when I bought some ham.'

'But the letters . . .'

'I never had your damn' letters,' she replied. 'I told your boy as much. He should have taken my word for it.'

Stead made as if to grab hold of her, but seemed to restrain himself, as another thought struck him. He glanced nervously around the room.

'Why have you brought me here, you wretched woman?'

'I think I can answer that, sir.'

The voice came from the far left of the room, as a figure stepped out of the darkness, pushing his way past the haunches of meat. Stead recognised the man instantly.

'Murdoch! What is the meaning of this!'

'Inspector Murdoch to you, sir,' said the detective. 'I should have thought the meaning was plain. You see, I wasn't entirely sure of Mrs. Tanner's account of this peculiar affair; not sure either what part she played in it – she's a tricky one, as you know. But she said she could prove it; and it sounds like she's been pretty straight with me.'

'This is ridiculous!' fulminated Stead. 'I have done nothing wrong! The woman lured me here. I merely played along with her scheme; I hoped to uncover the roots of her madness!'

'I suppose you think that there is no proof?' said Mrs. Tanner. 'That everything can be explained away, with the Viscountess gone? That no-one can hold you to account?'

'Well then, if you must, what shall you charge me with, eh?' said Stead, addressing the detective with renewed confidence. 'I should like to hear it.'

Murdoch was about to speak, but found himself interrupted.

'You don't need to hear nothing, Johnnie,' said another voice. 'Not from this fellow, leastways. Not if I have anything to do with it.'

Mrs. Tanner froze.

It was Jem Cranks, descending the stairs with a gun in his hand.

CHAPTER FORTY

'Here we are again, missus,' said the boy, pointing the gun in Mrs. Tanner's direction. 'I don't reckon there'll be a third time, eh? You should have known it was all chaff, John – what did you expect of this one! I told you, didn't I!'

'A pleasure to see you, my dear boy,' said Stead.

'I suppose you came down through the attic,' said Mrs. Tanner, cursing herself for not foreseeing the boy's arrival.

'Johnnie here reckoned he might need an helping hand. He weren't wrong, neither, was he, missus?' said Cranks, visibly elated by his success. 'Never thought you'd bring a Peeler, mind. Now the question is, I reckon, who do I pop – the Peeler or the whore?'

'You do either, my boy,' said Murdoch, 'and they'll fit a rope around your neck quicker than you can blink.'

'My old man always said I was born to be hanged,' said Cranks, cheerfully. 'Now, Johnnie, what d'you reckon?'

'I cannot say,' replied Stead. 'They are both such pleasant individuals.'

'"Cannot say"? Very sensible,' said Murdoch,

glancing at Mrs. Tanner. 'Oh, I'd keep quiet, if I were you, too, my friend.'

'Here, what d'you mean?' demanded Cranks.

'He doesn't want to be accessory to a felony, my boy,' continued the detective. 'He doesn't want to swing with you. Maybe just a long stretch in the jug if he keeps it shut. He'll say it was all your idea; never wanted anything to do with it. Now, you get him to speak up, if you like. You try it. But I don't reckon he will; he's had time to think it through. For one thing, he knows a fellow like me won't turn up here all on his own; he knows there's a dozen coppers waiting outside. And if he's going to get caught, I'll bet he doesn't want to risk his own neck, not for your sake he won't.'

'You're lying, Inspector,' said Stead. 'There's no-one outside. I would have seen them.'

'Hear him out, Stead,' said Mrs. Tanner, sensing the detective's plan. 'What will happen here? Do you really think you'll get away on the slates? The boy might manage it; but you're not built for that game. Besides, you've said all along it was the boy that killed Grubb and the girl; that's what you told us, wasn't it? That you weren't to blame? And I'm sure Mr. Murdoch knows it wasn't your doing.'

'I'll vouch for it in court,' said the detective. 'If you give yourself up here and now.'

'What have you been saying?' said Cranks, a hint of uncertainty in his voice.

'He told us all about it,' said Mrs. Tanner. 'How you made him swear he wouldn't tell about Grubb; how you did for poor Miss Wright when his back was turned.'

'Nonsense!' exclaimed Stead. 'Jem, my boy!'

'I ain't nobody's boy,' said Cranks, his hand wavering

between pointing the gun at Mrs. Tanner and his accomplice.

'Didn't you hear him when you came down the stairs?' continued Mrs. Tanner. '"I left her to the boy." He'll be happy to let you get scragged, don't you worry. A shame really, seeing as you're willing to risk your neck for him and all.'

'Now, Stead,' added Murdoch, quickly, 'it's all up with you, you know it. We've heard the confession. Help us take the boy and it'll go better for you.'

As the detective spoke, there was a loud banging in the back yard, and the sound of splintering wood.

'And that's my lads, bang on time,' said the detective. 'Better think fast, eh?'

Jem Cranks suddenly looked panicked, retreating a few steps up the stairs, still holding the gun out before him.

'I ain't nobody's boy!'

Stead turned; the sound of the policemen descending the ramp outside echoed through the room.

'Come on, Jem,' said the mesmerist, hastily, trying to ascend the stairs after him. But the movement was too quick. Whatever Stead's intentions, the boy cried out – whether in anger or fear it was impossible to say – and then came the report of the pistol.

Stead spun round as the bullet tore through his face in an explosion of blood and bone. He already appeared quite devoid of life as his body fell back down the stairs, landing heavily on the stone-flagged floor.

The boy disappeared from view, back the way he had come, just as two uniformed constables burst through the cellar doors. The sight of the dead man seemed to stun them both into inactivity, as they gazed in mute horror at the corpse.

'About time!' muttered Murdoch, gesturing towards the stairs. 'After him, you fools! He's going for the roof!'

The two policemen, recovering themselves, needed no further encouragement and set off on their pursuit. Inspector Murdoch, for his part, remained quite still, and breathed a long sigh of relief.

'Are you all right, Inspector?'

'To tell the truth, my dear, I thought one of us was for it. You did nicely; I couldn't have asked for better, not from one of my own men.'

'I am accustomed to living on my nerves. Although, I thought you said a dozen men?'

'I exaggerated.'

She bent down, looked at Stead's prostrate body and sighed.

'You won't catch the boy, you know. He's too fly.'

'Perhaps not,' said Murdoch. 'But we'll get him, don't you worry.'

'I leave that in your hands.'

'God help us! There'll have to be an inquest, of course. Lord knows what the press will make of it, once it's all tied together with Berkeley Square.'

Mrs. Tanner turned to the policeman, looking him in the eye.

'Inspector, you said yourself I have been honest with you. I have a favour to ask. Arthur told me you might keep our connexion a secret. That you might say you employed me as your adjunct.'

'That was before tonight!'

'Does that matter? Which will sound better in the newspapers – that I persuaded you to come here tonight, or that it was your own idea? Describe me as a retired actress, if you will; that will suffice. Only, keep our secret? I do not wish to damage him. Arthur will recompense you for it.'

'You're no fool, ma'am,' said the detective, 'I'll give you that. It goes against the grain, mind you . . .'

'Of course, Inspector.'

'The thing is, though,' continued the detective, 'the one thing I can't fathom is how he did it. How did he get Her Ladyship to confess, when she was hell-bent on seeing him to the gallows?'

'It wasn't mesmerism. I think she wanted the interview with him that day to pour salt on the wound; to see him squirm. She was bitter about how he had abused her trust. But my guess is that Stead knew something; something unexpected. I don't know what it was; but it was something she was willing to die to protect. They did a deal; she would take the rightful blame, for his silence. I think the letters might reveal it, if I had them.'

'Ah yes, those blessed letters. And would you tell me what it was, if you did have them?'

'I think, Inspector, we will never know.'

CHAPTER FORTY-ONE

The conjoined inquest into the deaths of Lord and Lady DeSalle, followed by that into the murder of one John Stead, in a butcher's cellar upon Leather Lane, provided fodder for the press for a solid fortnight. Following the testimony of Inspector Murdoch of Scotland Yard, there was little question that the mesmerist 'famed for his practical demonstrations of that dubious science' had practised an extravagant fraud, abetted by the family's solicitor, that had led to both murder and suicide. The doctor's complicity with Mr. Wilmot of Dovey's Chambers was further confirmed by the appearance of a man's body, not far from Vauxhall Bridge, drowned in the river. Respectably dressed, with distinguishing features all but destroyed – as the corpse had become squeezed between two coal barges – the body was still possessed of a watch, engraved with the lawyer's name. A third coroner's jury was sworn: the verdict, suicide.

One remarkable feature of the case, which garnered much comment, was Inspector Murdoch's employment of a female, a former actress who went by the name of Mrs. Richmond, to gather intelligence about the fraud, in the guise of a mesmeric patient. Some praised the intrepid young woman, and commended

339

the detective on his ingenuity; others, of a more conservative bent, wrote condemnatory letters to *The Times*, fearful that the move foreboded a legion of female spies being let loose upon the capital and an encroaching tyranny, worthy only of the Continent, enforced by 'detectives in petticoats'. The opinion of Mrs. Richmond herself, however, was not forthcoming. Nor was that of Arthur DeSalle, the new Viscount, who promptly removed himself from Society, and retreated to his family estate, as soon as the demands of the law had been met.

Upon Leather Lane, the salient features of the *DeSalle scandal* were rather lost, amidst a general impression that *something queer had gone on*. Few truly believed that George Sanders had accidentally obtained possession of a lawyer's treasured papers; that it was this which had led to the horse-meat riot and, ultimately, to the bizarre chain of suicide and murder. Indeed, the story had a tendency to alter with each telling, until half-a-dozen different rumours prompted the worthy butcher to post *The Times* account of each inquest in his shop-window, to which he directed his customers. It was fortunate, perhaps – or at least a testimony to Inspector Murdoch's ability to economise with the truth – that none of them seemed to connect a certain Mrs. Richmond with a certain Mrs. Tanner. Certainly, if George Sanders knew any better – if any information had been vouchsafed to him, when he loaned his cellar to Inspector Murdoch – he had the decency to keep it to himself.

The coffee-house upon the corner of Leather Lane and Liquorpond Street, meanwhile, remained closed. Mrs. Tanner stayed largely in her rooms in Calthorpe Street, visited only, on occasion, by Norah Smallwood and Ralph Grundy. It was a full six weeks after the last inquest, when the West End gossip had finally turned to other subjects, that a third visitor began to appear: a handsome young man who came only at night.

For Arthur DeSalle had returned to London.

⸻

'Arabella is determined to come to town. She says the manor is full of ghosts and cold draughts.'

Sarah Tanner watched her lover from the comfort of the bed. As he put on his boots, she wondered idly why she liked to watch him dress; it only meant he was leaving her, after all.

'So will I still have your company?'

'Whenever you desire it,' said DeSalle, turning round, and bestowing a brief kiss on her lips. 'I can stay longer, if you like.'

'No, I told you, I am expecting Norah. You had better go.'

'Are you sure?' he said, reaching out to caress her. She smiled and rolled away, out of his reach, wrapping the sheets about her body.

'You have had enough of me tonight.'

'Never.'

She sat up and kissed him again.

'Go,' she said, at last.

He bid her good-bye, making a considerable show of his reluctance. Once she heard the front door slam shut, she hurried to the window, pulling back the curtain a small fraction. She watched him stroll down the darkened street and, not for the first time, worried for his safety. Indeed, although Calthorpe Street was on the borders of Bloomsbury, it lay in the shadow of the Middlesex House of Correction and partook of the grim atmosphere that hung about the prison; and, as with many streets in the vicinity of a great gaol, it was, upon occasion, the haunt of thieves and villains.

She left the house some ten minutes later. If Arthur DeSalle had lingered in the street – if he had followed her – he would have swiftly realised that he had been deceived. For she did not meet Norah Smallwood, nor attempt to seek her out; rather, she turned her steps southwards, skirting the high walls of the prison, towards Gray's Inn and Holborn, until she came to Feathers Court, and the house of Charles Merryweather.

She stepped inside and found her old acquaintance pacing the hall.

'Miss Mills,' said Merryweather, with unaccustomed gravity.

'Is everything arranged in Camberwell?'

'My dear Sarah,' said Merryweather, 'I have done what I can. It was not a simple matter.'

'How many cracksmen can there be in Lambeth?'

'More than you might think; I had to lay it on thick to find a willing party.'

'You'll be paid back in full, Charlie, don't you worry. You have the keys?'

'Yes, there – take them. I am glad to be rid of them. The lease is for the month, if that makes any difference to you.'

'I only need one night. And the fanlight?'

'I am assured a blind man could put it loose.'

'Then I am set.'

'Sarah – I speak as a friend – are you quite sure what you are about?'

'Quite. I will not hide myself away any longer.'

Although little more than a mile west from the densely populated streets of Lambeth, the village of Camberwell was untouched by the ever-growing metropolis. True, a handful of new houses encroached upon the village green, but the sweeping terraces, beloved of suburban builders, had yet to appear; there were no factory chimneys; no railway clearances; and the fields about the parish church were green grass, rather than churned and burnt into clay brick.

And yet some were determined to change the district. For the green fields and pleasant air made it agreeable to City men, who might welcome a property in the country, a short ride – by metropolitan standards – from the Exchange and the Bank. And so, down country lanes and side-roads, a few grand villas had begun to appear, faced with stucco and pilasters, ready to be rented to gentlemen for whom one hundred pounds per annum would be no great burden.

It was outside one of these newly minted houses, in the small hours of the night – the same night Sarah Tanner had bid a premature good-bye to Arthur DeSalle – that two figures made their appearance. One was a boy of no more than fifteen or sixteen years, the other a man, some ten years older. They gave the appearance of being 'on the tramp' and yet, if anyone were to observe them closely, they would have noticed that both were close-shaved and carried none of the paraphernalia of pitiable bags and belongings, beloved of the regular vagrant. Moreover, as they came to the house in question, they came to an abrupt halt and dropped back from the road, crouching down in a ditch that lay opposite.

Their conversation was too low to be heard; but,

at length, the boy rose from his hiding-place and clambered back up to the road. He walked over to the front gate of the house – for a low wall had been built to mark its garden, though the ground had yet to be cultivated – strolling with a casual air, brisk but not hurried. He looked back at his companion, and the man nodded. The boy let himself through the gate, and up the steps that led to the porch and recessed front door. Again, he looked over his shoulder and received a second nod. He rapped sharply on the knocker.

No reply.

The boy waited a minute; perhaps two.

Still no reply.

Then, of a sudden, he scrambled up, somehow bracing one foot upon the knocker, wedging his body against the side of the porch. He pulled something from the bag strung over his shoulder – a piece of cloth or paper – which he placed over the fanlight, as he took a small sliver of metal and began to work away at the putty that held it in place. The glass gave way in seconds; and, within the blink of an eye, the boy somehow managed to lower the loosened pane into the interior of the house, and follow it himself, without hardly a sound.

His companion watched the boy's progress. By rights, as a responsible cracksman, he was obliged to remain where he was and keep watch. But he had the promise of twenty guineas that said otherwise; and so, with a heartfelt sigh, he got up and turned back to Camberwell Green.

❧

Jem Cranks replaced the fanlight from inside the hall. He was an accomplished thief, and the darkness did not trouble him. Nonetheless, once he felt certain that his entrance had not caused any disturbance, he pulled out a small tin cylinder from his bag, struck a match and lit the candle fixed within it. The cylinder was perforated with holes, and one side left open, so that it formed a dark lantern, whose dim beam could be pointed in whatever direction was required. Holding it by the hook strung through the lid, he began to explore the house.

To his annoyance, he found the ground floor all but empty. Although he had been told that the place had been newly built, he had been assured that it had just been acquired by a wealthy widow; that she had removed her possessions to the house the day before; and that she had left them unguarded, to visit a sick relative. To find nothing but bare boards and closed shutters – it riled him.

It was only his professional reputation amongst the Lambeth mobsmen who, on occasion, made use of his remarkable agility, that encouraged him to try the first floor.

He crept cautiously up the stairs. He consoled himself with the thought that a room on the upper floor might serve as the lady's bedroom; that a jewel-box might not be out of the question.

He tried the first room. His disappointment at finding it unfurnished was, however, soon replaced by surprise. For the door slammed shut behind him. His first instinct was that it was merely the wind; a trick played by draughts in the empty house.

Then he heard the woman's voice, and saw the figure waiting for him in the darkness.

'For the third time, then, Master Cranks,' said Mrs. Tanner. 'And most definitely the last.'

345

CHAPTER FORTY-TWO

He held the lantern aloft, peering at the woman before him.

'Damn me,' exclaimed the boy.

'Who did you expect?' said Mrs. Tanner.

'A widow woman,' said the boy, still open-mouthed.

'Is that so? Well, I expect your pal spun you a good tale.'

'Oh, he threw in the hatchet all right, missus. And here's me, believing every word, like a proper flat. He told me there'd be all sorts of flash for the taking and – I was only just thinking – this place ain't right. I almost reckoned I had the wrong house.'

'It's the right house,' she replied. 'And your friend will be half-way back to Lambeth by now, with twenty guineas for his trouble.'

'Is that right? Well, I'll have words with him tomorrow. Where's the Peeler, then?'

She shook her head. 'Just you and me, Master Cranks.'

The boy grinned. 'Then you're a bigger fool than I thought, missus, that's the truth.'

He reached inside the bag as he spoke, and pulled out the same small pistol she had seen in George Sanders' cellar, levelling it directly at her head.

'How about I put another hole in that pretty face, eh? What do you say to that?'

'I'd say it's just for show, Master Cranks. I'd say, if it were loaded, you'd be liable to have blown yourself to bits when you jumped that fanlight. That, and be hung for carrying it, if anyone ever laid hold of you.'

'You so cock-sure, then, missus?' said the boy, his finger caressing the trigger.

She shrugged.

'Bang! You're dead!' said Cranks, with a grin. But there was no sound; no explosion. Despite herself, Mrs. Tanner shuddered.

'Oh, you should see your face, missus!' exclaimed the boy, tossing aside the gun. 'Not that you ain't wide awake, don't get me wrong. You're a good'un, no mistake about it. Prime! But you won't get the better of Jem Cranks, not if I can help it.'

She looked at the boy's hand. No sooner had he dropped the gun than it contained a knife, pulled from his pocket. With an ease that betoked an unfortunate degree of familiarity with the weapon, he flicked the sheath from the blade. The metal glinted in the candle-light.

'I can match that,' replied Mrs. Tanner, stepping back a little. She held out her arm defensively, brandishing the sharp stiletto she had kept concealed in the folds of her dress. The boy, however, showed no fear.

'Is that all?' said Cranks. 'Didn't you bring a barker this time? I reckon you ought of, 'cos don't think I won't do for you, missus, just 'cos you're a woman. You proper deserve it an' all.'

'What, like you did for Wright?'

'That slavey? Well, that's hardly worth mentioning. Someone had to shut her up.'

347

'And what about poor Joe Drummond?'

'Him? Thought he could play the big man, didn't he? Only he weren't so big as all that, turns out.'

'Tell me,' she said, keeping her distance, as the boy tried to edge towards her, 'where did you meet Stead – at Vauxhall? Pimping boys and telling fortunes?'

'I never played that game, missus. Some of my mob did, mind, and good luck to 'em. But Johnnie Stead was all right, he was, back in the day; not bad company for an old'un. And he gave us little errands, now and then.'

'And what about your sister?'

'Helen? Well, she's always had the gift, see? That's how Johnnie got his start in life, with the mesmerics. Lor! And she told me not to come tonight an' all! Reckon I should have listened.'

'You think she has mesmeric powers?'

'Think! Just! How do you reckon old Johnnie got himself a living – he couldn't do it – not Johnnie! He could manage a bit of blarney, but he couldn't put 'em under good and proper – not without our Helen! Who do you think put 'em under the spell for him?'

'I don't believe it.'

'I don't much mind, missus,' said the boy, edging forward a little more. 'Now, why don't you drop that pig-tickler, eh? Let's settle this once and for all, eh?'

'And what will you do then?'

'Whatever I fancy, I reckon.'

'Very well,' she said.

But as she let go of the blade, she flicked her wrist, sending it flying, straight as an arrow. The boy's face barely had time to register his astonishment, as the dagger lodged in his neck.

The sound that escaped his mouth was terrible, a dreadful shriek of despair. He dropped his weapon, his hands instinctively reaching for the wound. The blood seemed to foam and bubble over his fingertips, an unstoppable crimson tide that refused to be quenched, as he fell to the floor, his breath coming in desperate agonising gasps.

Sarah Tanner walked over and knelt beside him. The lantern had fallen beside him, the candle still burning in its tin container. She could see by its light that the boards were already soaked in his blood. His eyes seemed to plead with her.

'Joe Drummond was one of the kindest, best men I have ever met,' she said, quietly. 'I am not sorry.'

Then she rose to her feet and left the room.

———

Wrapped in her shawl, she left the house by the kitchen-door, for safety's sake, through the garden and over the adjoining fields, rejoining the road at Camberwell Green. It was a troublesome journey in the darkness but she did not notice the mud on her skirts, or the water that seeped into her boots. Her mind was filled with black thoughts. She had hoped the night would put an end to certain fears; they seemed instantly replaced by others.

It was only as she reached the far end of the Green that she stopped. For standing there, alone on the deserted ground, was a woman whose pale, ghostly face she recognised.

Helena Smith. Helen Cranks.

The name did not matter.

Sarah Tanner's stomach turned, as the woman rushed towards her.

'You!' exclaimed the sick-nurse. 'I told him! I told him not to come!'

'I have no time for this,' said Mrs. Tanner, trying

to push past. 'And if you expect me to believe you are some prophetess, you are quite mad.'

'You killed him, didn't you?' said Miss Smith, bitterly. 'I warned him! Poor lamb!'

Sarah Tanner had resolved to say nothing; and yet every instinct made her cry out.

'"Poor lamb"! He deserved it. God forgive me, he deserved it. If ever any creature deserved to be despatched to his Maker, your brother was that man.'

'A mere boy!' she sobbed.

'A murderer!'

'And what are you, then, ma'am?' said Miss Smith, spitting in her face.

Sarah Tanner shook her head, pushing her interlocutor firmly aside, striding onwards. Helena Smith did not follow, but stayed on the grass, her face drenched in tears, her eyes bright with anger. And yet, a perverse smile seemed to play upon her lips.

'It won't be the fellow what she wants,' she muttered under her breath. 'Not by a long chalk.'

CHAPTER FORTY-THREE

The New Dining and Coffee Rooms re-opened quietly, without fanfare, two days later. Trade was slow for a few days, until the excellence of Mrs. Hinchley's breakfast, and the cheapness of Mrs. Tanner's coffee, drew the costers back to their old haunt.

It was one evening shortly after the opening, however, when the shop lay quite empty – with Ralph Grundy given leave to pay a celebratory visit to the Bottle of Hay, and Norah Smallwood busy in the kitchen – that a particular customer entered the establishment. His suit was of the worst cut; his boots scuffed and worn; even his hat had a distinctly shabby and battered appearance. And yet, it was not so much the apparel that made Sarah Tanner laugh out loud, but the man inside it.

'You!' she exclaimed.

'Hush!' said Arthur DeSalle. 'You will give me away!'

'I did not expect to see you here, Arthur. You had better not let Norah see you – she will be in fits. But you promised me some weights and a sack of potatoes. And there is no neckerchief – you will not pass for a coster at all, I'm afraid. It is too bad!'

'I said I would come and see your establishment, did I not?'

'And this is your best disguise?'

'Please, Sarah, do not toy with me. I had two reasons for coming – apart from amusing you with my incompetence in the art of deception.'

'Do you like my shop?'

'It is charming. Sarah, please . . .'

'What, then?'

DeSalle blushed. 'I cannot come later tonight; Arabella is unwell. I fear I must remain by her side.'

She stiffened a little. 'A note would have sufficed.'

'You have not heard my second reason,' said DeSalle, growing more grave as he spoke. 'Here, you must read this. It came in the post today.'

The item in question was a rather dirty-looking piece of paper: a hand-written note by someone whose hand was spidery and indistinct.

Your Lordship,

I do not heed the insinuations of the press and, after good advice, I have the pleasure to forward the following. I have in my possession letters which belong to a certain party that must be yourself. If you would care to recompense me for their recovery, please leave five pounds at the receiving-house, Whiskin-street, Clerkenwell, for M. Hoping you find this in the enjoyment of good health with all well wishes.

'Good Lord,' said Mrs. Tanner, 'the fabled letters. It appears they've turned up.'

'Turned up?' said DeSalle. 'Sarah! It is blackmail!'

'Well, of a rather unconvincing nature.'

'That depends what these wretched documents

contain! I had thought all this was done with! Is it Miss Smith?'

'No, I don't think so. Merryweather tells me she has left London.'

'But how can you be sure?'

'She would demand more money. If they have great value, this person knows nothing of it.'

'So what should I do?'

There was something so pathetic in the sight of her lover in his shabby costume that Mrs. Tanner could not help but smirk.

'It is no laughing matter!' protested DeSalle.

'I did not say it was. I doubt this will be hard to resolve. I will think on it; do not pay the woman yet.'

'"The woman"? Then you think it *is* Miss Smith?'

'It looks like a woman's hand to me, that is all. Ah, I think Norah is done in the kitchen – you had better go. Leave the note with me, it may contain some clue. Will I see you tomorrow night?'

'Tomorrow night, then,' said DeSalle, hurriedly turning on his heels.

'Who was that?' said Norah Smallwood, as she saw the back of Arthur DeSalle's head disappear down Leather Lane. 'Didn't he want nothing?'

'Just directions,' said Mrs. Tanner. She turned to grab her shawl from the hook. 'I'll be back in half an hour.'

Sarah Tanner had no need to ponder the mystery of the note. She had deduced its author almost instantly by the simple fact that she knew the geography of Clerkenwell. In truth, she had resolved to recover the lost property – the letters which had caused so much misery – and present them to Arthur DeSalle upon their next meeting. She might have told her lover as much in the coffee-house, but she was inclined to keep him waiting: whether it was punishment for his absence that night, or to impress him with her skills in detection, she herself could not have answered with absolute certainty.

She walked from Leather Lane through to Clerkenwell, not to Whiskin Street, but a narrow court adjoining the road, known to the locals as Plumber's Place. And, in that court, she found the dry lodgings belonging to one Margaret Maggs. The landlady was deep in gossip with one of her tenants when Mrs. Tanner entered her parlour.

'Mrs. Maggs, may I have a word in private?' she said.

'Do I know you, ma'am?' said the redoubtable female in question.

'We have met. You may recall you showed me the room of your former lodger, Charlie Grubb.'

'Ah!' exclaimed Mrs. Maggs, as she recalled it. 'Poor Charlie! Well, you must forgive me, ma'am – there were many curious parties that week. How can I oblige you?'

'It concerns some correspondence; intimate correspondence.'

The landlady positively blanched. 'I'm not sure what you mean, ma'am.'

'I think you do, ma'am. Is there somewhere we might go . . . ?'

Mrs. Maggs looked at the trio of lodgers who sat playing cards, as if unmoved from the very day on which Sarah Tanner had first visited the lodging-house, and then hurried her visitor from their presence.

'My own rooms, ma'am,' said the landlady, ushering Mrs. Tanner through a nearby door. 'It doesn't do to discuss business in public, after all, eh? Have a seat . . .'

'Business, ma'am?' said Sarah Tanner, as powerfully as she could manage. 'I will not sit. If you think that I have come here, on behalf of a certain party, to pay money for certain items, you are much mistaken.'

'Mistaken?' said the landlady, nervously.

'As agent for – let us not name names – I am here, ma'am, to demand return of certain letters in your possession, stolen by a certain youth. And, if you don't oblige me, I will be obliged to give you in charge.'

Mrs. Maggs, for all her bulk, positively quivered.

'But, ma'am, really—'

'I am sure I can find a constable quite easily.'

Wordlessly, defeated, the landlady hurried to a desk that sat in the corner of her room, and recovered a sheaf of old papers, bound with a red ribbon.

'Here, ma'am. Take 'em. For His Lordship, with my compliments. I never meant nothing by it. Charlie liked 'em and he let me have 'em to read – I only meant – if His Lordship was minded to offer some token . . .'

Mrs. Tanner took the letters from the landlady's outstretched hand.

'A word of advice, ma'am,' she said. 'Stick to dry lodgings and give up blackmail.'

And, with that, she turned on her heels and left, leaving Charlie Grubb's erstwhile landlady and confidante quite speechless.

———

Mrs. Tanner hurried back to Leather Lane, elated by her success. At several points her curiosity all but overwhelmed her. Nonetheless, she suppressed the urge to read the contents of the mysterious bundle until safely in the confines of her own home. At last, returning to the coffee-house, she concealed the letters in her dress and went directly upstairs, unwilling to share the discovery with Norah Smallwood, locking her bedroom door behind her.

She undid the ribbon and picked up the first sheet of paper, devouring the contents.

It made no sense.

They were letters, written by the young Lady DeSalle, signed simply C. for Caroline, addressed to her husband. She had anticipated something of the kind; but it made no sense.

My dearest William . . .

She read them one after the other.

I long for the time when I may see you again . . .

There were passionate; fervent. The private sentiments of a young woman devoted to her husband.

None was worth dying for.

She read them a second time. She spent an hour or more, growing increasingly perplexed and frustrated. There was nothing damning in them; nothing whatsoever. They were written from villas in Naples and Rome; her husband clearly had some private business that involved travel in Italy.

Then, at last, it struck her. Two simple lines.

I long for our wedding day.

Where was the other?

Even in these last two weeks we have been parted little Arthur has grown so much!

It was the date of each letter; it suddenly fitted together in her mind: half-a-dozen passing references to the birth of a child; to his first weeks of infancy. All of them came before that line.

I long for our wedding day.

It struck her like a thunderbolt. They were not

married when the child was born. Something had been arranged in Italy; it did not matter precisely what – the letters were the sole proof. That was what Lady DeSalle had sacrificed herself for: the mesmerist had uncovered the secret, even if the evidence had been lost, thanks to Charlie Grubb's incompetence. What was it the Viscountess had said?

I have always done what I have thought best for the family.

Arthur DeSalle was not the legitimate heir to his house in Belgravia; to the house in Berkeley Square. He had no claim to the lands; to the title; to all the privileges of his class, that he took for granted.

He was nothing whatsoever.

That was what his mother had hoped to spare him. What was she to do?

EPILOGUE

She sat upon the bench in St. James's Park, looking up and down the path by the lake. She had hardly slept; all night she had thought of the letters and their possible consequences. The previous day, when she first read Mrs. Maggs's note, she had intended to present them with a flourish to Arthur DeSalle; a token of her love, her loyalty. She had not given any serious thought to their contents; she had not imagined what they might mean. Now they seemed horrible to her; an awful burden. She was almost tempted to crush them in her hands; to throw them into the lake.

No.

She had resolved to tell him the truth; DeSalle deserved that much. She could not bear to wait the whole day; she knew his routine, his route between Belgravia and the Reform Club. She would greet him in the park; they would talk. She would tell him that his position in Society meant nothing – absolutely nothing – to her; that she would love him whether he retained his title or told the world the truth.

What would he tell his wife?

Did it give her some perverse pleasure to think that, with ridiculous integrity, he might abandon it all; that he might even abandon Arabella – that *she* might be reduced from Viscountess to a mere nobody.

She did not care to admit it to herself.

She had been sitting there for half an hour when she saw him. He was walking by the lake, on the far side. She rose to draw his attention then promptly sat down, cursing her own stupidity. She had not foreseen that he might have company. A woman walked beside him, arm in arm; a maid-servant trailed behind. It took her a second or two to realise what it meant.

It was his wife.

She had hoped never to see Arabella DeSalle. Even at two hundred yards' distance, she could see that she was beautiful, and the very sight pained her.

But there was something more. It seemed ridiculous at first, quite impossible; she almost smiled to herself at the thought of it. And yet it became more transparent, with every step the woman took. It was plain in the unfashionable cut of her gown; in the flush upon her cheeks; the slight constraint in her step. The way she paused to gaze across the water, leaning on her husband's arm, her hand resting conspicuously upon her belly.

Sarah Tanner rose from her seat and hurried across the park. She tried to contain her emotion; to tell herself it wasn't true.

The woman – whom she despised with all her heart – the creature whom he had swore meant nothing to him – was to bear his child.

———

That evening, Arthur DeSalle appeared outside a certain house in Calthorpe Street. He was surprised to discover a suite of rooms within, hired at his own expense, had been abandoned by their tenant. He

360

found a brief note on the mantel, wishing him congratulations on his wife's interesting condition, and a bitter oath that the author would never desire to see him again.

That night, the Viscountess DeSalle received a package, delivered by the final post of the day.

It contained a bundle of letters.

ALSO AVAILABLE IN ARROW BY L.M. JACKSON

A Most Dangerous Woman

The first in a series of mysteries featuring lady detective Sarah Tanner

It was said that she had the good manners of a respectable upper servant but was far too young to have been pensioned; that she spoke as if she had received an education, but knew the costers' slang as if she were born-and-bred to it; and that she not only had no husband – which was a commonplace on Leather Lane – but seemed never to have possessed one. . .'

When the mysterious Sarah Tanner opens her Dining and Coffee Rooms on the corner of Leather Lane and Liquorpond Street, her arrival amongst the poor market-traders causes something of a stir. Few doubt that she has 'a past'; no-one could have predicted how it will return to haunt her. . .

When an old friend is brutally murdered, Sarah Tanner is the only witness. Unable to turn to the police, she finds herself drawn back into the dark underworld of the Victorian metropolis. Relying on her wits, and trading on her past, Sarah Tanner risks her own life on a desperate quest for justice and vengeance.

'Evokes the colour and danger of Victorian London with a master's touch . . . an exhilarating experience' *Daily Express*

arrow books